Understanding

Phonetics

Understanding Language series
Series editors:

Bernard Comrie, Max Planck Institute for Evolutionary Anthropology, Leipzig, Germany
Greville Corbett, Surrey Morphology Group, University of Surrey, UK

The Understanding Language series provides approachable, yet authoritative, introductions to major topics in linguistics. Ideal for students with little or no prior knowledge of linguistics, each book carefully explains the basics, emphasising understanding of the essential notions rather than arguing for a particular theoretical position.

Understanding

Phonetics

Patricia Ashby

**Understanding
Language Series**

Series Editors:
Bernard Comrie
and
Greville Corbett

Routledge
Taylor & Francis Group

LONDON AND NEW YORK

First published 2011 by Hodder Education

This edition published by Routledge
2 Park Square, Milton Park, Abingdon, Oxon OX14 4RN
711 Third Avenue, New York, NY, 10017, USA

Routledge is an imprint of the Taylor & Francis Group, an informa business

Copyright © 2011, Patricia Ashby.

The advice and information in this book are believed to be true and
accurate at the date of going to press, but neither the authors nor the publisher
can accept any legal responsibility or liability for any errors or omissions.

British Library Cataloguing-in-Publication Data
A catalogue record for this book is available from the British Library.

ISBN: 978 0 340 92 82 71

Typeset in Palatino Light by Dorchester Typesetting Group Ltd

Cover photo © Roulier/Turiot/Photocuisine/Corbis

Typeset by MPS Limited, a Macmillan Company

Contents

Preface

Phonetics is something that all of us do, every day, every time we open our mouths and speak. We even do it when we listen to other people speaking. But we do it all subconsciously. Studying phonetics as a discipline raises this to conscious awareness.

Phonetic data embraces every sound of every living language – some 5,000 to 8,000 at the present count – and the subject has two distinct sides to it: theory and practice. These often complement each other, and this book, with its accompanying website (www.routledge.com/cw/ashby), is designed to give you experience of both. A further fact about the subject is that, although the majority of students who study it come from the arts and humanities, phonetics is actually quite a scientific discipline.

When students first hear about phonetics, the amount of work (theory and practice) together with its scientific nature can sometimes seem like a double whammy. However, speech is fascinating, and if you are even just a tiny bit curious, phonetics has a tremendous amount to offer.

The size of the subject also needs to be kept in perspective. How big is your mouth? Relatively speaking, mouths are small. They contain just a few organs with which we are already moderately familiar: lips, teeth, tongue, and the roof of the mouth, and down the throat to the larynx. Phonetics simply makes very careful observations about what this small number of organs does when we speak. Engaging in practice, alongside learning the theory, usually helps to clarify and reinforce these observations. This volume offers you the opportunity to do this, providing numerous practical, skills-based exercises (in the book itself) and parallel ear-training activities (see accompanying website). Exercises are integrated through the text and should be attempted as part of reading the book, especially if you are studying independently. The ear-training exercises (and web-based feedback and explanations that accompany these) will help your learning in several ways. They will reinforce the theory with the experience of listening to some of the effects being described. They will also help you to use the symbols, to write these in transcription. And they will help you to think in terms of sound rather than spelling – especially important when working on English, which is taken as our shared or common language throughout.

As far as the science is concerned, at least when you first start to study the subject, you will probably find it is actually less daunting even than your experience of science during secondary education. There is a little bit of anatomy (but remember how small the mouth is!) and a little bit of physics – that is about all.

What the present volume aims to do is to show you how speech sounds are made, giving you a thorough grounding in basic distinctions and sound types, before offering more advanced insights into the wide range of variation observable in the pronunciation of both vowels and consonants. Examples are drawn from a range of languages from across the world and are compared and contrasted with our shared language of English. You will learn to describe and represent these sounds (through transcriptions and diagrams) and to recognise them (by means of ear-training and by interpreting the acoustic representations offered in spectrograms). Representation of sounds throughout relies on using the symbols of the International Phonetic Alphabet (see page xvi) and, deriving from this, a set of commonly used symbols for transcribing English (page xv).

A huge number of people have contributed in many ways to the information provided here, offering advice, ideas and examples. My thanks are due first and foremost to the series editors, Bernard Comrie and Grev Corbett whose patience, encouragement, enthusiasm and support has been of immeasurable importance, and to the in-house, practical editorial support from staff at Hodder Education, especially in the early stages, Tamsin Smith, and latterly, Bianca Knights and Lavinia Porter.

Beyond Hodder, my thanks go colleagues, family, friends and students, including Michael Ashby, David Geall, Gösta and Barbro Bruce, Paul Robertson, Kayoko Yanagisawa, John Wells, Brian Mott, Kaseam Jongpitakrat, Elfriede Tillian, Minna Salonen, Kristina Starikova, Jill House, Maud Tyler, Marianne Sharp, Elena Loy, Janet Fraser, Martha Figueroa-Clark, Xosé Regueira, Arthur Abramson, Adrian Fourcin, Evelyn Abberton, Beverley Collins, Inger Mees, Rob de Koning, Núria Gavaldà, Joan Carles Mora, Dick Hudson (who first suggested my name to Hodder Education to write this volume) and most especially to Masaki Taniguchi who painstakingly read and corrected every inch of the first draft of the manuscript with the eyes of an eagle. All of these people have advised and helped me, but I alone am responsible for any remaining errors.

Finally, my thanks also to my daughter, Christabel Ashby, who not only gave me her support, but who kindly agree to let me use her head in a very literal way (in X-ray form in Figure 3.2), to my sons, Jonathan and Dominic Ashby, and to Bogna Lesniewicz.

Patricia Ashby
London
March 2011

Acknowledgements

Grateful thanks are due to Laryngograph Ltd for permission to reproduce the precision stroboscopic images and linked laryngograph (EGG) waveforms in Figure 2.2 (page 17) and Figure 2.5 (page 20).

Figure Exercise 9.1 Pattern Playback image 15 used with kind permission of Haskins Laboratories, New York.

The International Phonetic Alphabet (2005) is reproduced by kind permission of the International Phonetic Association (Department of Theoretical and Applied Linguistics, School of English, Aristotle University of Thessaloniki, Thessaloniki 54124, Greece) and to Barbro Bruce, widow of the late Gösta Bruce, for her help and kindness in permitting reproduction of the image in Figure 10.5 (page 170).

Thanks are also due to Elsevier (Figure 3.2 on page 32), University of Chicago Press (Figure 6.5 on page 90), Cambridge University Press (Figure 6.6 on page 91), Blackwell (Figure 6.8 on page 93), Hodder Education (Figure 8.14 on page 139), and Springer Verlag (Figure 10.6 on page 172).

Every effort has been made to trace and acknowledge ownership of copyright. The publishers will be happy to make arrangements with any copyright-holder that it has not been possible to contact.

Symbols for Transcribing English

Following WELLS, J.C. (2008) *The Longman Pronunciation Dictionary*. London, Longman.

All examples in this list are based on Modern RP (MRP) pronunciation.

Vowel symbols

iː	see	/siː/	ʌ	cup	/kʌp/
ɪ	sit	/sɪt/	ɜː	bird	/bɜːd/
i	happ<u>y</u>	/ˈhæpi/	ə	<u>a</u>bout	/əˈbaʊt/
e	ten	/ten/	eɪ	say	/seɪ/
æ	cat	/kæt/	əʊ	go	/gəʊ/
ɑː	calm	/kɑːm/	aɪ	five	/faɪv/
ɒ	got	/gɒt/	aʊ	now	/naʊ/
ɔː	saw	/sɔː/	ɔɪ	boy	/bɔɪ/
ʊ	put	/pʊt/	ɪə	near	/nɪə/
uː	too	/tuː/	eə	hair	/heə/
u	situation	/sɪtʃuˈeɪʃn̩/	ʊə	pure	/pjʊə/

Consonant symbols

p	pen	/pen/	s	source	/sɔːs/
b	bad	/bæd/	z	zoos	/zuːz/
t	tea	/tiː/	ʃ	shoe	/ʃuː/
d	did	/dɪd/	ʒ	vi<u>s</u>ion	/ˈvɪʒn̩/
k	cake	/keɪk/	h	hat	/hæt/
g	got	/gɒt/	m	man	/mæn/
tʃ	chain	/tʃeɪn/	n	no	/nəʊ/
dʒ	jam	/dʒæm/	ŋ	sing	/sɪŋ/
f	fall	/fɔːl/	l	leg	/leg/
v	van	/væn/	r	red	/red/
θ	thin	/θɪn/	j	yes	/jes/

THE INTERNATIONAL PHONETIC ALPHABET (revised to 2005)

CONSONANTS (PULMONIC)

© 2005 IPA

	Bilabial	Labiodental	Dental	Alveolar	Postalveolar	Retroflex	Palatal	Velar	Uvular	Pharyngeal	Glottal
Plosive	p　b			t　d		ʈ　ɖ	c　ɟ	k　g	q　ɢ		ʔ
Nasal	m	ɱ		n		ɳ	ɲ	ŋ	N		
Trill	ʙ			r					ʀ		
Tap or Flap		ⱱ		ɾ		ɽ					
Fricative	ɸ　β	f　v	θ　ð	s　z	ʃ　ʒ	ʂ　ʐ	ç　ʝ	x　ɣ	χ　ʁ	ħ　ʕ	h　ɦ
Lateral fricative				ɬ　ɮ							
Approximant		ʋ		ɹ		ɻ	j	ɰ			
Lateral approximant				l		ɭ	ʎ	ʟ			

Where symbols appear in pairs, the one to the right represents a voiced consonant. Shaded areas denote articulations judged impossible.

CONSONANTS (NON-PULMONIC)

Clicks	Voiced implosives	Ejectives
ʘ Bilabial	ɓ Bilabial	’ Examples:
ǀ Dental	ɗ Dental/alveolar	pʼ Bilabial
ǃ (Post)alveolar	ʄ Palatal	tʼ Dental/alveolar
ǂ Palatoalveolar	ɠ Velar	kʼ Velar
ǁ Alveolar lateral	ʛ Uvular	sʼ Alveolar fricative

OTHER SYMBOLS

ʍ Voiceless labial-velar fricative

w Voiced labial-velar approximant

ɥ Voiced labial-palatal approximant

ʜ Voiceless epiglottal fricative

ʢ Voiced epiglottal fricative

ʡ Epiglottal plosive

ɕ ʑ Alveolo-palatal fricatives

ɺ Voiced alveolar lateral flap

ɧ Simultaneous ʃ and x

Affricates and double articulations can be represented by two symbols joined by a tie bar if necessary.

k͡p t͡s

VOWELS

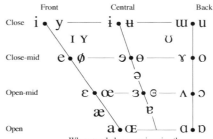

Where symbols appear in pairs, the one to the right represents a rounded vowel.

SUPRASEGMENTALS

ˈ Primary stress

ˌ Secondary stress

ˌfoʊnəˈtɪʃən

ː Long　eː

ˑ Half-long　eˑ

˘ Extra-short　ĕ

| Minor (foot) group

‖ Major (intonation) group

. Syllable break　ɹi.ækt

‿ Linking (absence of a break)

DIACRITICS

Diacritics may be placed above a symbol with a descender, e.g. ŋ̊

̥ Voiceless	n̥　d̥	̤ Breathy voiced	b̤　a̤	̪ Dental	t̪　d̪
̬ Voiced	s̬　t̬	̰ Creaky voiced	b̰　a̰	̺ Apical	t̺　d̺
ʰ Aspirated	tʰ　dʰ	̼ Linguolabial	t̼　d̼	̻ Laminal	t̻　d̻
̹ More rounded	ɔ̹	ʷ Labialized	tʷ　dʷ	̃ Nasalized	ẽ
̜ Less rounded	ɔ̜	ʲ Palatalized	tʲ　dʲ	ⁿ Nasal release	dⁿ
̟ Advanced	u̟	ˠ Velarized	tˠ　dˠ	ˡ Lateral release	dˡ
̠ Retracted	e̠	ˤ Pharyngealized	tˤ　dˤ	̚ No audible release	d̚
̈ Centralized	ë	̴ Velarized or pharyngealized	ɫ		
̽ Mid-centralized	e̽	̝ Raised	e̝　(ɹ̝ = voiced alveolar fricative)		
̩ Syllabic	n̩	̞ Lowered	e̞　(β̞ = voiced bilabial approximant)		
̯ Non-syllabic	e̯	̘ Advanced Tongue Root	e̘		
˞ Rhoticity	ɚ　a˞	̙ Retracted Tongue Root	e̙		

TONES AND WORD ACCENTS

LEVEL			CONTOUR		
e̋ or	˥	Extra high	ě or	˩˥	Rising
é	˦	High	ê	˥˩	Falling
ē	˧	Mid	e᷄	˦˥	High rising
è	˨	Low	e᷅	˩˨	Low rising
ȅ	˩	Extra low	e᷈	˧˩˧	Rising-falling
↓ Downstep			↗ Global rise		
↑ Upstep			↘ Global fall		

1

Starting phonetics

This chapter will look at what we already know about phonetics, exploring writing and spelling, texting and talking. It looks at the relationship between speaking and spelling and between speech sounds, letters of the alphabet and symbols. The IPA chart and transcription are introduced and the different types of phonetics (articulatory, acoustic, auditory), accents, our attitudes to what people sound like, and the phonetics/phonology interface.

1.1 WHAT WE ALREADY KNOW

1.1.1 Writing

Before we look more deeply into phonetics, it is worth finding out what we already know about this subject. Far from being a strange and different discipline, phonetics touches our everyday lives in a huge number of ways and has done so since the moment we were born (and maybe even earlier, while we were still in the womb). Phonetics, of course, is the study of speech sounds, but before we can really get to grips with these, we need to dispel a few myths about writing and spelling, and explore the relationship between the spoken and written forms of languages.

Most of us learn to speak very early in our lives but at school we all grapple with the intricacies of writing. Around the world, the first writing system many of us use is based on applications of the **Extended Latin Alphabet** (ELA). (If you are not sure what this means, check it out by looking at the fonts and symbols available on your computer.) Our familiarity with this alphabet, and with other alphabets such as the Greek alphabet, depends very much on where we live in the world. In the Faroe Islands, for example, shapes such as æ, ø and ð are part of everyday orthography (see Figure 1.1). In Greece, ɛ, β and ɸ are taken for granted in the same way. It is shapes like these from the ELA plus a few extras from the Greek alphabet that we use to 'write phonetics'. We give the name **transcription** to this writing and instead of referring to letters, we call the shapes that we use **symbols**.

Figure 1.1
Faroese street sign meaning 'Doctor's surgery'.

One advantage to transcribing is that once you have learnt the various symbols of the **International Phonetic Association**'s alphabet[1] (reproduced in what is called the **IPA chart** on page xiv), you can write down what people are saying regardless of the language they are speaking. This is a massive bonus! You can write down what people are saying not only in English, French and Spanish, but also in Chinese, Korean, Russian, Arabic or Cherokee without ever having to learn a new writing system at all. With training, you can learn to write down the speech sounds of any one of the 5,000 to 8,000 living languages spoken in the world today.

1.1.2 Spelling

Writing is one thing, but spelling is quite another. Some languages have what we call 'phonetic spelling' – when you write words in normal orthography, it is almost the same technique as transcribing them because particular letters of the alphabet or specific groups of letters always refer to the same sound. In fact, the correct term for this is **phonemic spelling**. So, in languages like Malay, for example, or Italian, once you have learnt the spelling-to-sound rules, you can often say words out loud and sound quite authentic even without knowing the language itself. Dutch, too, has a reasonably phonemic spelling system and many syllabaries are phonemic in structure, but perhaps the most phonemic spelling system of all is the Mkhedruli alphabet used to write Georgian (see Figure 1.2). Developed as early as the third century AD, every distinctive sound has its own orthographic representation. In comparison, a language like English is a learner's nightmare and this is true whether you are a native-speaker at school learning to spell and read or a non-native speaker learning to read, write and pronounce the language.

> ჩრდილოეთის ქარი და მზე კამათობდნენ თუ რომელი იყო უფრო ძლიერი. ამ დროს გაიარა
> ერთმა ნაბადწამოხურულმა მგზავრმა. ისინი შეთანხმდნენ უძლიერესად ეცნოთ ის,
> რომელიც მგზავრს პირველი მოახდევინებდა ნაბადს. ჯერ ჩრდილოეთის ქარმა დაუბერა
> მთელი ძალ-ღონით, მაგრამ რაც უფრო ძლიერ უბერავდა, მგზავრი მით უფრო მაგრად
> ეხვეოდა ნაბადში. ბოლოს ჩრდილოეთის ქარი დაცხრა. ახლა მზემ გამოაბრწყინა და
> დააცხუნა. მგზავრმა ნაბადი მაშინვე მოიხადა. ამრიგად, ჩრდილოეთის ქარი იძულებული
> გახდა ედიარებინა, რომ მათ შორის მზე უფრო ძლიერი იყო.

Figure 1.2 Example of Georgian writing from *The North Wind and the Sun*.[2] *Source*: Shosted & Chikovani (2006).

---

[1] The International Phonetic Association, instituted in 1886, is a professional organization of phoneticians.
[2] This Aesop's fable, *The North Wind and the Sun*, is used by the IPA as a test passage, translated into the target language and then recorded. A range of recordings from the IPA's *Handbook* can be freely downloaded from http://web.uvic.ca/ling/resources/ipa/handbook.htm.

Ex 1.1

Look at the following short utterances written in Georgian:

(1) ნელა

(2) დალაქი

(3) გუდა

(4) ზარი

(5) ცერი

Unless you know the language and have learnt how to read it, you will not be able to read (1)–(5) above. However, once they are re-written, using *transcription* (based on broad phonetic symbols for Georgian) you will find you can easily begin to read them and say them aloud. You won't sound exactly like a native speaker of the language, but at least you can give it a try:

(1) [nela] *slowly*

(2) [dalaki] *barber*

(3) [guda] *leather bag*

(4) [zari] *bell*

(5) [tseri] *thumb*

Hint: [e] is similar to the sound in English *bed*, [ɑ] is similar to the sound in English *palm*. (Note the convention of placing phonetic transcriptions inside a pair of square brackets.)

A language more familiar to many of us is Italian. In Italian, *c(c)* followed by <a>, <u> or <o> reflects the [k]-sound (like the second sound in the English word *skin*). In English, however, this same sound can be spelled *c(c)* in *cake* or *occur*, *k* or *ck* in *kick*, *(c)q(u)* in words like *racquet, bouquet, unique, queue* (which starts [kj-] when we say it, as if it ought to be spelled <ky>) or *quiet* (which starts [kw-], as if it was spelled <kw>). But in phonetic transcription (sometimes also called 'phonetic spelling') every time you hear a [k]-sound, you write a k-shape – Italian *casa* would look more like <kasa> and English *cake, occur* and *kick* (provided we just concentrate on the [k] sound) more like <kake, okur, kik> while *racquet, bouquet, unique, queue* and *quiet* would be transformed into something more like <raket, bouket, yunike, kyue, kwiet>. Of course, there are still glaring problems in the English words, but the Italian example is now almost a proper phonetic transcription, [kasa].

The vagaries of English spelling were encapsulated once and for all by the spelling-reformer and playwright, George Bernard Shaw, who invited us to read the English word *fish* spelled *ghoti*: effectively a [f]-sound as at the end of words like *cough* or *enough,* followed by an [ɪ]-sound like the **vowel sounds** in *women* (the first of which, even though it sounds the same as the vowel in *sit*, is unhelpfully spelled with the letter <o>) and a [ʃ]-sound like the one at the beginning of *sharp* which we find spelled <ti> in *station*. If only we spelled as we transcribe, [fɪʃ] (*fish*), [kɒf] (*cough*), ['wɪmɪn] (*women*) and ['steɪʃən] (*station*) would all start to look much more straightforward and more directly related to what we actually hear when we say them.

> **Ex 1.2**
>
> **Try to work out what this sentence says. (Transcription is far more intuitive than spelling.)**
>
> [ɪf aɪ 'swɪtʃ ət ðɪs 'pɔɪnt tə fə'netɪk træn'skrɪpʃən | ju 'maɪt bi sə'praɪzd tə 'faɪnd ju kən 'stɪl 'riːd ə 'lɒt əv wɒt aɪ 'raɪt]

> **Ex 1.3** **This awareness of sound/spelling relations is behind the product name of an ice-cream called Phish Food. Can you explain this? How does it sound when we say it and why can the manufacturers spell it this way?**

1.1.3 Speech sounds

So far, we've taken for granted the concepts of *letters* on the one hand and (*speech*) *sounds* on the other. The short transcriptions in the above paragraphs look more or less transparent next to the orthographic versions of the words they represent. But there are some interesting differences in the two versions and these differences are a direct product of the fact that there are different sorts of speech sounds – the previous paragraph, for example, makes reference to 'vowel sounds'.

Speech consists of alternations between two major sound-types: vowels and **consonants**. In some orthographies, these two sound-types are represented systematically by vowel letters and consonant letters. In others, however, like English, there is some overlap. The sound on the end of *funny*, for example, is a consonant letter *y*, but when we say the word aloud, we pronounce a vowel sound, [i]. The next thing we need to do, then, is to make sure we can keep the ideas of letters and sounds separate (in other words, forget about spelling) and then to ensure that we can recognize some of the different types of sounds – consonants as opposed to vowels, and certain different types of vowel sound.

If we take the English word *women* that we looked at above, the alternation of sounds matches the clues we get from the spelling: consonant (*w* sounding [w]), vowel (*o* sounding [ɪ]), consonant (*m* sounding [m]), vowel (*e* sounding [ɪ] again), consonant (*n* sounding [n]). If we represent each consonant sound by C and each vowel sound by V, we can describe the pattern of this utterance as CVCVC and that matches what we saw in the transcribed form ['wɪmɪn]. Of course, it is always the case that different accents of English might have slightly different ways of pronouncing some of the sounds – especially vowel sounds – but for the moment, I will stick with what we might call the codified norm, **Modern Received Pronunciation** (MRP) or **Standard Southern British English** (SSBE) (Cruttenden (2008)). The actual pronunciation is not important here and regardless of the accent we have, the consonant and vowel categories of the sounds will be the same.

Some of the other examples have spellings which are much less closely related to the sound pattern: *cough*, for example. Here, although the spelling starts with a single letter *c* corresponding to the [k]-sound we identified which is a consonant sound, we can only hear one vowel-sound in this word (an [ɒ]-sound, like the sound in MRP *hot* or *off*), so we need to ignore completely the rather unnecessary *ou* spelling. The problem with the final *gh* has already been discussed – these letters reflect the single consonant sound [f]. So *cough* has the sound pattern CVC which parallels the phonetic transcription [kɒf].

Greater disparity can be noted in *station*. When spoken, the pattern we hear in this word is CCVC(V)C. Initial *st* is relatively unproblematic – we can identify a [s]-sound and a [t]-sound. But in many accents of English, including MRP, if you listen carefully to the next sound (represented in the spelling by *a*) it changes quality. That gliding or changing sound quality is a special sort of vowel, a two-part or two-sound vowel, technically called a **diphthong**. It is one kind of **complex vowel**. This changing quality is recognized in the transcription by a special two-part symbol [eɪ]. So far then, we have CCV-. The next two letters (a consonant letter *t* and a vowel letter *i*) have already been recognized as combining to represent a single consonant sound [ʃ]. So this leaves *on*. Here, there is another conundrum. If you go round listening to how people say this word, some use a vowel sound and finally a consonant sound, saying something like [ən] while others omit the vowel altogether and just say the last consonant, [n]. This gives us two possible sound patterns to listen out for: CCVCVC and CCVCC. Both variants are possible and both are recognisable and acceptable. (Vowels which do not glide, like the vowels in *women* or the vowel in *cough*, are single-quality vowels called **monophthongs** – monophthongs are **simple vowels**.)

Ex 1.4	Can you say which of the following words have a simple vowel (monophthong) and which have a complex vowel (diphthong)? (Your answer will depend on your accent, but non-native speakers are advised to stick to MRP.)			
1 beach	2 fine	3 pound	4 breeze	5 boy
6 day	7 head	8 young	9 through	10 no

Ex 1.5	Write the CV-patterns for each of the following English words:			
1 spin	2 cream	3 tomato	4 Spain	5 wrought
6 attack	7 psychic	8 cupid	9 Anglo-Saxon	10 announce

Clearly, it doesn't make sense to say that we speak using letters of the alphabet. We spell using them, but we speak using speech sounds or **phones**. The relation between these sounds and the alphabet letters used in romanized representations of languages varies in closeness. In English, although spelling can occasionally help, the relationship on the whole is often rather remote. When we are looking at the different sounds in specific languages, another name we often use instead of phone is **segment**.

Another feature of a language like English is that some pronunciations correspond to multiple spellings. We have words that look different but which sound exactly the same. Such words are called **homophones** (from Greek 'homo' *the same* and 'phone' *sound*). The plural of the letter name *C* (*Cs*) and the words *seas, sees* and *seize*, for example, are all pronounced [siːz] in MRP. Other examples would be *rowed* and *road* [ɹəʊd], *file* and *phial* [faɪl], *passed* and *past* which, again in MRP, would be something like [pɑːst], or *two, too, to* which could all be pronounced [tuː]. Worse still, we have words that look the same (called **homographs**) but which have more than one way of being pronounced – *bow,* for example, can be said [baʊ] if we are talking about bending from the waist, or the front end of a boat, but if we are talking about an elaborate knot in a piece of ribbon, or about a piece of musical equipment, then we say [bəʊ].

Ex 1.6	Say if the following word pairs are homophones or not in your accent.		
1 rain, reign	2 tense, tens	3 write, right	4 cue, Q
5 glace, glaze	6 age, H	7 frees, frieze	8 lock, loch
9 mouth, mouthe	10 way, weigh		

Ex 1.7	In many accents of English, each of the following words has at least one homophone – give examples.				
1 eye	2 tacks	3 stair	4 which	5 taught
6 site	7 bail	8 hi	9 awe	10 Y

1.1.4   Texting

In spite of the remoteness, spelling doesn't stop us from being very sensitive to sounds, even if we are not always responding at a particularly conscious level of awareness. The centuries' old **rebus** puzzles (using pictures and letters combined with plus and minus signs to encode words and messages) rely on this tacit awareness, as in Figure 1.3.

The same sort of phonetic awareness underpins texting. For many of us, texting is now part of our daily life. Our text messages show our phonetic awareness in two ways. The most obvious is the way we capitalize on homophones to reduce the number of letters we need to key into our message: R U comin 2 nite? Wil U B l8? (*Are you coming tonight? Will you be late?*) Such text messages capitalize on the homophonous pairs *R* and *are* (which can both be pronounced [ɑː]), U and *you* (pronounced [juː]), *2* and *to* ([tuː]), *B* and *be* ([biː]), and the patching of the letter *l* with the number *8* ([eɪt]) to coin *late* ([leɪt]). Together with our awareness of the possibility of g-dropping at the end of words like *coming* (giving the pronunciation often represented in literature as *comin'*), our understanding

Figure 1.3
Rebus puzzle: *I can hear you.*

that *nite* and the mis-spelled *wil* will be understood/pronounced exactly as if they were spelled *night* and *will* respectively, this is all part of our existing knowledge of phonetics.

We also know that when we send a *txt msg* our reader will supply correctly the missing sounds…

1.1.5 Talking

Far from clearly articulating every sound when we speak, in rapid informal talking, we tend to engage in a sort of verbal form of texting.

If I quickly tell someone *I'm going to be late*, what comes out is very unlikely to bear much resemblance to the **citation form** of each word that you might find in a pronouncing dictionary (a dictionary such as Wells (2008), for example, [aɪ æm 'gəʊɪŋ tuː biː 'leɪt] – see below for an explanation of the stress mark [']). Even at our most formal, we make all sorts of adjustments to this string when we speak – [aɪm 'gəʊɪŋ tə bi 'leɪt], for example (where [ə] represents the sound at the beginning of a word like *above* [ə'bʌv]). Much more likely, however, in rapid informal communication are extremely reduced variants such as [əm 'gənə bi 'leɪt] or even [əŋənəbə'leɪt].

What is amazing is that there is nothing wrong with a message like this at all and that in spite of its apparent remoteness from our starting point (the citation forms of the words) we still understand each other perfectly.

1.1.6 Syllables and stress

We also know one or two other things about the spoken form of our language. These are quite tricky linguistic concepts but for our present purpose it will be enough to remember what was learnt at school. We know something about the notion of the **syllable** and something about what phonetics calls **stress**. This knowledge often relates to studying poetry – giving lines of verse a particular **rhythm**, for example. We can only do that if we get the number of syllables and the number and distribution of stresses or rhythmic beats correct.

One of the best ways to illustrate how this works in English is to look at the structure of the **limerick**. Years ago, I taught for a time at the University of Reading and while there, my students wrote two limericks – one about phonetics and one about me! The one about me went:

> There was a young teacher of sounds
> Who from larynx to lips knew no bounds.
> Her whole oral cavity
> Caused enormous hilarity;
> The class laughed so much they lost pounds.

In discussions of poetry, you often see the rhythmic beats (the syllables on which you might tap your foot or clap your hands, if you were keeping in time to the rhythm) marked by an acute accent over the vowel: *There wás a young téacher of sóunds,* etc. Likewise, if you were asked to count the syllables, you might abstract the line as something like di-**da**-di-di-**da**-di-di-**da**, where each CV sequence represents a syllable and the stronger ones (the beats) have **da** while the weaker ones in between have di.

> **Ex 1.8   Continue identifying the stressed syllables in the limerick.**

> **Ex 1.9   Identify the stresses in the following limerick (the second written by my students).**
>
> When doing transcription in phones
> I tend to get lost on the tones.
> The stress is quite clear –
> Well, it is to my ear.
> Thank goodness for Daniel Jones.
>
> *(Daniel Jones, 1881–1967, was the founder of modern English phonetics and the first professor of phonetics in the University of London at UCL.)*

> **Ex 1.10   The limerick as a poetic form can be defined in terms of its rhymes and stress pattern. Use the data you have to explain the stress pattern of limericks.**

Now, if we look again at the line itself and try to work out its CV-structure as was done in Exercise 1.5, we will find:

There	was	a	young	teach er	of	sounds
CV	CVC	V	CVC	CVC-V(C)	VC	CVC(C)C
di	**da**	di	di	**da** di	di	**da**

Each one of the da's and di's lines up neatly with a single V in the real CV-structure which leads us to the idea: one vowel means one syllable. So, whatever still needs to be sorted out regarding the consonants (you will have noticed a couple of Cs with brackets round them), we can say that in English, this line has eight syllables. We can also say that three of them carry a rhythmic beat/stress. Phonetics has a special symbol for marking this prominence, called a **stress mark**. You will find it under Suprasegmentals on the IPA chart (page xiv) – a small raised vertical line – and this is placed immediately before the complete stressed syllable (not just the vowel, but also any consonants that satellite around it), giving: there 'was a young 'teacher of 'sounds.

Speakers of different languages perceive syllables differently, however. *Ice-cream*, which most native-speakers of English agree has two syllables (VC-CCVC), is often perceived by native-speakers of Japanese as having five! The same is true of the English seaside resort *Skegness* – two syllables for the average English holiday-maker, but five for a speaker of Japanese.

1.2   THREE TYPES OF PHONETICS

1.2.1   Articulatory phonetics

So far, we've been talking about speaking, saying words aloud, and thinking about how one word shares characteristics of pronunciation with another word, and so forth. We have explored some of the confusions that abound in English spelling and we have discovered what a lot we already know about phonetics. If we delve a little more deeply into what phoneticians do with this knowledge, we will find that there are generally three different approaches that can be taken or three different ways in which we can look at a speech sound and at speech.

Describing how sounds are made is the business of **articulatory phonetics** which informs theories of **speech production**. We know a lot about this and such knowledge lies behind the organization of the IPA chart (page xiv). Learning all about the articulation of speech sounds can sometimes seem a rather daunting proposition. But if you bear in mind that all you are doing is learning about the movements made by the tongue and lips and a certain amount about the anatomy of the inside of the mouth and throat – the vocal tract – then that can help to keep it all in proportion ... it is a minute fraction of the knowledge you would need to be a doctor, for example!

Moreover, you will find that you already know some articulatory phonetics. What is necessary is to learn some new vocabulary in order to be able to verbalize your knowledge, and to become more aware of movements, gestures and feelings in your vocal tract that we otherwise take for granted.

Ex 1.11

1. Look in a mirror and repeat several times *ba-ba-ba...*, then *ma-ma-ma...*, then *pa-pa-pa...*. What can you see happening to make the consonant sounds [b], [p], [m]? Describe this.
2. Repeat the sequence *la-la-la* several times. You probably won't be able to see much this time, but think about what you can feel when you make the [l] sound. Describe this.
3. Go back to the sequences in 1 above. Gently pinch your nostrils and then say the three sequences again. Do you notice anything different? Try to describe what you notice.

Making accurate descriptions of the production of speech sounds can sometimes be done from first principles – extrapolating from our knowledge of the articulatory organs and linking this to what we can see, hear and/or feel. Sometimes, though, we may rely on physical measurements of one sort or another in order to clarify or confirm what we suspect is happening. A very useful account of such possibilities can be found in Ladefoged (2003).

Articulatory phonetics is the most widespread type of phonetics taught, underpinning both other types (acoustic and auditory), and is studied not only by linguistics students but also by students of speech and language therapy, many language students as well as some medical students, voice students, drama students, and students of singing, to name but a few.

1.2.2   Acoustic phonetics

One aspect of the instrumental measurements we can make of speech sounds is related to physics and involves measuring sound waves – the invisible part of speech, the disturbances in the air between us that are caused by the actions of the speaker and which are picked up or heard by the ear of the listener. Acoustic measurements are often used to support articulatory and auditory judgements.

Acoustic measurements can be made fairly easily these days using a computer, microphone and freely downloadable software such as **WASP** or **Praat**. Such programs enable us to process recordings of speech and analyse the waveforms in great detail. The branch of phonetics that deals with the physical nature of speech sounds is called **acoustic phonetics** or the **physics of speech**.

Ex 1.12   **If you have a chance, download one of these programs from the internet and make a short recording (say *pa ba ma*, for example, from Exercise 1.12 or record your name) and then have a look at the different pictures the program can create. Look at the speech waveform, the wideband spectrogram, and the Fx or pitch track, for example. The URLs are:**

1.   for WASP: http://www.phon.ucl.ac.uk/resource/sfs/wasp.htm
2.   for Praat: http://www.fon.hum.uva.nl/praat/

Many specialisms require knowledge of acoustic phonetics, from psychology through speech therapy and pronunciation training, to forensics. Increasingly today, interactive displays based on speech waveform analysis are being used in the classroom by language teachers to assist in fine-tuning pronunciation of foreign learners of languages (although, of course, all applications are also dependent on some knowledge of other types of phonetics as well).

1.2.3   Auditory phonetics

Listening to speech sounds and thinking about exactly what they sound like is something many phoneticians do routinely as part of their work. It can be called **auditory phonetics** and it underpins much of practical phonetic training or ear-training. This is useful because it also serves to remind us that speech isn't just something we produce but also something we hear and pay attention to, listen to. So phonetics is interested just as much in how we hear or perceive what is said as in how we say it in the first place. Another dimension of auditory phonetics is the study of **speech perception**.

In a linguistics degree, students might expect to undertake auditory phonetics in the form of ear-training, alongside production practice, learning to identify and make all the sounds of the IPA chart for themselves. This is useful for linguistics fieldwork, speech therapy, accent coaching, language teaching, and so on. In a psychology degree or an audiology degree, ear-training as such has little direct relevance and students tend to study the hearing mechanism (audiologists) and the effects of sounds on the brain (psychologists, neurologists, etc.); in such instances, it is the more theoretical dimension, the theory of speech perception, that is central.

1.3   ACCENTS AND ATTITUDES

1.3.1   Accents

While dealing with preliminary matters, it is worth spending a few moments thinking about regionalisms in speech, how we all sound different, and about our attitudes towards this variety.

Although this is not a book about accents (there is a large literature on this subject: Wells (1982); Foulkes and Docherty (1999); Hughes, Trudgill and Watt (2005), etc.), accents are an endless source of interest to people, and describing them is obviously a phonetic exercise. The two most widely described and documented English accents are MRP and **General American** (GAm); phonetics books published in the UK tend to use MRP as the English language accent of illustration while those published in the United States use GAm. This book will use mainly MRP.

Our accent is often largely determined by where we grow up. This is true of almost any language. By virtue of going to school in London, I ended up with a very different accent from my immediate family who came from the north of England. I had the same accent as them until I went to school and then, after a few years, my speech habits matched to those of my peer group (and were different again from the regional accent associated with the locality in which I then lived, suggesting that not only region but also class contributed – my first school was a private school). My accent now is mainly MRP.

What this shows us is that while accents are principally thought of as being a geographical phenomenon, they are also socially conditioned. Geographically, they are an independent part of a dialect – independent in the sense that a person might comply with the rules of standard English regarding grammar and lexis but may still speak with an accent.

Socially, an accent is often conditioned by some form of peer pressure - pressure to conform, for example, in the playground or the club, in much the same way as complying with dress code or the latest fashion. Younger people in particular do not want to stand out. Instead, they want to identify with the group they aspire to belong to and sounding the same when they speak is one way of achieving this. Indeed, this may be partly behind the new **Multicultural London English** dialect (MLE) and its pronunciation which is shared by an ethnically diverse speech community.

1.3.2   Attitudes

Accents may also be conditioned by a more negative form of pressure – we could call this 'desirability'. People vary enormously in their reaction to different accents. At its most extreme, they love or hate the way another speaker sounds. The English have a fondness for Welsh, Irish and Scottish-English accents; they are less well disposed to some of the English urban accents, however. While the former are often perceived as desirable and the speaker with one of these accents becomes a desirable person, some urban accents are regarded as much less desirable and their speakers are regarded negatively as a consequence. There is a certain amount of prejudice around which is triggered by how we speak – **accent*ism*!**

The crucial point here, however, is that unless we are using phonetics as a means to an end in a study of phonaesthetic judgements, for example, phonetics is not about evaluating accents or making any kind of judgement about them. It is not the job of phonetics to say how a language should be spoken; phonetics is in no way **prescriptive**. Phonetics is a **descriptive** discipline. The role of phonetics is simply to describe what is pronounced, nothing more and nothing less.

1.4 PHONETICS AND PHONOLOGY

1.4.1 The relationship

Phonetics and **phonology** are indissolubly linked but whereas you can study phonetics without ever really going into phonology, phonology is closely dependent on phonetics for the data on which it relies to prosecute its arguments (Gussenhoven and Jacobs (2005)).

For example, both GAm and MRP can be said to have two p-sounds. There is the p-sound in *pin* and the p-sound in *Spain*. If you say these aloud or listen carefully to a native-speaker of either of these accents saying these words, you will hear an h-sound following the p-sound in *pin* (we represent this as [pʰɪn] in phonetic transcription – note again the use of square brackets to show the reader that this is, indeed, a phonetic transcription) but there is no h-sound in *Spain* (which accordingly looks different when transcribed, giving [speɪn]). Careful analysis of lots of similar examples will confirm that in words like *pin, pear, pot, pie, Peter*, speakers of these two main accents pronounce [pʰ] while in words like *Spain, spin, spare, spend, spy*, they pronounce just [p]. This is a phonetic description of the pronunciation.

However, I can switch these two variants round and say *[pɪn] and *[spʰeɪn] (linguistics uses a precursive asterisk to denote a non-grammatical form) without changing the meaning of either of the words. This means that [p] and [pʰ] must have something in common because if I replaced the p-sound with a t-sound, then the meaning would change because I get *tin* and *stain* ([tʰɪn] and [steɪn]). This is of great interest to phonologists. Evidence like this enables them to conclude that although there is more than one way of pronouncing it (the phones [p] and [pʰ] are just two of many), English has actually only got one p-unit, one overarching unit that can bring about a change of meaning and includes these two variants. They call this unit a **phoneme** and the different ways in which it can be pronounced are its **allophones**. We can therefore say that MRP and GAm have a phoneme /p/ (note how the brackets have changed – phonemic transcription is distinguished from phonetic transcription by being enclosed in slant brackets) which is realized in a number of different ways, including the allophones [p] and [pʰ]. This also permits a more simple transcription of *pin* and *Spain*, /pɪn/ and /speɪn/; the way in which /p/ is actually pronounced doesn't affect meaning and so we don't need to show all the detail at this level. We are therefore able to keep the citation form of words (the form given in a pronunciation dictionary) simple. Phonology is thus dependent on phonetics, but one step more abstract. Phonetics is an extremely concrete discipline, by comparison.

1.4.2 Pronunciation dictionaries

There are a number of these on the market. The one used as a reference source for this present text is written by John Wells (Wells (2008)). Called the *Longman Pronunciation Dictionary*, this dictionary is often referred to by phoneticians as the LPD. If you look up the words *Spain* and *spin* you will find transcriptions which are identical to those given above. If you look up some longer words, you will also find information about syllables (this dictionary leaves a space between syllables to show you where the boundary falls) and stress. Even without knowing any more phonetics, you can look up the transcribed form of almost any English word, discovering the pronunciation of the word if you don't already know it.

Ex 1.13	Look up the following words in LPD. Copy the transcriptions given and see if you can figure out the most common way of pronouncing them in MRP. (The first variant is always the most usual form; if a double bar occurs in the entry, ‖, what follows is GAm pronunciation.)

| 1 anemone | 2 Wroclaw | 3 BBC | 4 inculpatory | 5 exit |
| 6 unknown | 7 Legh | 8 once | 9 oleic | 10 cholla |

Ex 1.14	Field Notebook: Phonetics in One Word

Entry 1 To use the theory you have just learned, you can write a Field Notebook, applying your knowledge to the detailed phonetic description of the word *completes*.

Go to www.routledge.com/cw/ashby for instructions and feedback.

1.5 SUMMARY

- Even without training, we have extensive passive knowledge of phonetics in general and of the sound system of our language in particular; this knowledge is an extremely valuable resource.

- We need to cultivate active awareness of both the similarities and the differences between speech and writing.

- When we set out to study phonetics more deliberately, we learn to make conscious this passive knowledge and to describe sounds from the articulatory, acoustic and auditory viewpoints.

- We need to be aware that speakers belong to different speech communities and have different accents. All accents are equal to the phonetician although it is helpful to make descriptions and comparisons against a widely available codified norm when dealing with a specific language.

- Phonetics inputs to phonology. Phonology streamlines all the detailed phonetic data about the pronunciation of a language, grouping variants into phonemes (more abstract units that cause a change of meaning).

Ear-training

Once you have studied this chapter carefully, continue the development of your practical skills by attempting the ear-training exercises for this chapter, available as recordings at www.routledge.com/cw/ashby.

FURTHER READING

Further very simple introductory accounts to speech and phonetics can be found in many phonetics textbooks, including: Chapters 1 and 2 in Ashby (2005); Chapter 2 in Ladefoged (2001), which also explains the different transcription conventions used by American and British authors; and Chapter 1 in Ashby & Maidment (2005), Lodge (2009) and Cruttenden (2008).

Cruttenden (2008) also introduces the idea of the phoneme and the place of phonetics in linguistics. Linguistics textbooks, too, often cover this ground. For an example, see Chapter 1 of Fromkin *et al.* (2006), but be aware that this volume uses an American system of transcription, so symbols will not always match those you find in British publications. At a more advanced level, you might enjoy reading Part 1 of Laver (1994).

The role of the laryn›

Introducing the sources of sound used in speech, this chapter begins a journey through the vocal tract, starting at the bottom with the larynx or voice box as it is known in lay terms. This structure (visible only as our Adam's apple) houses the vocal folds, responsible for voicing sounds (Aah!) or making them voiceless (Shh!), for creating different voice qualities (termed 'normal', 'creaky', 'breathy', etc.), for making the pitch of our voices go up and down (an ability we use to the full in intonation), and even for being a specific place in the vocal tract where we make certain recognizable speech sounds.

2.1 WHAT IS THE LARYNX?

We need to start this description with a small amount of anatomy. For general linguistic purposes, a small amount is enough.

You often see the **larynx** (a term familiar to us from when we lose our voice and are told we have *laryngitis*) described as a box made of cartilages. To an extent, this is true. Figure 2.1 shows this box-like structure made up of cartilaginous 'walls'. The front wall is the **thyroid cartilage**, or 'shield cartilage' in lay terms, which is responsible for the 'Adam's apple' (the thyroid prominence) and which is located at the front of your neck. The reason for the name 'shield' is not just because of its protective role, but also because the cartilage itself has depth (top to bottom) and curves round at the sides, reminding us of the appearance of a riot shield. Behind the thyroid prominence, on the inner surface of the cartilage is the anchor point for the front ends of the **vocal folds**.

The thyroid cartilage is located at the top of the **trachea** or 'wind pipe' – the cartilaginous tube that channels air in and out of the lungs. (You may have heard of a disorder of the trachea called *tracheitis*.) The trachea itself is constructed by superimposed, incomplete rings of cartilage, open at the back (like inexpensive jewellery rings that we can squeeze to fit our fingers and which have an opening on the underside) which are sheathed in a membrane, completing the tube-like effect and preventing air from escaping. The very top cartilage, however, is different. It is a complete circle and is known as the **cricoid cartilage** or 'ring cartilage' in lay terms. Again, this lay terminology has a reason: the cartilage reminds us of a signet ring – the wider part of the band (corresponding to the visible face where the initials would be engraved on a piece of jewellery) is located

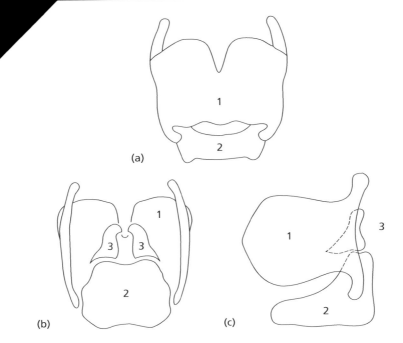

Figure 2.1
The larynx structure (a) front view (b) rear view (c) side view. *Source*: Laver (1980: 100).

at the back of the trachea and narrower band (corresponding to the underside of the ring) at the front.

The thyroid cartilage locates above the narrower, front face of the cricoid cartilage (which now becomes the foundation or open 'floor' of the box) and curves around the sides, leaving an opening at the back in which two further cartilages sit, above the wider part of the cricoid cartilage ring, making, effectively, a rear wall. These are the **aretynoid cartilages** – a matching pair of small rather triangular or pear-shaped cartilages which constitute the back anchor point for the vocal folds – one attached to each fold.

The vocal folds – fleshy folds of tissue – have depth (like the thyroid cartilage, to which they attach at the front) and are effectively hung like a pair of very substantial curtains across from the front to back of this structure. Muscles attaching to the aretynoid cartilages move these in various directions and are the main force for positioning the folds in an open (**abducted**) or closed (**adducted**) position. When open, the space between the folds is called the **glottis** (visible in the third frame of Figure 2.2).

This whole structure is the larynx, the cartilaginous housing with the internally positioned folds.

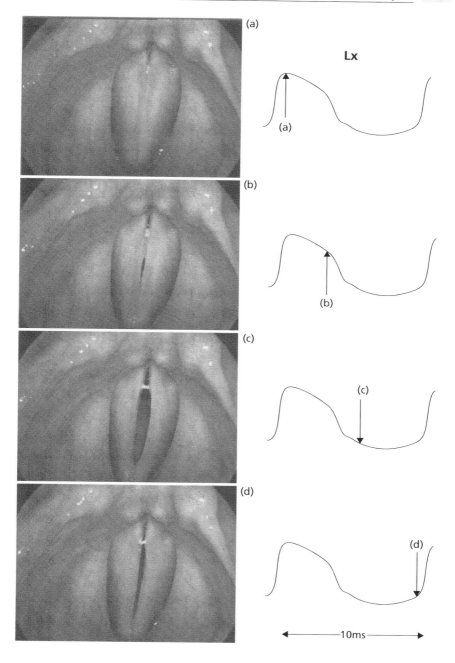

Figure 2.2
(a) – (d) The vocal folds. *Source*: Laryngograph Ltd.

2.2   THE LARYNX AND VOICE

2.2.1   The egressive pulmonic airstream

The larynx, or more specifically the interaction between the vocal folds and the **egressive pulmonic airstream**, is responsible for **phonation**, the **sound source** which is termed **voice** in speech.

In Chapter 1, we talked about speakers and listeners. The very fact that the listener can hear speech depends on the presence of a moving stream of air. If I hold my breath and then go through the motions of talking, that is all it is – going through the motions. There will be nothing meaningful to hear because the articulatory movements are gratuitous. As long as I am holding my breath and no air is leaving my body, I am just miming the articulations and there is nothing for the movements to act on and modify and no energy to carry these effects to the listener's ear.

> **Ex 2.1**   **Try it – hold your breath and at the same time 'say' something. You may hear your lips or tongue making faint percussive sounds, but you certainly won't hear speech.**

Various airstreams are used in speech but the basic one, used in every single language, is the egressive (moving outwards) pulmonic (from the lungs) airstream. When we speak, we first inhale, filling our lungs with air, and then we engage in something reminiscent of what swimmers call 'trickle breathing'. We expel the air in a carefully controlled fashion at a rather slower rate than if we were just breathing out for normal breathing. This maximizes the air and allows us to speak for some time without needing to breathe in again. The expulsion is controlled or regulated by action of the muscles moving the diaphragm and by the various pairs of muscles that act on the rib cage (principally here, the sets of intercostal muscles).

The pathway for the airstream is thus: out from the lungs, up the trachea and via the larynx into what are called the **supraglottal cavities** (the cavities above the glottis: the **pharynx** (the throat), the **oral cavity** (the mouth) and the **nasal cavity** (the nose) which collectively form the **vocal tract** (the part of our body in which vocalization – speech – occurs). You can see the whole of this pathway in Figure 2.3.

2.2.2   Normal voice

How we sound for the greater part of the time when we are speaking a language like English is a function of what is variously called **normal**, **chest** or **modal voice**. Normal voice is the result of the vocal folds vibrating in a particular way. For this to happen, as soon as the speaker has inhaled, the aretynoid cartilages draw the folds (and themselves) together but not so tightly that they cannot be forced open by the pressure exerted by air which is then expelled from the lungs.

The vocal folds, remember, have depth. The aretynoids cause them to close in depth, like a pair of curtains with the edges touching all the way from top to bottom as in the first diagram in Figure 2.4. When the egressive pulmonic airstream reaches the bottom, it is strong enough to start pushing the folds apart from the

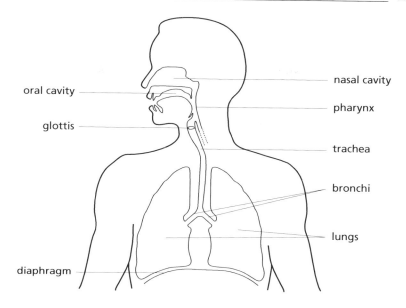

Figure 2.3
The vocal tract – a pathway for pulmonic egressive airflow.

bottom edge and, gradually, it pushes them apart in depth as it reaches the top of the obstruction. It is acting against the force being exerted by the aretynoids in doing this – remember, they are trying to hold the folds together, touching each other. (You can follow these stages in the second and third diagrams in Figure 2.4.)

When the air finally escapes out of the top, it is rather like when we push and push against a resistant object (trying to push a broken down car, for example, or open a stuck door). When the object finally gives, we momentarily move forward at faster than normal speed. The airstream does this, too, and the effect is to leave behind it a momentary drop in pressure in the fully re-opened glottis. This means that the

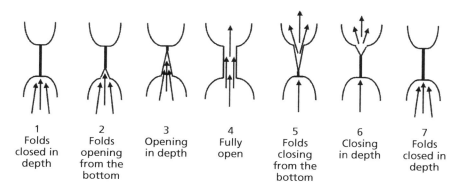

Figure 2.4
The vibratory cycle for normal voice.

effort being made by the aretynoids is now strong enough to enable the folds to close again. Elastic recoil brings the bottom edges back together (that is where the pressure drop is first felt) and then the effect passes up the folds to the top, bringing them back together in depth. This is a complex process which I have deliberately simplified – the pressure drop means there is also a small suction effect (known as the **Bernoulli effect**) that reinforces the drawing back together of the surfaces – but this essentially describes the process of the production of normal voice. (These final stages are depicted in the last three images in Figure 2.4, where 1 and 4 correspond to frames (a) and (c) in Figure 2.2.)

What we have put into words is just one **cycle** of vibratory activity. If we count these cycles (using a speech analysis program such as WASP or Praat, for example), we find that they repeat on average 100–120 times per second for adult male voices and 200–240 times per second for adult female voices. In children, it can be as many as 300 times per second. We hear this as **pitch** when we listen to speech and deliberately varying the rate of vibration of our vocal folds makes our voices go up and down in pitch, adding **intonation**. Basically, the faster the rate of vibration, the higher the pitch of the voice. In physical terms, we talk about the **frequency** with which the cycle repeats and this measurement is expressed in **Hertz** (**Hz**). One Hz is one cycle per second. An average male voice, therefore, has what we call a **fundamental frequency** (**Fx**) of 100–120 Hz (that is, 100–120 cycles per second), while the Fx of an average female is about an octave higher at 200–240 Hz. This movement is too fast to see with the naked eye although it is possible to film it using a stroboscopic (intermittent) light source; it has a beautiful undulating appearance. (Films can be accessed on the internet.)

The cycle produces a rather triangular looking waveform, called the **larynx waveform** (**Lx**) the shape of which can be seen in Figure 2.5. The gentler angle in the opening phase is indicative of the exertion required to push the folds apart (meaning the movement is slower, occupying more time), while the sharper angle on the closing phase is indicative of the much quicker drawing back together when the sudden drop in pressure occurs and no resistance is offered. (Compare this with the images and annotated waveform in Figure 2.2.) The repeated shape shows that Lx is what is called a **periodic waveform**. Periodic waveforms are ones in which an identifiable pattern repeats through time and we can count the repetitions. As we've just said, this pattern repeats at different average rates depending on the age and gender of the speaker.

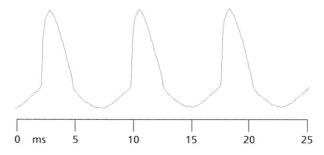

Figure 2.5
The larynx waveform for normal voice. *Source*: Laryngograph Ltd.

The presence or absence of voice makes an important difference between speech sounds and later on we will see that the periodicity we have just identified as being a characteristic of Lx will be evident in all voiced speech sounds.

Ex 2.2   Rest your fingers lightly against the front of your neck and describe exactly what you can feel when you perform the following activities:

1. Open your mouth and sigh, making a sort of h-sound.
2. Say a long, slow *aah!*
3. Say *ssh!* and then imitate the sound of a snake, making a long drawn out s-sound.
4. Imitate the sound of a bee, making a long drawn out z-sound.
5. Make a long drawn out m-sound.

Almost certainly, while doing this exercise, you will have detected a buzz or vibration against your fingers for 2, 4 and 5 but nothing at all for 1 and 3. 2 invites you to make a vowel sound, and if you compare this with any other vowels you can think of, you will find that they all tend to buzz. What this tells us is that vowels almost always have vocal fold vibration. We call them **voiced** sounds.

The rest of the sounds you tried were all consonant sounds and the presence or absence of buzz will have varied. This is because some consonants are voiced, like the vowel sounds (in this exercise, you can tell that m-sounds and z-sounds are both voiced), while others are produced using an open glottis which makes them buzz-free, or **voiceless**.

We can distinguish some consonants from each other simply by comparing voicing. In English, for example, *pan* with a p-sound at the beginning is different from *ban* with a b-sound – the meaning of the word is changed by whether or not the vocal folds vibrate at all in the first segment. Another such pair is the s-sound in, for example, *Sue, racer* or *bus* and the z-sound in *zoo, razor* or *buzz*. This is common in a huge number of languages: French, for example, has p/b contrast (*pain* (bread) and *bain* (bath)), and f/v contrast (*fin* (end) and *vin* (wine)), etc., Dutch also has a p/b contrast (*pak* (suit of clothes) and *bak* (bin)), a t/d contrast (*tuin* (garden) and *duin* (dune)), and so forth.

Ex 2.3

1. Try to say a prolonged s-z sequence, not moving your mouth or stopping, but just switching voicing on and off to change from the s-sound to the z-sound and back to the s-sound again: sssssszzzzzzzsssssszzzzzz
2. Once you have managed this, try it with f-v.
3. Try switching on the voice while saying *ssh!*
4. Try to prolong the sound at the beginning of MRP *think* – is it voiced or voiceless? Make the sound and then change the voicing... does MRP have this new sound or not? (If yes, find a word where it is used.)

This dichotomy is reflected in the IPA chart (page xiv). In the main table, you will see that some cells have two symbols in them while others only have one. In the very first cell, you can see the symbol [m]. This represents the m-sound in a word like *Mummy*. It is located at the right-hand side of the cell and this is the location associated with voiced consonants. The fact that there is nothing at the left-hand side of this cell is interesting. It tells us that almost all m-sounds are voiced; although we can easily make them, languages rarely use voiceless ones. Because of that, the IPA does not need to provide a special symbol for a voiceless m-sound and the space at the left of the cell is empty.

In the cell below, however, you will find [p b]. This tells us that the only basic difference between a p-sound and a b-sound is in terms of voicing (we can hear this in English if we compare the name *Harper* with voiceless [p] between the vowels with *harbour* which has voiced [b] in the intervocalic position, although in other positions in English words, the difference becomes less clear-cut). For our present purposes, though, we can quite correctly say that the p-sound on the left of the IPA chart cell is voiceless while the b-sound on the right is voiced. The fact that both options are represented means that this is a contrast which is widely used in languages and so two different symbols are definitely needed.

Ex 2.4   **Look carefully at the Consonants (pulmonic) table within the IPA Chart on p. xiv and find six more examples of sounds that are typically only voiced and six more examples of sounds that are commonly found in voiceless/voiced pairs.**

Ex 2.5   **Note that from now on, if you are in any doubt about the way in which words are pronounced by speakers of MRP, you should consult a dictionary such as Wells (2008). (This book endeavours to follow the advice offered there.)**

1.   Which of the following utterances begins with a voiceless consonant?

1 phial	2 banana	3 heartache	4 pneumatic	5 embargo
6 knock	7 charade	8 Xerox	9 write	10 honest

2.   Which of the following utterances have a voiceless consonant between the two vowels?

1 easy	2 clothing	3 pleasure	4 mission	5 breathy
6 leather	7 racer	8 tougher	9 classy	10 fever

3.   Which of the following utterances have a voiceless consonant at the end?

1 rays	2 worse	3 wise	4 faces	5 breathe
6 off	7 does	8 cloth	9 dose (of medicine)	10 of

Ex 2.6   **Take the utterances in Exercise 2.5.3 and change the voicing of the last sound. Which ones are still proper English words and which words do they become?**

Example *hers* ends in a voiced sound; if this becomes voiceless, we get the word *hearse* (the car that carries the coffin at a funeral).

Ex 2.7 Take the list of symbols used for transcribing English (page xiii) and divide the consonants into two sets, voiceless and voiced.

Ex 2.8 Change the voicing of the underlined consonants. Say them aloud – which new English word do you get?

1 beg	2 wait	3 few	4 chump	5 thy
6 lacy	7 reviews	8 bigger	9 fuzzy	10 etching
11 fleece	12 cart	13 ice	14 ridge	15 host

Ex 2.9 Go through the following text and identify all the voiceless consonants.

I love reading the little cameos in the National Trust magazine about its various properties. Some of the names are wonderful. Polesden Lacey, Quebec House, Orford Ness. And then there's Canons Ashby House. I wish that was *my* address! A delightful Elizabethan manor house.

Ex 2.10 Try to match the voiceless consonants in Exercise 2.9 to the correct symbols on the list of symbols for transcribing English (page xv).

Example [t] in *little*, [k] in *cameos*

A final practical skill here is to make **voicing diagrams** which show the switching on and off of the voice. These are a form of **parametric diagram** which record the action of the vocal folds. The vibrations associated with the presence of voicing are represented by a zig-zag line and voicelessness is shown as a flat line (schematically representing a speech waveform). Utterances are divided into columns with one column per segment, as in the voicing diagram for *chintzy* (Figure 2.6).

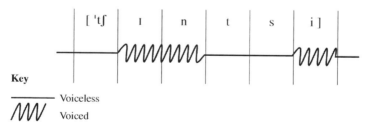

Figure 2.6
Parametric diagram showing vocal fold action during production of the utterance '*chintzy*'.

Ex 2.11 Draw voicing diagrams for each of the following utterances. (Check the transcription of each item in Wells (2008) first and then check the voicing status for each sound against your answer for Exercise 2.7.)

1 ether	2 sobbing	3 misty	4 laughter	5 umbrella

2.2.3   Creaky voice

Normal voice is just one way in which the vocal folds can be made to vibrate. There are several other so-called states of the glottis utilized in speech production. Another is the setting required for a different phonation type called **creaky voice** (see Figure 2.7). Some languages exploit this phonation type deliberately, but in English you will only hear it routinely as a function of extremely low pitch. Having said that, for some speakers of English, creaky voice is part of their idiolect. Some speakers tend to cultivate a very 'creaky' way of speaking. You will encounter it particularly if you listen to female speakers of American English. Americans refer to this sound as **glottal fry** and the quality is sometimes an indicator of social status. The big differences between creaky voice and normal voice are that the vibratory cycles tend to be irregularly spaced in creaky as opposed to regular in normal voice and that the frequency is always very low.

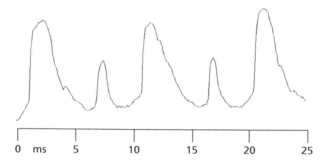

Figure 2.7
The larynx waveform for creaky voice.

To produce creaky voice, the adjustment of the folds made by the aretynoids is a little bit different. This is represented in Figure 2.8. The folds are still drawn

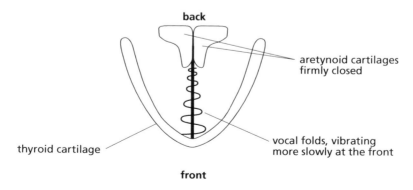

Figure 2.8
The glottal setting for creaky voice.

together, but they are allowed to vibrate very slowly at the front (near where they attach to the thyroid cartilage). If this happens on its own, with the rest of the folds remaining closed, you hear a sound termed creak. However, when the rest of the length of the folds continues to vibrate normally, this becomes what is called creaky voice. You can try this out by speaking as low as you possibly can and then try to go even lower – this generally results in creaky voice.

The table of **diacritics** on the IPA chart (page xiv) provides a symbol that can be used to indicate creaky voice – a **tilde** placed below a symbol. So, if I wanted to show voice quality changes that might occur in English when I say a long drawn out exclamatory *Aah!* with the pitch going from high to very low in my voice range, I can transcribe this using the vowel symbol [ɑ], starting with normal voice (so, nothing to add to the basic symbol) and turning into creaky voice, [ɑɑ̰] (with the tilde placed below the second half of the vowel). (Note that the two symbols joined by an over-tie diacritic here show that the vowel is continuous and rather long in duration.) Diacritics, then, are small additional symbols that are added to the main symbol shapes to modify the sound being represented.

Languages which use creaky voice systemically are rare but it is found in a number of north African languages, the most well-known of which are probably Hausa and Margi (both spoken in Nigeria). These have been documented by Ladefoged who describes the phenomenon as **laryngealization**, demonstrating, for example, a contrast such as Margi [jà] *to give birth* and [j̰à] *thigh* (where the change in meaning is brought about entirely by the addition of creaky voice to the [j]-sound (like the first sound in English *yes* [jes])) or [bábál] *open place* and [b̰áb̰àl] *hard* (Ladefoged 1971:15). (Note that the accents above the vowels are **tone marks**, with the acute accent representing a high tone and the grave a low tone; these can also be found on the IPA chart, page xiv, under the heading Suprasegmentals – Tones and Word Accents).

Creaky voice is also used in Danish where it is responsible for the linguistic characteristic known as **stød** in which a short interval of creaky voice affects the end of certain longer vowel sounds or **sonorant** consonants (see page 62) when they follow shorter vowels. Sonorant consonants are typically those which appear as 'voiced only' entries in the IPA chart (m-sounds, n-sounds, l-sounds, vowels, etc.). The Danish phonetician, Fischer-Jørgensen (1985: 59) gives examples where the meaning of a word changes when creaky voice is added: [vɛn] *friend* but [vɛ̰n] *turn!* (imperative), [du] *you* but [dṵ] *tablecloth*, etc.

2.2.4   Breathy voice

Whispering and sighing are forms of breathiness, but these are also voiceless. To achieve this effect, the aretynoids draw the folds together, closing the folds themselves firmly, so that they resist the pressure from the egressive pulmonic airstream, but maintaining a gap between the two cartilages to enable the air to escape continuously at this point.

Breathy voice, however, is produced when the closure of the folds is less firm and the airstream not only escapes continuously between the open aretynoids, but also sets the folds vibrating (see Figures 2.9, 2.10). You might expect to hear this exceptionally if someone is speaking while a bit out of breath, but in English it also occurs fairly routinely in rapid speech when the h-sound is used between two vowels in words like *ahead* or *behind*. This voiced h-sound has its own symbol: [ɦ]. (The ordinary voiceless h-sound is represented by [h].) Breathy voice is also occasionally referred to humorously as 'the voice of passion' and is, again occasionally, idiolectal in that it is a quality cultivated deliberately by some female celebrities.

Breathy voice is also used systemically in a number of languages and is especially characteristic of many of the Indo-Aryan languages (such as Hindi, Bengali, Gujarati, Urdu and Assamese) which have series of so-called **murmured** consonants (**voiced aspirates** is another name for these). Gujarati also has breathy-voiced or murmured vowels which contrast with plain (normal voice) vowels. Ladefoged provides some examples (from Gujerati) of the way these change meaning, including the group [bar] *twelve* (where the utterance is made up of plain, non-murmured sounds) but [ba̤r] *outside* with a breathy voiced or murmured vowel and [bʰar] *burden* with a breathy voiced or murmured consonant. (Breathy voice is indicated in transcription of vowels by the diaeresis diacritic being placed below the symbol representing the affected sound; this can be found on the IPA chart, page xiv, in the Diacritics table.)

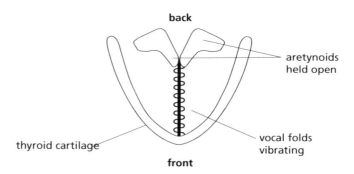

Figure 2.9
The glottal setting for breathy voice.

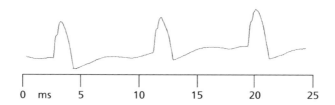

Figure 2.10
The larynx waveform for breathy voice.

2.3 THE LARYNX AS A PLACE OF ARTICULATION

A detailed account of place of articulation is the focus of the next chapter, but for now suffice it to say that such places are points in the vocal tract where a gesture is made that results in a particular speech sound. The glottis is one such place and sounds made by the glottis are called **glottal**. You will find symbols associating with glottal articulations in the very last column of the pulmonic consonant matrix on the IPA chart (page xiv).

We have already mentioned the different h-sounds that are used in English – the regular voiceless [h] as in *hello, here, hot* (see Figure 2.11) and the voiced version of this, [ɦ], heard in words like *ahead, behind* and *rehearse*. At the same time, the glottal setting for [ɦ] was described (open aretynoids and vibrating vocal folds). To produce the voiceless variant, a different setting is required in which the folds and aretynoids are drawn near to each other, but not touching, leaving a very small space between them such that as the egressive pulmonic air forces its way through, it becomes turbulent or 'disordered' and makes an h-sound. (This feature, too, is described in more detail later.)

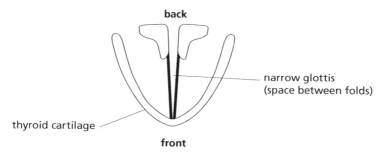

Figure 2.11
Glottal setting for [h].

Figure 2.12 represents a further possibility when the aretynoids and the folds are held together so firmly that they resist the pressure exerted by the pulmonic air

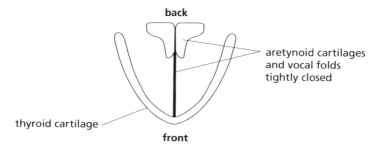

Figure 2.12
Glottal setting for [ʔ].

which becomes trapped below in the sub-glottal space (in the trachea, in fact). When this happens, we articulate the sound known as the **glottal stop**. This is widely used and will be found in languages across the world. It is very characteristic of all London Englishes (Cockney, MLE, Estuary) and is often represented in literature by authors attempting to create an impression of such accents by replacing certain *t*'s with an apostrophe as in *wha' a lo' of ho' wa'er* (*what a lot of hot water*). The process involved here has an extremely graphic name: **t-glottalling** (see page 43 for more about this.)

Like the h-sounds, the glottal stop also has its own symbol, [ʔ]. (Don't confuse this with a question mark – there is no dot at the bottom.)

2.4   THE LARYNX AS A PITCH MODULATOR

We have already talked about pitch and its relationship to the rate of vibration of the vocal folds. Languages exploit this in two principal ways.

Some languages use it to make distinctions between different words. This is a lexical use of pitch and such languages are called **tone languages**. Tone languages are found all over the world, but they are particularly prevalent in East and South-East Asia where you find all the different Chinese languages (Modern Standard Chinese, Cantonese, Hokkien, etc.), Thai, Burmese and so forth. Tone languages are also found in Africa (Hausa, Zulu, etc.) and in the Americas where some of the indigenous American Indian languages are tone languages (Navajo, Chatino, etc.).

How lexical tone works can be illustrated by this example from Thai. For a single syllable [kʰaː] (which sounds a little bit like the English word *car* spoken with an Australian accent), the pitch on which the syllable is spoken changes and for each different pitch pattern, there is a different meaning. Standard Thai has five tones: high [ˉ], mid [>], low [_], rising [/], and falling [\], so [kʰaː] spoken with a high tone, [ˉkʰaː] means *to get stuck*, but with a low tone, [_kʰaː] it means *galangal* (a ginger-like spice). When it is spoken using the mid tone, [>kʰaː], it becomes the first person singular pronoun, *I*, with a rising tone, [/kʰaː], it means *to engage in trade* and with a falling tone, [\kʰaː], *leg* (after Tingsabadh and Abramson (1999)).

In a language like English, pitch changes map over a longer phrase (called the **intonational phrase**). Here, a falling tone *car* gives the listener the impression of a statement (*it is a car*) while a rising tone /*car* is more likely to be interpreted as a question (*is it a car?*). The same syllable spoken with a mid tone >*car* sounds as if the utterance is incomplete (maybe the speaker forgot what they were going to say next), and so on.

2.5   VOICE AND THE IPA CHART

If you have completed all the exercises in this chapter, you will already be familiar with the representation of the voiceless/voiced opposition in the IPA chart. We said that: sounds whose articulation is identical except for the behaviour of the vocal folds, like a p-sound and a b-sound, for example, are represented in a single cell on the IPA chart. This represents all the shared characteristics but by placing the pair, as appropriate, on the right and the left of the cell reflects presence and absence of vocal fold vibrations. So, symbols at the left of the cell represent voiceless sounds and those at the right represent voiced ones. As we also said earlier, in some instances, because the voiceless version of a particular articulation is very rarely used in languages, the voiceless half of the cell is left blank. In one instance (at the top of the last, glottal column in the main table), the voiced part is not only left blank, but it is also shaded out. This indicates that it is physiologically impossible to voice this sound – you will recognize the symbol as the glottal stop which we have described as requiring an articulatory setting such that the folds are held tightly together and resist pressure from the egressive pulmonic airstream. It follows, therefore, that they cannot simultaneously vibrate and so no voicing can be produced – [ʔ] cannot be voiced.

Should it be necessary to transcribe a voiceless sound when there is no symbol provided, the IPA chart offers us a zero-voicing diacritic – a tiny zero which is placed below the symbols for the voiced sound and effectively renders this voiceless. So, [m] is the voiced sound at the beginning of *my*. If I wanted to transcribe a voiceless one of these (some languages, Burmese for example, do have voiceless m-sounds), I would need to put the tiny zero underneath the symbol: [m̥].

Whether a consonant sound is voiceless or voiced is extremely important and always features in the name of the sound. It is the first element in what are known as Voice-Place-Manner (VPM) labels. The next step will be to supply information to fill the remaining place and manner slots.

Ex 2.12   Field Notebook: Phonetics in One Word

Entry 2 Use the theory you have just learned in order to continue writing your Field Notebook, applying your knowledge to the detailed phonetic description of the word *completes*.

Go to www.routledge.com/cw/ashby for instructions and feedback.

2.6   SUMMARY

- This chapter has addressed the question *what is the larynx?* It has described the larynx structure and identified two crucial speech organs: the vocal folds and the glottis.

- We have explored the concept of voicing, introducing the voiceless/voiced dichotomy and looking at some different phonation types.

- The glottis as a place of articulation was discussed.

- The role of the larnyx in the production of tonal contrasts and intonation (including the relation between measurable frequency and perceptual pitch) was explored.

- The representation of voice in the IPA chart was explained and this was also linked to Voice-Place-Manner labelling of consonants.

Ear-training

Once you have studied this chapter carefully, continue the development of your practical skills by attempting the ear-training exercises for this chapter, available as recordings at www.routledge.com/cw/ashby.

FURTHER READING

Further elementary study of the voice and the role of the vocal folds in speech production can be found in: Chapter 2 of Cruttenden (2008); Chapter 3 of Ashby (2005); Chapters 2 and 6 of Ashby & Maidment (2005); Chapter 2 of Lodge (2009); Chapter 4 of Ogden (2009); and Chapter 7 of Laver (1994).

Discussion of phonation types can also be found in Chapter 6 of Ladefoged (2006). Much more advanced here is Laver (1980).

3

Place of articulation

This chapter introduces the organs of speech, studying how these relate to the concept of place of articulation. A distinction is made between active and passive speech organs. Places are rather like 'ports of call' around a coastline. In speech production, these 'ports' or places are the passive articulators found along the upper surface of the vocal tract – they always stay in the same position, they cannot move. They are 'visited' by active articulators. Specific reference is made throughout to the sounds represented in the pulmonic consonant matrix on the IPA alphabet chart.

3.1 THE ORGANS OF SPEECH

3.1.1 The vocal tract

The speech organs in which we are primarily interested here are found in the supra-glottal cavities – the cavities immediately above the glottis. After flowing between the vocal folds, the first space the egressive pulmonic airstream enters is the pharynx, otherwise known as the **pharyngeal cavity** (or **pharyngal** cavity – both variants will be found in the literature, although the IPA chart uses *pharyngeal*). This is your throat, of course, but the more technical term tends to be familiar because of the diagnosis *pharyngitis* when we have a sore throat.

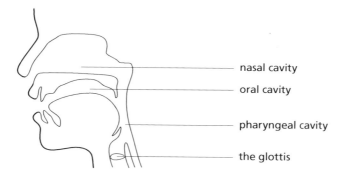

Figure 3.1
The supraglottal cavities.

At the top of the pharynx is a choice. At this point, the airstream can enter and pass through one or both of the nasal and oral cavities – the nose and the mouth. The oral cavity is bounded on the visible, outward side by the lips.

It is worth noting that the primary function of the so-called speech organs is not speech production at all, of course! Each contributes first and foremost to our survival, enabling breathing, biting, chewing and swallowing amongst other things. The fact that we have also learnt to use them to communicate is ingenious and fascinating.

Within the supra-glottal cavities, the different parts of the anatomy (identified in the X-ray image reproduced in Figure 3.2) have names used by phoneticians to identify **places of articulation**. Before going ahead with a more detailed explanation of place, it is worth learning the basic terminology, learning the names.

3.1.2   Active and passive articulators

A quick glance at Figure 3.2 reveals two types of speech organ: organs we can move (often voluntarily and in a controlled fashion) and organs that are fixed or stationary. In speech terms, these are referred to respectively as **active articulators** and **passive articulators**.

The idea of voluntary movement is particularly relevant to the oral cavity where the moveable or active organs associate mainly with the lower jaw while the immovable ones associate mainly with the upper jaw. In phonetics, all this information is usually represented in diagrammatic form, in drawings we call **vocal tract drawings**. Figure 3.1 above is an example of this tradition.

The technical name for such a drawing is **mid-sagittal section** – a slice straight down the middle of the speaker's head going from back to front (rather than side to side). This book will use the more transparent name, vocal tract drawing, however. All phoneticians learn to reproduce such diagrams when representing the juxtaposition of the different articulators for any given consonant. (Vowel sounds, as we will see later, are generally represented by a different sort of diagram.)

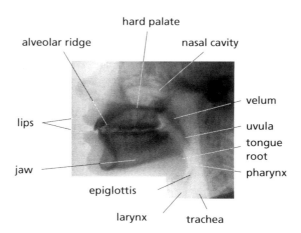

Figure 3.2 The vocal tract. *Source:* Ashby (2006: 365).

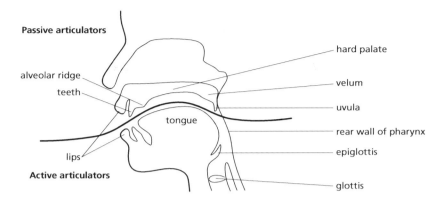

Figure 3.3
Vocal tract drawing showing active and passive articulators.

In Figure 3.3, we can see that most of the organs above the wavy line are fixed, passive points in the structure of the tract. The organs below are generally moveable – some are extremely flexible (like parts of the tongue) while others are less so (the tongue root and epiglottis).

3.1.3   The tongue

The extreme flexibility of the tongue makes it inappropriate to treat it as a single organ of speech. Certain parts of the tongue can move relatively independently of each other and it is best to regard each part as a separate active articulator. Accordingly, we can see from Figure 3.4(a) that from the tip (visible when you stick your tongue out) to the root (invisible) we need to distinguish six different parts. The **tip** (technically the **apex**, the pointed termination of this highly complex muscular structure) and the **blade** (the bulk immediately behind the tip) are the unattached portion. Behind these, where the tongue starts to be anchored to the floor of mouth, is what we call the **front**. You can quite easily see the front when you open your mouth and look in the mirror. The last visible part, underneath the velum at the back of your mouth, is actually called the **back** and the term **centre** can be used to describe a mid-way point between the front and the back. Invisible, and forming the front wall of the pharynx, is the most firmly anchored part of all, the tongue **root**.

Even these six divisions, however, are not quite enough. In Figure 3.4(b), a view of the tongue from above, the **side rims** are labelled. These, too, can be voluntarily moved and this ability is also exploited in the production of speech sounds. Further flexibility derives from the possibility of creating depressions of various types, usually described as **grooved**, down the **central line** of the tongue (also called the **median line** or the mid-sagittal line), so this too needs to be recognized and has been identified and labelled in Figure 3.4(b).

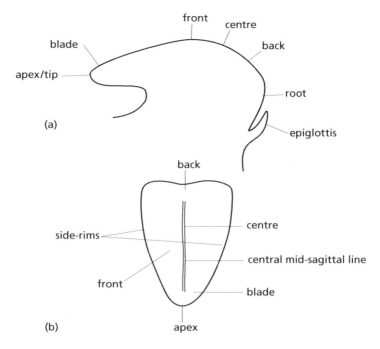

Figure 3.4
Mid-sagittal (a) and superior (b) views of the tongue.

3.2   THE PRIMARY PLACES OF ARTICULATION

3.2.1   Identifying places

For the greater part, places of articulation are (passive) points along the upper surface of the vocal tract which are approached (and sometimes actually contacted) by the corresponding active articulator during the production of a speech sound. When the speech organs are in the rest position, there is an inherent alignment between points on the upper and lower surfaces, and the 'corresponding active articulator' means the moving articulator on the lower surface of the vocal tract that is in an inherent relationship with the point on the upper surface.

> **Ex 3.1**   **Sit quietly for a moment with your mouth shut, relax and breath through your nose. Try to describe exactly what you can feel inside your mouth—what is happening with the articulators.** *Try this before you read on.*

Generally, people find that the **lower lip** is in contact with the **upper lip** and, for many speakers, is also lightly in contact with the upper incisors (the upper front **teeth**). There may be a slight gap between the upper and lower teeth, but the jaw is clenched sufficiently to keep the mouth shut. The **tongue tip** is often touching the back of the lower incisors and the part immediately behind the tip can be felt against the bony ridge behind the upper incisors (the **alveolar ridge**). You will probably also note that the edges or **side rims** of your tongue are in contact with the upper and/or lower molars and that the tongue feels large enough to fill most of the oral cavity. The fact that you are breathing through the nose while you feel all this demonstrates that the velum and the glottis are both open – there is an unobstructed passage from the nostrils to the lungs. This is the **rest position**. (For more information about the behaviour of the velum, see Sections 4.1.1 and 4.1.2.)

3.2.2 Place names

Another important idea that is visible in Figure 3.3 is this inherent alignment between the active and passive articulators that we have just implied in the description of the rest position. The lower lip and incisors are immediately below the upper lip and incisors (regardless of whether the speaker's mouth is open or closed). Likewise, the tip of the tongue (the bit you can see if you stick your tongue out just a small amount, technically termed the apex) is at the back of the incisors. (Remember that in the rest position we felt the lips touching and the tongue tip down behind the lower front teeth.)

If we now consider the remaining parts of the tongue (identified in Figure 3.4), we can see that the (active, moveable) blade is directly below the (fixed, passive) alveolar ridge and the area immediately behind it, the **postalveolar** area; behind that, the front of the tongue is below the **hard palate**; the centre lines up approximately below the intersection where the palate changes from hard to soft; the back is below the **soft palate**, or **velum**, and adjacent to the **uvula**; the root is opposite the rear wall of the pharynx. These relationships are taken for granted when we start to delineate what we call place of articulation.

Basically, a place of articulation is any passive point that is approached or contacted by its relevant active organ. The place names in Figure 3.3 correspond to the places identified along the horizontal axis on the IPA chart (see Figure 3.5).

Only the most common articulatory places are represented in this matrix. One place not included is the infrequently used, and therefore rather rare place, **epiglottal** (see below). Its rarity and its often close association with the adjacent location **pharyngeal** enable the IPA to economize on space required for the matrix and epiglottal sounds will be found under the list of **Other Symbols**. Another is the equally rare **linguolabial** or **apico-labial** gesture (see below).

3.2.3 A summary of active to passive relationships

These gestures can be tabulated and illustrated using sounds represented in the IPA alphabet as in Table 3.1.

As we can see from these summaries, the tongue is exceptionally flexible. For this reason, it rarely makes sense to talk about it as a single organ of speech. Although we do not make overt reference to the moving part when describing articulations, it is essential to get used to thinking about the tongue in terms of its various

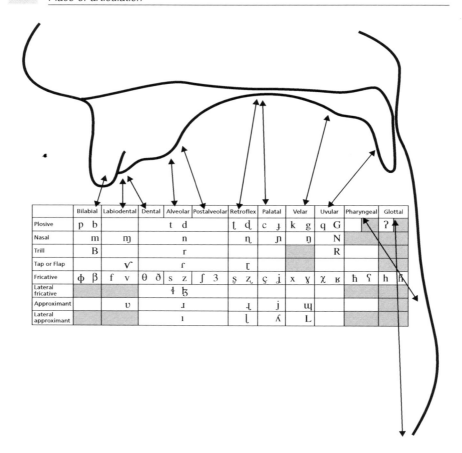

Figure 3.5
Alignment of vocal tract with the horizontal axis of the IPA chart.

different parts. The tip and the blade, for example, can move fairly independently of the main body of the tongue. They can move forward towards the front teeth, protrude between the teeth, retract slightly, even curl over backwards. Just as Table 3.1 explains that 'retroflex' is a sort of shorthand for *apico-palatal,* so 'dental' is shorthand for *apico-dental* and velar for *dorso-velar,* etc. The side rims, too, have some independence. They can rise to contact the upper molars or remain low on one or both sides at the same time. Additionally, any part of the upper surface of the main body of the tongue can rise up towards whichever part of the roof of the mouth – the palate – is above, rising from just a small amount to a movement sufficient to bring the active part into complete contact with the passive articulator.

What must be understood here is that the tongue as a single mass does not move backwards and forwards in the mouth. Tongue body movement involves mainly vertical movements (upwards and downwards) of different points along the upper surface of the organ, including the side rims.

Table 3.1
Places of articulation

Articulators	Place of articulation	Examples (from MRP unless otherwise stated)
Passive: *Active*:	BILABIAL	[m p b] as in *mum, pop, bib*
Passive: upper incisors (front teeth) *Active*: lower lip	LABIODENTAL	[f v] as in *fife, viva*
Passive: upper lip *Active*: tongue tip	LINGUOLABIAL	Tangoa [t̼] (*Extremely rare sound*)
Passive: upper incisors *Active*: tongue tip	DENTAL	[θ ð] as in *think, the*
Passive: alveolar ridge *Active*: tongue tip and/or blade	ALVEOLAR	[n t d s z l] as in *nine, tot, dad, sauce, zoos, loll*
Passive: rear of the alveolar ridge *Active*: tongue tip	POSTALVEOLAR	[ɹ] as in *red roses*
Passive: hard palate *Active*: tongue tip (Note *the tongue tip is stepping out of line here, away from the inherent rest-position relationship between active and passive articulators*)	RETROFLEX (Note *This rather impressionistic term is used instead of the literal place names such as:* apico-palatal, sub-apico-palatal, etc.)	[ɭ] (GAm r-sound)
Passive: hard palate + rear of alveolar ridge	PALATOALVEOLAR (*Sub-category of Postalveolar*)	[ʃ ʒ tʃ dʒ] as in *sheepish, pleasure, church, judge*
Active: front + tip/blade of tongue *Passive*: front of hard palate + rear of alveolar ridge	ALVEOLOPALATAL (*These sounds are represented under 'Other Symbols' on the IPA chart.*)	Polish [ɕ ʑ] Serbian [tɕ] Japanese [dʑ]
Active: front of tongue *Passive*: hard palate *Active*: front of tongue	PALATAL	[j] as in *yes*
Passive: soft palate (velum) *Active*: back of tongue	VELAR	[ŋ k g] as in *sing, kick, gag*
Passive: uvula (= extreme end of soft palate) *Active*: back of tongue	UVULAR	French [ʁ] German [ʀ]
Passive: rear wall of pharynx *Active*: root of tongue	PHARYNGEAL	Arabic [ʕ] (the *ayn*)
Passive: aretynoid cartilages *Active*: epiglottis	EPIGLOTTAL	Agul [ʜ ʡ] (*Extremely rare sounds*)
The vocal folds	GLOTTAL	[h ʔ] as in *ho'*

3.3   THE IPA CHART

3.3.1   Labial articulations

The passive places on the horizontal axis of the IPA pulmonic consonant matrix (the large grid at the top of the IPA chart) can be grouped by active articulator. The first two columns, **bilabial** and **labiodental**, rely on the active contribution made in particular by the lower lip. This is the phonetic information that phonologists rely on to define the feature [LABIAL]. Bilabial means 'both lips', whereas labiodental (again deriving from Latin) means 'lip-teeth'.

Universally, we can say that virtually all languages have bilabial sounds. (There are only four, possibly five, exceptions to this – all are indigenous North American Indian languages discussed by Maddieson (2008c) – Tlingit, Chipewyan, Oneida, Wichita and, depending on interpretation, Eyak.) It is also true that this very simple gesture is easily mastered and is one of the first recognizable sounds produced by infants in the process of speech acquisition.

Whereas in bilabial articulations, the lower lip approaches the upper lip, in labiodental articulations, the lower lip moves up to form a relationship with the upper front incisors (Figure 3.6). These are both primary articulatory gestures and no participation by any other articulator is involved. (The exact nature of the relationships between the pairs of articulators here and at all the other places of articulation will be described in the next chapter when we look at manner of articulation.)

Ex 3.2   **The following words are among the first 50 or so words that children learn to pronounce when they are acquiring English. A lot of them have labial articulations. Put a ring around each one that contains a labial consonant. (If you are unsure, think about what you can feel and watch yourself in the mirror as you say each word aloud.)**

ball	dog(gie)	give	bye-bye	cat
sit	baby	all-gone	Mummy	up
peep-o	no	yes	shoe	bikkie/biscuit
more	Daddy	milk	stop	down

In how many of the words have you spotted a labiodental sound?

The lips are independent of gestures made elsewhere in the vocal tract and for this reason can **coarticulate** (articulate at the same time) with gestures made at other places, perhaps to add lip-rounding, for example.

Ex 3.3   **Watch yourself in a mirror as you say the word *see-saw*. Pronounce it very carefully, at a slow speaking speed. Compare the two s-sounds and describe what you can see happening at the lips. *Do this before you read on.***

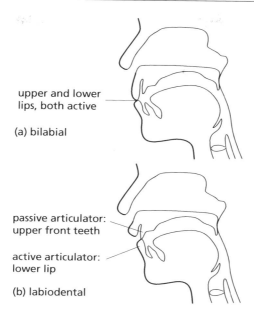

upper and lower
lips, both active

(a) bilabial

passive articulator:
upper front teeth

active articulator:
lower lip

(b) labiodental

Figure 3.6
Diagrams showing the juxtaposition of active and passive articulators in (a) bilabial and (b) labiodental articulations.

If you watch carefully in the mirror, the chances are that you will notice the lips behave a little differently, being more neutral (even a bit spread in contour) in the *see* syllable and moving towards a more rounded shape in the *saw* syllable. If that happens, we say the [s] in *saw* is labialized (has added lip-rounding) which we symbolize by adding a diacritic in the form of a superscript [ʷ]: [sʷ]. We will return to this idea later.

3.3.2 Lingual articulations

3.3.2.1 Coronals

The tongue, as we have said, is immensely complex and flexible. It is not surprising, therefore, to find that it participates in a range of different articulations. As we have already seen, each part of the tongue has an inherent relationship with different passive articulators and these relationships will now be seen to result in the production of different groups of sounds. Gussenhoven and Jacobs (2005: 7) note that the American linguist, Clements, refers to the tip and blade of the tongue together as the **crown**. The British tradition here, however, follows IPA terminology and refers always and only to the tip and the blade. However, the notion of 'crown' allows phonologists to group together all the articulations made with the tip and/or blade of the tongue and to identify them by the single feature [CORONAL].

Such thinking also appears to motivate the grouping of the next three columns on the IPA chart. You will notice, if you look, that there is a large column embracing dental, alveolar and postalveolar and that this is only overtly subdivided into the three specific places in one row, the row labelled 'fricative'.

The grouping of these three places in this way and the provision (except for fricatives) of only one symbol (or one pair of symbols) in each row is motivated by the fact that, in general, languages tend to select one (or maybe two) of these places rather than using and contrasting all of them. Multiple symbols in most rows, then, would be superfluous, **redundant**. Most English accents, for example, use an alveolar t-sound (tongue tip on the alveolar ridge) in *tea, otter, sit,* whereas French usually makes the sound at the dental place (tongue tip to the back of the upper front teeth) as in *thé, auteur, cette* ('tea', 'author', 'this'). Given that neither language contrasts a dental-t with an alveolar-t, the one symbol will suffice. In Irish English, however, many speakers will use both varieties – in an expression such as *thin tin*, you will find the pronunciation of the first word begins with a dental-t and the second with an alveolar-t. So, since the IPA chart only provides one symbol, if we want to show this difference we need to apply a diacritic to change the basic place value of the symbol. [t] can be thought of as the average value here, a voiceless alveolar sound (located to the left under the alveolar column heading). To move this forward to the dental position, we add what is often called the **dental diacritic** (technically 'subscript bridge', following Pullum and Ladusaw (1986)) which looks like a tiny drawing of a tooth, below the basic t-symbol: [t̪]. This can be done to any alveolar symbol to show that the primary constriction between the tongue tip or blade and the passive articulator is with the (back of the) upper front teeth rather than with the alveolar ridge itself. The Irish English pronunciation of *thin tin*, therefore, would look and sound something like [t̪ɪn tɪn].

It is also worth noting here that the basic alveolar symbols can be used to represent postalveolar articulations by applying a **retracted** diacritic which is, effectively, a minus sign placed beneath the symbol. So, [t̠] is a voiceless postalveolar sound. (This is actually what happens when we articulate the t-sound in *try* – you may be able to feel this yourself if you say the expression *try Thai,* slowly and carefully and think about what you can feel at the very beginning of each word – concentrate on where the tip of your tongue touches the roof of your mouth.)

Ex 3.4	Say the following English words to yourself and see if you can work out the place of articulation of the first consonant. Also decide whether the sound is voiced or voiceless.

(Not everyone will get exactly the same answers – sometimes the place of articulation will depend on your accent.)

see	taste	mnemonic	do	ride
think	zoo	date	that	brown
look	never	moon	please	Thomas
cease	xylophone	pink	view	physics

Ex 3.5 Try saying the following short text aloud and see if you can feel the various alveolar consonants – identify them as you go. You may even be able to retrieve the phonetic symbol for the sounds from the alveolar column on the IPA chart (in the pulmonic consonant matrix).

David told Tina the date of the next outing to London Zoo. He'd like it if she was able to meet up with them there for a photo shoot. It would be a good chance to get some new photos for the noticeboard at the club.

3.3.2.2 Dorsals

Referring back to Figure 3.4 again, we can see that the main body of the tongue (where the muscle starts to be more fully attached to the lower jaw and begins to lose some of its flexibility) is divided by phoneticians into the front, centre and back. These are again grouped by phonologists and described as sharing the feature [DORSAL]. Dorsal articulations are much less visible to the observer, occurring further back in the vocal tract, using the palate as the passive articulator and including palatal (the front of the tongue articulating with the hard palate), velar (the back of the tongue articulating with the soft palate or velum), and uvular (the back of the tongue again, but this time articulating with the uvula).

As we saw with the coronal articulations, the precise point at which a gesture is made may be retracted or advanced from the primary position indicated by the symbol. Within this group of sounds, that is particularly true of velar articulations. To experience this for yourselves, say the phrase *car key* slowly and thoughtfully, concentrating on where you can feel the tongue making contact at the back of the mouth; then compare *car* with *cot*. It is certainly the case that you will feel the contact a bit further forward along the palate for *key* than for *car*. We can thus describe the variant of [k] in *key* as being **advanced**. This time, we will use the regular **advanced** diacritic, placing a small plus sign below the main symbol: [k̟]. For many speakers, too, there is different feedback in terms of point of contact for *car* and *cot* – the contact in *cot* may be slightly more retracted, [k̠]. This gives us a range from what is often called **pre-velar** [k̟] through velar proper [k] to **post-velar** [k̠] (this last with the retracted diacritic beneath the main symbol). More detailed distinctions of this kind are possible for most places of articulation. All these different lingual gestures can be seen in Figure 3.7.

Ex 3.6 Can you think what is wrong with the notions *pre-bilabial* or *post-glottal?*

Ex 3.7 English has five consonants made by the tongue body – these are velar [k] as in *cake*, [g] as in *gag*, [ŋ] as in *king*, palatal [j] as in *yes* and labialvelar [w] as in *want*. Can you spot these dorsal articulations in the following text?

I hear you took a taxi to Loch Ness from where you were staying. Did you get any sightings of the monster? Did you go on the boat trip? You get some beautiful views doing that. Michael took loads of photographs with his new Pentax when we went. I think it's an excellent excursion.

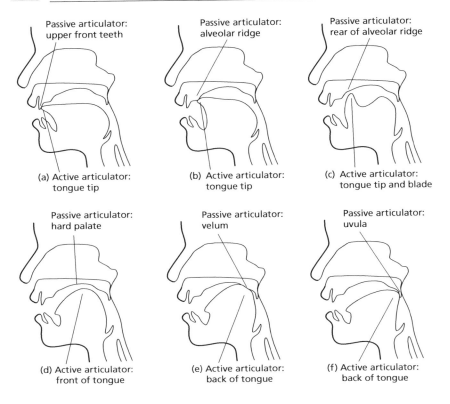

Figure 3.7
The juxtaposition of active and passive articulators in lingual articulations: (a) dental, (b) alveolar, (c) postalveolar, (d) palatal, (e) velar and (f) uvular articulations.

3.3.2.3   Radicals

The term **radical** refers to the root of the tongue and as the name implies, like any root, very little movement can occur (Figure 3.8). The tongue is pretty firmly fixed at this point and such movement as there is results from tensing and relaxing the muscles that essentially form the front wall of the pharyngeal cavity. Such gestures are required to produce pharyngeal consonants. These are quite rare sounds in the world's languages, being most commonly found in Afro-Asiatic languages such as Arabic, Somali and Tigre. They are also found in at least one Amerindian language, Nootka, several Northwest Caucasian languages including Kabardian, the Dhagestanian language Lak, and in the Indo-European Kurdish.

A further place of articulation in the radical region is **epiglottal**. These sounds are even less widespread than pharyngeals. Some data collections (Maddieson (1984), for example) include no epiglottals at all while others (Ladefoged and Maddieson (1996)) cite only two languages, Agul (a Daghestanian language) and Dahalo (Afro-Asiatic, spoken in Kenya). The IPA chart provides for three different epiglottal sounds. However, because of their rarity, no column is allocated in the main matrix and, instead, the representations are listed under the Other Symbols section of the chart.

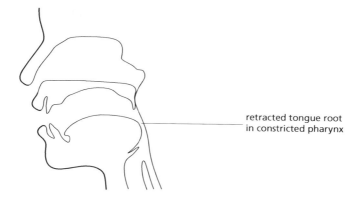

Figure 3.8
Shows retracted tongue root in constricted pharynx.

3.3.3   Glottals

In addition to the roles of the larynx as a sound source producing voice of different types and as a pitch modulator (described in Chapter 2), the glottis also functions as a place of articulation. Sounds produced in the larynx, at the glottis, are identified by phonologists by the feature [LARYNGEAL].

Two possible glottal speech sounds are well-known. They are the h-sound, [h], and the sound often called the glottal stop or the *glottal catch* that is so characteristic of popular London speech (represented orthographically by an apostrophe: *wha' a lo'* (*what a lot*) or *wa'er* (*water*), for example) and transcribed [ʔ]. Whether or not a speaker of English uses these sounds tells us something about their accent – popular London, for example, tends to be an **h-dropping** accent (meaning speakers don't pronounce the [h] at the beginning of words like *here, house, who*), but it makes wide use of the glottal stop, regularly replacing t-sounds at the ends of syllables with it (*what* [wɒʔ], *fit* [fɪʔ], *winter* ['wɪnʔə], etc.). Replacing final t-sounds by [ʔ] is called t-glottalling.

Ex 3.8   Use the following sentences to begin to find out about your own accent of English.

1.   Listen carefully to yourself as you say the following sentence aloud. Try to decide whether you have an h-pronouncing or an h-dropping accent:

Harriet hit Henry hard over the head with her* handbag.

2.   Listen carefully again and say the following sentence aloud to decide whether or not you are a speaker who makes regular use of t-glottalling:

There are quite a lot of little streets in the centre of Stratford.

* Note that anybody can drop the h-sound at the beginning of this word – this is not accent-dependent.

3.4 OTHER PLACE-ASSOCIATED VARIABLES

3.4.1 Apical and laminal

What cell entries in the IPA chart do not show is that coronal gestures can be made by either the tip or the blade of the tongue, described respectively as **apical** and **laminal** articulations. In spite of being closely linked anatomically, the tip and the blade are able to articulate separately with any one of these three passive points. This already makes for an increased range of articulatory variation that is not immediately visible from the chart itself: apico-dental and lamino-dental, apico-alveolar and lamino-alveolar, apico-postalveolar and lamino-postalveolar.

This added subtlety is useful when attempting to characterize between-speaker differences in the realization of the s-sound in British English accents, for example. The difference lies in which part of the tongue they use to articulate with the alveolar ridge. Some make this with an apico-alveolar gesture, while others use the blade of the tongue, making a so-called laminal [s] with a lamino-alveolar gesture, [s̻]. Although it is true to say that probably only one known language, Basque, relies on this distinction to make a contrast (change the meaning of an utterance), the IPA still makes it possible to be absolutely precise in transcription about which gesture is in question. Use of the **subscript box** diacritic as in [s̻] indicates laminal, and use of the **subscript inverted bridge** diacritic as in [s̺] indicates apical.

Ex 3.9	Say the following (adapted) tongue twister aloud to yourself, slowly, and try to determine whether you are making an apical gesture or a laminal gesture when you articulate the s/z-sounds:
Sister Suzy's sewing suits for sailors.	

3.4.2 Dental and interdental

Although adequate for the distinctions needed to answer the questions in Exercise 3.4, the distinctions between dental, alveolar and postalveolar places are still not quite enough.

While we are able to describe how the vast majority of speakers of British English varieties make the th-sound at the beginning of *think* – speakers of most British varieties of English tend to use the tongue tip against the back of the upper front teeth in a straightforward apico-dental gesture – we cannot yet describe how many speakers of American English (especially those from the Midwest and West Coast) articulate this sound. Midwesterners are recorded as having the tip protruding slightly between the teeth in an **interdental** gesture (Ladefoged (2001)). There is no specific way of symbolizing this difference which is not known to be used to make an actual contrast in any language. However, it can be argued that since the interdental gesture uses the surface of the tongue blade against the upper front teeth rather than the absolute tip, there is therefore an apical *vs* laminal distinction here ([θ̺] *vs* [θ̻]), rather like the variation noted for [s]-articulations at the alveolar ridge. Midwestern American pronunciation is laminal compared with British accents which are apical.

Ladefoged and Maddieson (1996:15) demonstrate interdental (lamino-dental) by means of an advanced diacritic, a subscript plus, [t̟]. However, while capturing the degree of advancement, this fails to express overtly the laminality of the gesture which can be captured overtly by use of the subscript box diacritic.

3.4.3 Linguolabial

This same reliance of the IPA pulmonic consonant matrix on inherent active-to-passive relationships also means that it does not capture another extreme (albeit rare) gesture of which the very flexible tip and blade of the tongue are capable. This is the linguolabial gesture, where the tip or even the blade of the tongue steps completely out of its inherent relationship with the upper front teeth and the alveolar ridge and protrudes sufficiently to contact the upper lip. Each, separately, can articulate with the upper lip at the labial position. In Table 3.1, Tangoa (one of just a handful of languages, all of which are spoken in Vanuatu) was mentioned as using the linguolabial place of articulation.

The IPA provides the **subscript seagull** diacritic to represent this extreme gesture, placing it beneath the basic alveolar symbol such that [t̼] represents a voiceless linguolabial sound (See Table 3.1 and Table 3.2).

Ex 3.10	Use a mirror to help you try out the range of tongue-tip gestures, starting with [tɑː] (like English slang *Ta!*), then dental [t̪ɑː] (or [θɑː] if you can't manage a t-sound here yet), interdental [t̟ɑː] (or try [θ̟ɑː] first, if you find this one is also a bit tricky, and then gently increase the pressure of the tongue on the teeth) and lastly, linguolabial [t̼ɑː].

3.4.4 Retroflex

Interestingly, the IPA pulmonic consonant matrix does include one non-aligned gesture, in the column headed retroflex. Retroflex sounds are much more common than many of the other consonantal gestures that we have just been talking about and because of this, they need to be included explicitly in the pulmonic consonant matrix. For sounds made in this column, the tip and blade of the tongue are curled up and back-over in such a way that they articulate with the hard palate. A more transparent name for this would be apico-palatal. However, as we have said, place names do not, in general, make overt reference to the active articulator, only to the passive target. By coining the very graphic name *retroflex* the IPA has been able to identify this group of sounds using a single term, just like all the other places along the horizontal axis of the chart. The difference, of course, is that unlike all the other names (which identify specific locations), this one describes a type of gesture or movement being made by the tongue. Retroflexion may involve the use of either the upper or lower surface of the tongue tip and/or blade.

Retroflex consonants are particularly characteristic of many Indo-Aryan and Dravidian languages (Hindi and Bengali, Tamil and Toda, for example) as well as typifying the Standard Indian English accent. The General American r-sound is also often quite retroflex in nature.

Whereas linguolabial was the most forward (or **anterior**) gesture made by the tip and blade of the tongue, retroflex is the backmost (or most **posterior**). The full range of coronal possibilities, summarized in Table 3.2, is described and illustrated in much greater detail in Ladefoged and Maddieson (1996). In particular, there is a huge range of variation at the retroflex end of this scale. The most back extreme illustrated here, Toda, involves complete curling over of the tongue to articulate with the underside of the blade against the hard palate, sub-lamino-palatal. There are, however, many degrees of retroflexion before this extreme is reached.

Table 3.2
A simplified summary of coronal possibilities

Place:	linguolabial	interdental	dental	alveolar	postalveolar	retroflex
Symbol:	[t̼ d̼]	[θ ð]	[t̪ d̪]	[t d]	[t̠ d̠]	[ʈ ɖ]
Language:	Tangoa	Midwestern American English	French	British English	Ewe	Toda

---

Ex 3.11   Field Notebook: Phonetics in One Word

Entry 3 Use the theory you have just learned in order to continue writing your Field Notebook, applying your knowledge to the detailed phonetic description of the word *completes*.

Go to www.routledge.com/cw/ashby for instructions and feedback.

3.5   SUMMARY

- This chapter outlined the basics with regard to *place of articulation*, introducing the organs of speech in the supra-glottal cavities, identifying the active and passive articulators and specifying the inherent relationships that hold between them.

- Knowledge of the International Phonetic Association's alphabet chart (hereafter, the IPA chart) has been extended to include the horizontal axis of the pulmonic consonant matrix as well as selected diacritics and 'other symbols'.

- Places of articulation were grouped with reference to the active articulator(s) associated with them and the link made with certain phonological features.

- Additional articulatory characteristics associated with place of articulation and the extreme flexibility of the tip and blade of the tongue have been discussed.

 Ear-training

Once you have studied this chapter carefully, continue the development of your practical skills by attempting the ear-training exercises for this chapter, available as recordings at www.routledge.com/cw/ashby.

FURTHER READING

Specifically, the place of articulation is the focus of Chapter 5 in Ashby (2005) and Chapter 3 of Ashby & Maidment (2005). A rather more advanced and wide-ranging account can be found in Chapter 2 of Ladefoged & Maddieson (1996).

Further references can be found combined with references for the manner of articulation at the end of Chapter 4.

4

Manner of articulation

The places of articulation identified in Chapter 3 are approached in different ways by the active articulators, the different gestures producing different sound effects – different manners of articulation. Manners combine with voice and place to create individual speech sounds. Double articulations, and primary and secondary articulations are also introduced in this chapter, completing the range of terms needed to construct Voice-Place-Manner (VPM) labels. Ways of representing sounds are discussed (transcriptions, labels, diagrams), and instrumental-imaging of speech sounds (waveforms and spectrograms) introduced.

4.1 DIRECTING AIRFLOW

4.1.1 Oral, nasal and nasalized airflow

In the previous chapter, we saw that when the egressive pulmonic airstream reaches the top of the pharynx there is a choice of direction. This choice is determined by the position of the velum.

The default position of the velum in speech production is closed, forming velic closure (image (a) in Figure 4.1). Here, the velum is in the raised/closed position, directing all the air through the oral cavity and preventing access to the nasal cavity. This is the position of the velum for 'plosive', 'fricative' and the norm realization of 'approximant' consonants (all manners of articulation, described in detail below, and which appear in the vertical axis of the pulmonic consonant matrix on the IPA chart).These are **oral** speech sounds.

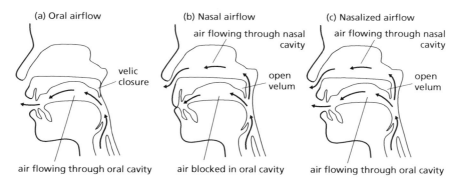

Figure 4.1
(a) Oral (b) nasal and (c) nasalized airflow.

When the velum is lowered/open, however, two further possibilities arise. Provided there is a complete obstruction to the airflow somewhere in the oral cavity (see image (b) in Figure 4.1, for example, where the lips are closed producing bilabial [m]), although the air can still enter the oral cavity, it cannot escape that way and instead, flows over the lowered velum to escape via the nasal cavity. Exclusively nasal airflow of this kind produces **nasal** speech sounds, illustrated in the second row of the pulmonic consonant matrix of the IPA chart. 'Nasal' is thus a manner of articulation, describing all speech sounds with exclusively nasal airflow.

4.1.2   Nasalization in speech

Sometimes, however, although the velum is open, the oral cavity also permits free air flow, as in image (c) in Figure 4.1. There is no oral closure. This produces sounds with a nasal resonance added to their basic oral characteristics. Such sounds are said to be **nasalized**. Vowels and approximant consonants are the sounds most commonly affected by nasalization and some languages do this deliberately (Hindi, for example, with [sɑs] 'mother-in-law' where the velum is closed, but [sɑ̃s] 'breath' where the velum is intentionally opened for the vowel, or French, with *paix* [pɛ] 'peace' but *pain* [pɛ̃] 'bread'). Nasalization thus creates further contrastive units of sound. When a sound is nasalized, we place a special diacritic above it in transcription to show this particular auditory quality: [̃]. (This is a new application of the tilde, first introduced below the symbol to indicate creaky voice in Chapter 2.)

In other cases, nasalization is a phonetic effect – the function of an oral sound occurring next to a nasal sound and the velum opening or closing a little slowly, the gesture overlapping (we say coarticulating) with the adjacent sound. In the English word *mad*, for example, the start of the vowel undergoes nasalization for this reason. Transcribed as [mæ̃d], this shows that the velum closes during the articulation of the vowel such that the resonance gradually changes from nasalized to oral. In the word *ban* [bæ̃n], the end of the vowel is nasalized, and the transcription shows that the velum starts to open during the articulation of the vowel. In the case of *man*, however, the velum can stay open throughout the whole utterance, bringing about a fully nasalized vowel, [mæ̃n]. In English, unlike French and Hindi, this does not change the meaning – nasalization here is not deliberate, it is simply a consequence of the phonetic environment. This behaviour of the velum is shown as a line representing velum action in the following parametric diagram (Figure 4.2) of the utterance *sent/scent* [sẽnt]. What can be seen here is that the velum is preparing for (anticipating) the [n] sound during the preceding vowel sound [e] but that it needs to be fully raised again in order to effect the transition from the nasal [n] to the oral [t]. ([t] belongs to a group of oral consonants described later in this chapter called **plosives**; plosives must have velic closure in order to be produced.)

Ex 4.1   **With the parametric representation of velum action in Figure 4.2 in front of you, can you work out the velum action line for the utterances *set*, *net* and *mend*? Try to transcribe these utterances and then draw appropriate velum action diagrams.**

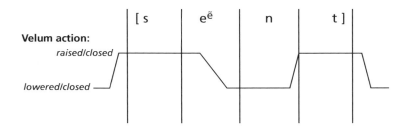

Figure 4.2
Parametric diagram showing velum action during the articulation of *sent*.

4.1.3   Central vs lateral airflow

Once flowing through the oral cavity, there is still a further possibility for diversion of the egressive pulmonic airstream. Oral consonants can be produced either with **central** airflow – the airstream passing straight along a central/median/mid-sagittal channel through the vocal tract, or with **lateral** airflow – air flowing across the lowered side rims of the tongue around some central obstruction. English l-sounds are one such variety of sound with lateral airflow – indeed, you may even be able to feel the action of the side rims if you compare *da-da-da* with your experience of saying *la-la-la* (Chapter 1). Think carefully about what you are feeling. (It is often easier to concentrate on feelings if you make the gesture in silence.) When I say *da-da-da* I can feel the side rims of my tongue against my upper molars as well as contact between the tongue tip and the alveolar ridge. But when I say *la-la-la*, I am only aware of the tongue tip touching the alveolar ridge – I can no longer feel the side rims of my tongue at all. What this different feeling means in practice is that the air cannot get across the side rims of my tongue for *da* but for *la* it can – l-sounds have lateral airflow.

4.2   REPRESENTING CONSONANTS

4.2.1   Transcription

There are a number of ways in which phonetics can identify or represent a speech sound. The quickest way is to note down the symbol: [m], for example, for the sound at the beginning of *Monday*. The sound:symbol relationship is unique – every symbol represents a different sound. The *Principles of the International Phonetic Association* tell us:

> When two sounds occurring in a given language are employed for distinguishing one word from another, they should whenever possible be represented by two distinct letters without diacritical marks.
> (*Handbook of the International Phonetic Association* 1999: 159)

4.2.2   Labelling

As well as a unique symbol, each sound has a unique, three-part name or label. For consonants, labels identify the voice of the sound (voiceless or voiced), the place at which the gesture responsible for the sound is made (place of articulation) and, lastly, the nature of the gesture itself (manner of articulation). We now know enough about the sound [m] to demonstrate this. We know that [m] is a voiced sound, bilabial (made by the two lips), and that all the air is directed via the nasal cavity, so the manner is nasal. The voice-place-manner label (VPM label) for [m] is therefore voiced bilabial nasal. Consonant names are always constructed this way, detailing voice, place and manner, in that order.

4.2.3   Diagrams

A more elaborate way to represent a consonant is to make a vocal tract drawing. The voiced bilabial nasal [m] is illustrated in the diagram in Figure 4.3. All the phonetic characteristics are represented: the vibratory activity of the vocal folds is shown, the closed lips reflecting the bilabial place of articulation, and the pulmonic airflow is represented by arrows, blocked at the lips in the oral cavity but passing freely over the lowered velum, thence through and out of the nasal cavity.

Vocal tract drawings and parametric diagrams are just two of a range of diagrams habitually used by phoneticians.

4.2.4   Instrumental outputs

Any speech sound can also be represented instrumentally in a variety of ways, including its **waveform** and its **spectrogram**. Such representations will be introduced

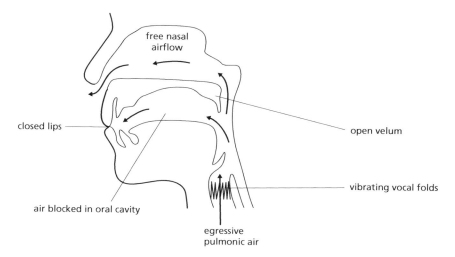

Figure 4.3
Steady state of the voiced bilabial nasal.

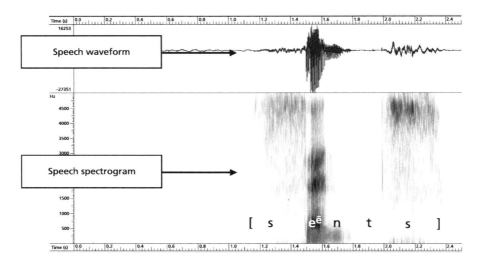

Figure 4.4
Speech waveform and spectrogram of 'scents'.

and discussed as appropriate, but their appearance can be seen initially in Figure 4.4 which shows the speech waveform and wideband spectrogram for one realisation of the utterance *scents*. These are exactly the types of image that you may have created when you did Exercise 1.12, the visible representations of the vibrations and disturbances made in the air when we speak. Speech is produced on a moving airstream which is modified by the articulators as it travels through the vocal tract. Each different speech sound is the product of different articulatory modifications, so the air that leaves the speaker's mouth has a unique pattern which relates directly to the articulatory gestures that produced it. It is this unique pattern that in turn impacts on the ear-drum; the brain recognizes the pattern and decodes it to tell the listener which sound has been said. With practice, we can learn to 'read' spectrograms and waveforms.

An excellent introduction to phonetics which is written specifically from the acoustic viewpoint is Ashby and Maidment (2005), and an excellent overview of these and other instrumental techniques and representations (including simple photography as a means of recording lip positions) can be found in Ladefoged (2003).

4.3   MANNER OF ARTICULATION

4.3.1   Nasal

Nasal consonants – those for which all the egressive pulmonic air is directed via the nasal cavity – are very common. Almost all languages have them.

Figure 4.5
Speech waveform for a sustained realisation of [m] (inset: enlargement showing periodicity).

(Maddieson (2008c) records just 13 languages or 0.04 per cent of the 2,650 mapped in the *World Atlas of Language Structures Online* (WALS) sample as having no nasals in their consonant inventories.) English has three: [m] as in *mummy*, [n] as in *none* and [ŋ] as in *thinking*. A fourth type, [ɲ], is found in languages such as Spanish (specifically Castilian Spanish unless otherwise stated), as in *mañana* 'tomorrow', French, as in *agneau* 'lamb' and Italian, as in *gnocchi* 'potato balls'. The difference between these sounds lies entirely in the place of articulation.

For all nasal consonants, as already said, the velum is in the lowered position, there is pulmonic egressive airflow and normally, too, the vocal folds will be vibrating. Nasals are almost always voiced sounds and the periodic nature of the sound source (meaning, evidence of the regular repeated pattern, generated by the cyclical opening and closing of the vocal folds) is clearly visible in waveforms of nasal consonants (see Figure 4.5). Voiceless nasals are extremely rare – exceptionally, Burmese has these in contrast with voiced ones: [ˆm̥a] 'strong' as opposed to voiced [ˆma] 'lift up' (Ladefoged (2001: 118)). (Note the application of the voiceless diacritic again here.)

We already know that [m] is produced using the lips. [n], by comparison, is made by raising the tip of the tongue to close firmly against the alveolar ridge and, at the same time, raising the side rims of the tongue to seal against the edges of the upper molars; these combined gestures form a complete obstruction to the airstream, again forcing all the air to flow through the nasal cavity, and producing a voiced alveolar nasal.

To produce [ɲ], the obstruction is further back in the mouth. If you consult the IPA chart, you will find [ɲ] in the palatal column. To make this sound, the tongue tip remains down behind the lower front teeth while the front of the tongue moves up and seals across the hard palate and the rear side rims rise and make a firm closure against the edges of the back upper molars, articulating a voiced palatal nasal.

Ex 4.2   Find the symbols [ŋ] and [N] on the IPA chart. What is the place of articulation for each of these sounds? Which active articulator will be used to create the obstruction in the mouth? Try to make these sounds.

Ex 4.3	Examine the following English data. (If you are a native speaker of English, in some cases – especially when it comes to velar nasals – your accent may differ from MRP; don't worry about that, but see if you can spot the differences as well.)
1.	Put a ring round all the words that contain a voiced bilabial nasal.
	Mary tipped out the contents of her mother's bag, looking for some small change for the meter – a comb, a mirror, an empty make-up purse, but no money!
2.	Put a ring round all the words that contain a voiced alveolar nasal.
	. . . ninety-nine, a hundred. One hundred steps! No wonder I've got aching knees!
3.	Put a ring round all the words that contain a voiced velar nasal.
	Are you hungry? I'm starving. I think I fancy something to eat, although I know it's not long till supper.

4.3.2 Plosive

Another manner of articulation that requires the formation of complete closure somewhere in the oral cavity (often referred to as a **stop** gesture) is the plosive sound type. A plosive is considered an **oral stop** while the nasal just described would be called a **nasal stop**. (Stop and its antonym **continuant** are terms used by phonologists to group these particular sound types.)

The plosive manner of articulation introduces one of the two remaining sound sources used in speech production. Vocal fold vibration has already been discussed as being one source of sound. The other two, both of which contribute to the manner of articulation, are **shock** and **turbulence** – plosives are the product of shock excitation. All three sources are important for making oral consonants but whereas vocal fold vibration occurs at the very start of the air's journey through the supra-glottal cavities – the airstream enters the cavities as an uninterrupted, voiceless flow or as a succession of pulses, voiced – these other two sources become involved at a later stage and each further modifies the voiceless or voiced airflow. Each is the product of a gesture being made by an active articulator.

At its most extreme, an active articulator moves towards a passive one and makes complete contact. This was true for nasals, but the difference now, for plosives, is that there is also velic closure. Once an additional closure has been formed, elsewhere in the oral cavity, the pulmonic air flows into a completely sealed chamber. The air can get into the chamber but it cannot get out, so air pressure in the chamber increases – **compression** occurs. Compression may be accompanied by limited vocal fold vibration (increased air pressure above the glottis impairs the folds' ability to continue vibrating normally for very long) or it may be a silent interval during which the vocal folds are held apart (an open glottis). Typically, this hold phase of plosives presents a flat line in the speech waveform, as can be seen in the waveform of the

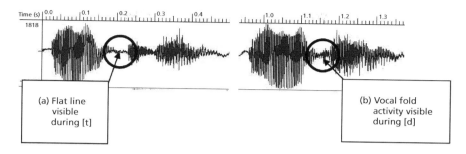

Figure 4.6
Speech waveform of plosives [t] and [d] in the utterances *otter* and *odder* (speaker PA).

utterance *otter* in Figure 4.6. In *odder* there is evidence of vocal fold vibration for voiced [d].

After a few milliseconds, the active articulator moves away from the passive articulator, releasing the compressed air. It is this separation that causes the sound source described as shock. It is heard by the listener as what we call audible **plosion**. This is a very, very brief, transient sound effect and can be seen as a tiny random, aperiodic displacement in the waveform.

What happens next depends on whether the active articulator moves a reasonable distance from the passive one, forming **wide approximation**, or whether it stays quite near to the passive point, forming **narrow approximation**. If the active articulator creates a wide opening following audible plosion, the sound produced will be a plosive. This articulation can be represented in a parametric diagram illustrating the roles of the active and passive articulators, as in Figure 4.7. Sounds made this way are located in the top row of the pulmonic

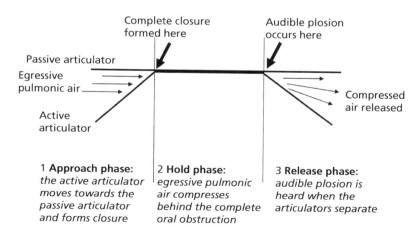

Figure 4.7
Parametric diagram of plosive articulation.

consonant matrix on the IPA alphabet chart (page xvi). In English, this is the way we articulate the sounds [p b] as in *pop*, *bib*, [t d] as in *tot*, *dad*, [k g] as in *kick*, *gag*. In each case there is velic closure and for [p t k] the vocal folds remain open, while for [b d g] the folds usually vibrate for normal voice. (Languages vary as to how much voice is employed in the production of so-called 'voiced' plosives, but the cardinal value of [b d g] – the sounds as represented on the IPA chart – is voiced.)

If we apply all this to the articulatory description of a single plosive, [k] for example, we will find that the velum rises and forms velic closure while the vocal folds remain open. The back of the tongue rises and forms a firm closure against the velum with the rear side rims rising and sealing against the backmost upper molars. The front, blade and tip of the tongue remain low, the tip behind the lower front teeth. Egressive pulmonic air compresses in the pharynx and in the small area of the oral cavity behind the complete velar obstruction. After a short silent interval of compression, the back of the tongue moves down away from the velum. Audible voiceless velar plosion is heard as the articulators first separate. This is followed by the strong expulsion of air.

The main characteristics of this articulatory sequence can be captured in a vocal tract drawing by representing the hold phase of the plosive and adding voicing and airflow information and appropriate labels, as in Figure 4.8.

Ex 4.4   Complete the VPM labelling of the following plosive consonants. Use the IPA chart to help you complete this table. The first one is done for you.

	Voice	Place	Manner
[k]	voiceless	velar	plosive
[p]			
[d]			
[c]			
[ɢ]			
[t̪]			

Ex 4.5   Identify the words that contain at least one plosive sound.

car	phlegm	pneumonia	atom	queue
Thomas	forgive	though	lamb	cease
bomb	orchid	X-ray	foreign	door
know	civilian	machine	Aleutian	lough

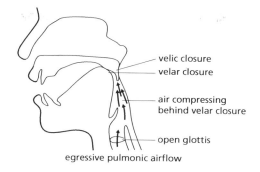

Figure 4.8
Hold-phase of voiceless velar plosive [k].

4.3.3   Trill, tap, flap

Shock is also the sound source for **trills** (repeated striking of the active articulator against the passive one), and for **taps** and **flaps**. Taps and flaps are instances of a single strike by an active articulator against a passive one. The fact that they share a row on the IPA Chart (see page xiv) is simply to save space. They are not one and the same thing. A tap is a deliberate gesture on the part of the active articulator, which moves to strike the passive articulator once – a bit like tapping once on a door. A flap, on the other hand, is a function of the active articulator being drawn out of its inherent alignment with a passive articulator and then being allowed to spring back to its original rest position, striking once against the relevant passive articulator as it does so.

These three percussive sound-types can be conveniently grouped together and are found in the third and fourth rows of the pulmonic consonant matrix on the IPA chart.

English does not use any of these sounds on a regular basis, but both alveolar and uvular trills and the alveolar tap are all found in other Englishes and European languages. The **voiced uvular trill [ʀ]** (in which there is velic closure and vocal fold vibrations while the uvula vibrates in the moving stream of air, repeatedly tapping against the raised back of the tongue) is used immediately before vowel sounds in German and in northern accents of Dutch. The voiced alveolar trill (also with velic closure and vocal fold vibrations, this time with the tongue tip vibrating in the airstream against the alveolar ridge) is used in Spanish (one of two r-sounds) as in *parro* 'grapevine' [para], Italian, and by speakers in southern accents of Dutch.

The voiced alveolar tap is the second Spanish r-sound (as in *para* 'for' [para]) (Figure 4.9). It is also used by speakers of Scottish English immediately before vowel sounds, and by speakers of South African English where it is the only type of r-sound used. These sounds are found, together with one or two others, in the third and fourth rows of the IPA chart. The others are the voiced bilabial trill [ʙ] in which the upper and lower lips are held lightly together such that vibration occurs

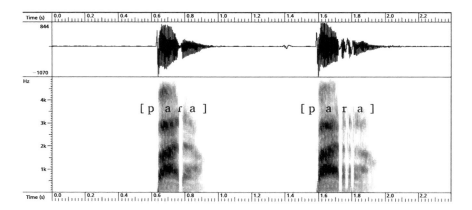

Figure 4.9
Speech waveforms and spectrograms of Spanish [para] 'for' and [parra] 'grapevine' (Speaker Núria Gavaldá).

as the air passes through between them (often used paralinguistically in English to express feeling cold – *Brr!*), the voiced labiodental flap [ⱱ] (a sound, only added to the IPA alphabet in 2005, in which the lower lip is drawn slightly into the front of the oral cavity and then 'flaps' back to its normal position, striking once against the upper front teeth as it does so; this is found in a number of Central and East African languages, including East-Chadic Kera and Nilo-Saharan Mangbetu), and the voiced retroflex flap [ɽ], widely used in Dravidian languages such as Tamil and Malayalam, in which the tongue tip rises and curls over backwards so as to point towards the hard palate and then 'flaps' back to the rest position, striking once against the back of the alveolar ridge as it does so.

The percussive and intermittent quality of such sounds is clearly visible in the spectrogram and speech waveform of an alveolar tap and trill in Figure 4.9.

4.3.4   Fricative

The manner of articulation we call **fricative** is the product of turbulent airflow. As with shock, turbulence can occur alone or it can combine with vocal fold vibrations. Occurring alone produces voiceless friction. Combined with vocal fold vibrations produces voiced friction – these effects were created in the production exercise carried out in Chapter 2, changing an s-sound into a z-sound and back to an s-sound again by switching the voicing on and off. Pure friction (voiceless friction, that is) has an entirely random waveform (see [s] in Figure 4.10) which is said to be **aperiodic** (it contains no measurable repeated pattern of any kind) while voiced friction still exhibits this random characteristic but underpinned by the additional presence of the periodic sound source which adds the voicing (see [z] in Figure 4.10).

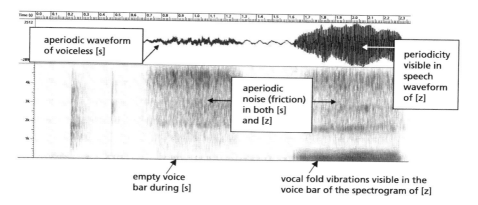

Figure 4.10
Speech waveforms of the sounds [s] and [z].

To generate turbulence, the active articulator approaches the passive one but stops just short of making a firm closure. Either a very small distance is left between the two surfaces (narrow approximation) or the contact is so light that the egressive airstream is able to force a gap, force its way through. The nature of this gesture means that as with plosives, the air pressure inside the vocal tract is somewhat higher than the ambient air pressure. The effect of forcing all the air through a space that is too small for it is like lots of people trying to get down the same small corridor at the same time – you are jostled from side to side, you stop and start, maybe even take a step backwards... exactly what happens to the air molecules in fricatives, so movements become disordered and random instead of the regular, repeated movements associated with periodic sounds.

There are a great many different fricative sounds and these are entered in the fifth and sixth rows of the pulmonic consonant matrix on the IPA chart. Looking at the entries in these rows tells us that friction can be generated at absolutely any place of articulation from bilabial at the front of the vocal tract to glottal at the back. When the tongue is the active articulator, frication can be generated using either central or lateral airflow.

Central fricatives far outnumber lateral ones. For this reason, central airflow is considered the default flow type and is not mentioned in the manner label itself. Central fricatives are simply described as 'fricative'. English [s] is a central fricative but we would label it simply as a voiceless alveolar fricative. You can check this by holding the s-position and sucking air in instead of blowing it out; you will experience a feeling of coldness along the middle of your tongue as the ambient air is drawn in. Similarly, if you can form an l-position and then breathe in and out, you will feel the same coldness but this time at the side(s) of your mouth. Looking at these two fricative rows in the IPA chart tells us that the vast majority of fricatives are central fricatives and only two are what are described as **lateral fricatives**. Both lateral fricatives are found in Zulu (the voiceless one spelled <hl> occurs twice in the name of the National Park *Hluhluwe* (IPA symbol [ɬ]) and the voiced one spelled

<dhl> in a word such as *dhlala* meaning 'to play' (IPA symbol [ɮ])). The voiceless one is also found in Welsh, indicated by the use of <ll> in the spelling. This is often seen in place names (have a look at a map of Wales) – *Llanelli*, for example, or *Llandudno, Llangollen* and so forth. [ɬ] is also indicated by the <lh> romanization of *Lhasa*, the capital of Tibet.

All lateral consonants are produced by lowering one or both of the side rims of the tongue at the same time as forming a complete central obstruction. For [ɬ] and [ɮ], the primary obstruction is at the alveolar ridge. The tongue tip rises and forms a central closure against the alveolar ridge. At the same time, one or both side rims remain near to, but not touching, the upper molars and the narrowness of the approximation causes the passing air to become turbulent and generates audible lateral frication.

Ex 4.6 The Japanese *hiragana* syllabary provides a separate written sign for each possible consonant + vowel syllable of the language. Study the small part shown here and use the VPMs for the consonants to help you answer the following questions.

Japanese *hiragana* syllabary

za	se	ko	zo
ざ	せ	こ	ぞ
ta	**ge**	**so**	**to**
た	げ	そ	と
ka	**de**	**ga**	**ze**
か	で	が	ぜ

(1) Which sign will represent [te]?

   (a) だ   (b) せ   (c) て

(2) Which sign is [do]?

   (a) の   (b) ど   (c) は

(3) One of the following is the disyllabic word /sake/ 'rice wine'. Which?

   (a) ざ   (b) さ   (c) さ
       け   び   け

Ex 4.7	**Complete the VPM labelling of the following fricative consonants. Use the IPA chart to help you complete this table. The first one is done for you.**		
	Voice	**Place**	**Manner**
[x]	voiceless	velar	fricative
[ɸ]			
[z]			
[h]			
[χ]			
[ʒ]			

4.3.5 Affricate

In the discussion of plosives, it was assumed that the articulators were making a wide central approach and a wide central release, as if the plosive was between two vowel sounds (as in *upper* or *robber*, for example). Sometimes, however, when the active articulator moves away from the passive articulator it moves only a minute distance, creating narrow approximation and generating an interval of audible local friction. Friction in such a position, occurring as a function of a very narrow release (often described as a 'slow release') of a plosive closure, creates a new manner of articulation, called **affricate**. Affricates, then, can be defined as a close-knit **homorganic** sequence of stop plus friction, agreeing in voice. 'Homorganic' means 'at the same place of articulation'. So we could have a sequence of voiceless alveolar plosive ([t]) followed immediately by voiceless alveolar fricative ([s]) and this could result in a voiceless alveolar affricate, [t͡s]. English has something like this at the end of words like *cats* or *fits*, but this is the accidental product of adding [s] to words that happen to end in [t]. German, however, uses [t͡s] deliberately, for example in the words *zwei* (two) [t͡svai], *Zimmer* (room) ['t͡sɪmɐ], etc.

As can be seen in Figure 4.11, the speech waveform and spectrogram of an affricate show the brief (flat) hold-phase in the waveform (corresponding to the empty space in the spectrogram) followed immediately by a short time of aperiodicity, the friction component. As with pure plosives and fricatives, affricates may or may not be accompanied by vocal fold vibration. Affricates also have increased intra-oral air pressure.

Affricates are not entered separately on the IPA chart because the symbols are coined by linking the appropriately related plosive and fricative symbols. English has two regular affricates, the voiceless palatoalveolar affricate [t͡ʃ] as in *church, archer*, and the voiced palatoalveolar affricate [d͡ʒ] as in *judge, edging*. Use of the over-tie diacritic to show 'a close-knit sequence' is not imperative, but it is good practice to distinguish ordinary sequences of plosive followed by fricative (as in *cat*

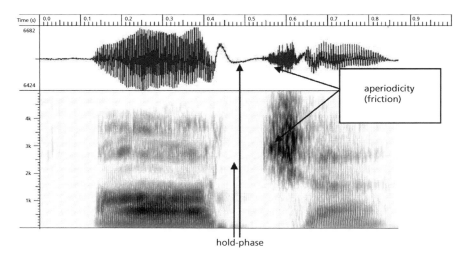

Figure 4.11
Speech waveform and spectrogram for the utterance *archer* ['ɑːtʃə].

shit ['kæt ʃɪt] or *what shell* ['wɒt 'ʃel]) from the close-knit relationship in *catch it* ['kætʃ ɪt] and *watch Elle* ['wɒtʃ 'el]. It is also worth observing that in an affricate, the hold-phase is usually shorter than the hold-phase in a plosive and the friction lasts for less time than the friction in an equivalent simple fricative sound. The relative timing of the phases can be demonstrated by adapting the parametric diagram just given for plosives, as in Figure 4.12.

Ex 4.8   Use the IPA chart to create symbols for the following affricates:

1 voiceless bilabial affricate   2 voiced uvular affricate
3 voiced velar affricate   4 voiceless dental affricate
5 voiceless palatal affricate

4.3.6 Approximant

One final manner of articulation affecting pulmonic consonants is a sound effect where (as with nasals) the only source of sound is vocal fold vibration. There is no physical noise present in the acoustic signal of these sounds – no audible friction, plosion, trilling or tapping can be heard. Sounds of this type are produced when the active articulator assumes a position of open or wide approximation below the passive one. This gesture is used to produce vowel sounds and also a variety of vowel-like oral consonants called **approximants**. The periodic nature of the resonance can be seen in the speech waveform of the utterance [ɑwɑ] (Figure 4.13).

Approximants can be made at any point in the vocal tract where voluntary narrowing is possible. There is no major impediment to the airflow and so, again, no audible friction and no particular increase in air pressure inside the vocal tract

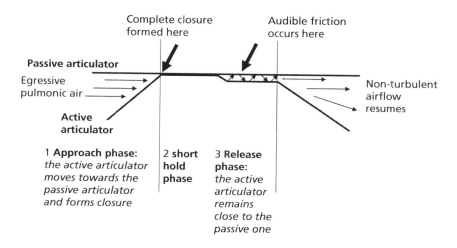

Figure 4.12
Parametric diagram of affricate articulation.

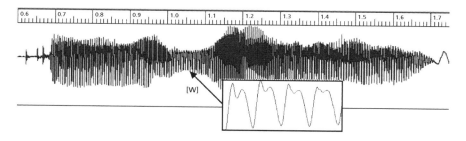

Figure 4.13
Speech wave form of [ɑwɑ] (inset: close-up of [w] showing periodicity).

(intra-oral air pressure). Phonologists use these phonetic characteristics to identify two main groups of speech sounds, distinguishing sounds which are [SONORANT] (all sounds with periodic waveforms and negligible increase in intra-oral air pressure – vowels, approximants and nasals) from those which are **obstruent** (sounds with heightened intra-oral pressure and with aperiodicity evident in the waveforms – plosives, fricatives and affricates). Phoneticians often borrow these terms from phonology and talk about sonorants and obstruents. If there is no ready-made approximant symbol on the IPA chart, a symbol can be coined by taking the voiced fricative symbol and applying a **more open** diacritic to represent a wider distance between the active and passive articulators – wide approximation instead of narrow approximation. We do this to transcribe the r-sound that is often used at the end of a word in German, a voiced uvular approximant, [ʁ], as in *vier* 'four'.

As with fricatives, airflow in approximants can be central (again the default airflow and unmentioned in the label) or lateral. The term **lateral approximant** will be found on the IPA chart (the name of the eighth row in the pulmonic consonant matrix) although in practice phoneticians frequently abbreviate this simply as **lateral**. English has three central approximants, [ɹ] as in *red*, [w] as in *wet* and [j] as in *yes*, and one lateral approximant, [l], as in *love* – the voiced alveolar lateral. Dutch, French and German also have just one lateral approximant. Spanish and Italian, however, each have two. In addition to alveolar [l], as in Spanish *la, el* [la, el] 'the' and Italian [lo, li] 'the', they also have the voiced palatal lateral, [ʎ], as in Spanish *calle* ['kaʎe] 'street' or Italian *figlio* ['fiʎo] 'son'. It should be noted, however, that it is increasingly the case that the Spanish variant is pronounced as a central approximant, giving ['kaje], etc. and that in a large number of Italian accents, there is considerable friction involved in the pronunciation of [ʎ], creating a voiced palatal lateral fricative (for which there is no established IPA symbol).

Laterals can be produced at any point in the tract where the tongue can make a central obstruction to the airstream.

Ex 4.9

Lateral approximants

1. Look at the IPA chart and work out the full VPM labels for each of the lateral approximants.
2. How could we symbolise a voiced dental lateral approximant?

Central approximants

Find the symbols for the following sounds:

1. voiced labiodental approximant
2. voiced retroflex lateral approximant
3. voiced palatal approximant
4. voiced velar approximant
5. voiced labialvelar approximant

Ex 4.10   Following the example, use VPM labels to assist in completing the following proportions.

For example:

	[p]	:	[k]	::	[b]	:	[g]
	voiceless bilabial plosive	*is to*	voiceless velar plosive	*as*	voiced bilabial plosive	*is to*	voiced velar plosive
1.	[b]	:	[m]	::	[ ]	:	[n]
2.	[t͡ʃ]	:	[t]	::	[ ]	:	[d]
3.	[m]	:	[n]	::	[b]	:	[ ]
4.	[j]	:	[ɰ]	::	[ɥ]	:	[ ]
5.	[z]	:	[d]	::	[ ]	:	[t]

4.4 DOUBLE AND SECONDARY ARTICULATIONS

4.4.1 A scale of strictures

The manners of articulation just described have involved three different degrees of **stricture** or approximation between the active and passive articulators. These are fundamental to distinguishing two different types of parallel articulations.

The narrowest stricture involved firm contact between the articulators. This was close approximation – a gesture of complete closure made (intermittently or for a sustained period of time) by the active articulator against the passive one. This was the case in the production of nasals, plosives and affricates (sustained closure), and trills, taps and flaps (intermittent closure) – the top four rows of the pulmonic consonant matrix. We can treat complete closure as being at the top of the scale of strictures.

The next two rows on the vertical axis of the matrix represent sounds involving narrow approximation – a narrow gap between the active and passive articulators of the sort that generated audible friction. On the mid-point of the scale, therefore, is narrow approximation.

Finally, with the distance increased to what is called wide approximation – the lowest point on the scale – the last two rows of the matrix represent resonant sounds known as approximants. Vowels also come into this category.

The vertical axis of the pulmonic consonant matrix can therefore be seen to be organized by degree of stricture and assigning rank to these (with the closest at the top and the most open at the bottom) creates a scale:

Scale of strictures:	Highest	1	complete closure
		2	narrow approximation
	Lowest	3	wide approximation

4.4.2 Double articulations

To increase the range of consonantal contrasts, languages occasionally use two places of articulation at the same time. This is what happens when we say [w].

We are now in a position to identify this as being a double-articulated approximant consonant. The two articulatory gestures (one at the lips, the other at the velum) both involve a stricture of wide approximation. Because the two parallel gestures are equal in stricture, the sound constitutes what is called a **double-articulation**.

The simultaneous use of two places of articulation means double-articulations cannot be entered in the main consonant grid on the IPA chart. Instead, they are listed separately among the 'Other Symbols'.

4.4.3 Secondary articulations

In the case of two parallel articulations which are unequal in stricture, we have **primary** and **secondary articulations**. The gesture which ranks highest on the scale of strictures is the primary articulation and determines the place of articulation of the consonant in question. The secondary gesture is an additional modification.

For example, in the word *see-saw*, when you looked in the mirror, you noticed that in *see* your lips remained in a fairly neutral position while in *saw* they assumed a more rounded contour. In both cases, we are dealing with a voiceless alveolar fricative, but in *saw* there is a parallel articulation of open approximation at the lips (right at the bottom of the scale of strictures) which results in rounding. The gesture between the tongue tip and alveolar ridge, however, ranks higher – a stricture of narrow approximation, at point 2 on the scale of strictures. The alveolar gesture is therefore primary, creating an alveolar consonant. The labial gesture becomes secondary and so the alveolar sound is described as being **labialized**. The effect is caused by the vowel sound, [ɔː], which involves quite strong lip-rounding and this is anticipated during the production of [s], giving [sʷ], a voiceless labialized alveolar fricative. The superscript [ʷ] is the diacritic which indicates **labialization**.

There are four secondary articulations. All involve adding a vowel-like gesture (an articulation of open approximation) to an articulation of closer stricture. The remaining three, **palatalization, velarization** and **pharyngealization**, will be discussed in Chapter 8. Any one of them can be produced deliberately, or can be (like the labialization of [s] in *saw*) a product of the phonetic environment in which a sound occurs.

Ex 4.11   Field Notebook: Phonetics in One Word

Entry 4 Use the theory you have just learned in order to continue writing your Field Notebook, applying your knowledge to the detailed phonetic description of the word *completes*.

Go to www.routledge.com/cw/ashby for instructions and feedback.

4.5   SUMMARY

- This chapter has developed our study of the behaviour of the active articulators in speech, describing in detail different manners of articulation, both in terms of the gesture used to make them and the sound effect achieved.

- Knowledge of the IPA chart was expanded with the vertical 'manner' axis of the pulmonic consonant matrix being viewed as a scale of strictures.

- Manner information was integrated with information about voicing and place carried forward from previous chapters and VPM labels constructed for pulmonic consonants.

- Different ways of representing speech sounds were also introduced including waveforms and spectrograms.

 Ear-training

Once you have studied this chapter carefully, continue the development of your practical skills by attempting the ear-training exercises for this chapter, available as recordings at www.routledge.com/cw/ashby .

FURTHER READING

Chapter 4 of Ashby & Maidment (2005) and Chapter 6 of Ladefoged (2005) discuss manner of articulation. Further elementary discussion of manner, combined with place of articulation, can be found in Chapter 4 of Cruttenden (2008), Chapter 7 of Ladefoged (2001), and Chapter 2 of Lodge (2009).

Further, more advanced reading can be found in Chapters 8–10 of Laver (1994), and Chapters 3–7 of Ladefoged & Maddieson (1996). Again, a different perspective (but still advanced) is offered in Ashby (2006).

Airstream mechanisms

Speech utilizes four different airstream mechanisms but only one of these – the pulmonic egressive airstream mechanism – is used regularly by all languages. The different mechanisms produce radically different sound types, effectively extending the range of manner variations described in Chapter 4. This chapter focuses on the three non-pulmonic airstream mechanisms and the sounds they are used to produce – sounds located in the non-pulmonic consonant table on the IPA chart, ejectives, implosives and clicks. The chapter also includes a discussion of the relationship between these non-pulmonic sound types and the concept of double articulation.

5.1 PULMONIC AIRSTREAM MECHANISMS

5.1.1 The universal airstream

The name, **pulmonic egressive airstream**, refers to the cavity in which air is stored (the lungs) and the outward direction of airflow, relative to the body (egressive).

All speech uses air from the lungs. For the vast majority of speakers, this egressive pulmonic variant is the only airstream mechanism they ever need. *Ethnologue* (Lewis 2009) statistics show that 60 per cent of the world's population speak one of 30 languages. None of these makes regular, systematic use (that is, as the only or main way of making a contrast) of an airstream other than pulmonic egressive (although see Maddieson's discussion of 'glottalized consonants', Maddieson (2008a)). That is not to say that speakers of languages like Modern Standard Chinese, Hindi, Spanish, English, Modern Standard Arabic and so on are incapable of making non-pulmonic sounds; all this generalization tells us is that such languages only have pulmonic sounds in their sound systems. We all can, and often do, make non-pulmonic sounds for various (often paralinguistic) reasons, such as when speakers of English want to express disapproval and make a so-called tutting noise, *tsk! tsk!*

One reason for such universal reliance on this airstream might be that the lungs are capable of supplying a considerable volume of air, expelled under pressure, enabling long stretches of speech without pause for replenishment. None of the other three mechanisms has this capacity.

5.1.2 The pulmonic egressive mechanism

The mechanism itself was described briefly in Chapter 2 during the discussion of normal voice. As it passes through the larynx, the egressive pulmonic air may be modified (as we said earlier), being broken into pulses by the vibrating vocal folds to add voice (for sounds such as [iː ɑː ɥ m b z]). Alternatively, it may flow without interruption through the open glottis and remain voiceless (for sounds such as [p s tʃ]).

5.1.3 Direction of flow

For normal speech purposes, the direction of flow is always egressive.

However, speech on an ingressive pulmonic airstream is not unknown and is documented as occurring both linguistically and, especially, **paralinguistically** – linguistically to bring about change of meaning, paralinguistically to achieve some other effect or as a function of deviant speech. Linguistic evidence is minimal, however, being confined to one speaker of one dialect of the Austronesian language Tsou (spoken in southern Taiwan) who was recorded as using two ingressive pulmonic fricatives in word initial position before a glottal stop (the voiceless glottal plosive): [f◄] and [h◄] (where I have coined a back-pointing arrowhead diacritic [◄] to indicate ingressive airflow, there being no directional diacritic of this kind on the IPA chart). Fuller (1990) records this speaker as producing utterances such as [f◄ʔúe] '*sweet potato*' and [h◄ʔúju] '*blood*' but using regular egressive variants in all other positions ([fó] '*meat/fish*', [mafuíŋu] '*woods*', [t͡suhúmu] '*water*', etc.).

Paralinguistically, this mechanism is used more widely, both as a function of running out of breath (when counting quickly to a high number in English – I have heard this when bank notes were being counted out loud in a finance office, for example) and for stylistic and/or attitudinal reasons (French *oui* 'yes' spoken ingressively is a frequently heard stylistic variant; English *yeah* (coll.) spoken ingressively as [j◄eə◄] comes across as conveying agreement but also a certain amount of irritation on the part of the speaker).

Sociolinguists and anthropologists have also noted use of pulmonic ingressive air to disguise the voice – ritualistic disguise such as its use by young men when speaking to their girlfriends in courtship customs in the Fensterle region of Switzerland (Dieth (1950)), for example, and among the Hanunóo in the Philippines (Conklin (1959)). Catford (2001: 30) also reports hearing its use for disguise purposes by mummers at a village festival in Cyprus. If you try talking while breathing in, instead of out, you will hear just how effective this is! It places limitations on the length of the utterance, but the speaker is certainly unrecognizable from their voice. Ingressive pulmonic phonation is also used sometimes as a therapeutic or remedial tool in the treatment of stuttering, dysphonia and other disorders.

There is an excellent and comprehensive overview of instances of ingressive pulmonic airstream use in Eklund (2008), and a very readable summary in Laver (1994:168–70).

5.2   GLOTTALIC AIRSTREAM MECHANISMS

5.2.1   Air storage and initiation

Working outwards from the lungs, the next cavity we encounter in which air can be contained and set in motion for the purpose of speech is the pharynx (see Figure 2.3).

Compared with the lungs, the capacity of the pharynx is very small. Additionally, it has a more limited means of setting the air in motion. (Remember, all speech is produced on a moving column of air, so there has to be an adequate means of initiation.)

We can see from Figure 2.3 that the only moveable articulator associated with the body of air in the pharynx, apart from the pharynx walls which have exceptionally limited movement, has to be the larynx. Larynx movement, too, is very restricted, but it is sufficient to be able to set the pharyngeal air in motion for a limited period of time. The larynx structure has the potential to be fractionally raised or lowered. Combining this with the valve-like nature of the vocal folds, a piston-like effect can be created which is comparable (in a very modest way) to the action of a bicycle pump. Such intervention is instrumental in either pushing air out from the pharynx (creating an egressive direction of airflow) or drawing air in (ingressive airflow). Both of these options are utilized in speech production.

The airstreams will be found to have two names in the wider literature. My preference is to name these airstreams after the initiator, using the adjective **glottalic**. This widely used option (see, for example, Catford 2001; Laver 1994; Ladefoged 2005) gives overt recognition to the contribution made by the glottis in the production of these sounds. The alternative, used among others by Kenneth Pike in the 1940s (see Pike 1943: 90), is **pharyngeal**, and names the mechanisms after the cavity in which the air is stored.

5.2.2   The egressive glottalic airstream mechanism

Outward airflow from the pharynx gives rise to a group of sounds called **ejectives**. These are the most widespread of the non-pulmonic consonants, occurring in about 16–19 percent of languages (Maddieson 2008a; Greenberg 1978). They are often familiar to English speakers who make not infrequent use of them when articulating utterance final voiceless plosives – expressions such as *Nope!* (for *no*), *Quite!* and one I heard one of my sons saying recently which involved the final [k] in *I told him to put it back!* My impression is that this adds (or can add) a certain emphatic or authoritative tone – the speaker is not expecting contradiction. So, what exactly are these sounds, and how are they made?

To produce an ejective, the articulatory process can be broken down into four consecutive steps:

1. The vocal folds are brought firmly together to form glottal closure (as in [ʔ]). Simultaneously, the speaker forms a more forward constriction, anywhere in the oral cavity; for the purpose of illustration, let us say that the back of the tongue rises and forms a firm closure against the velum (as when articulating the ordinary pulmonic [k] sound in Chapter 4, see page 56). Air is trapped in the pharynx and the rear part of the oral cavity, between the three closures (Figure 5.1).

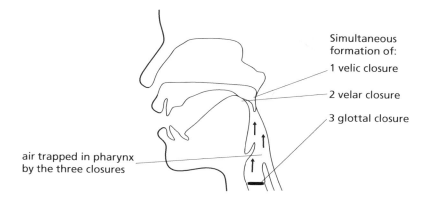

Figure 5.1 The glottalic egressive airstream mechanism: Step 1.

2. The larynx, containing the tightly closed glottis, rises fractionally, compressing the air trapped in the pharynx by reducing the amount of space (Figure 5.2).

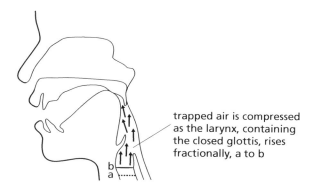

Figure 5.2 The glottalic egressive airstream mechanism: Steps 2 and 3.

3. Immediately, the more forward closure is removed – in this example, the back of the tongue moves down, away from the velum – releasing the small quantity of compressed air which is literally 'ejected' under pressure from the pharynx (Figure 5.3).

4. Immediately, the vocal folds re-open, the larynx lowers to its original position and routine pulmonic egressive airflow resumes.

Because of the closure of the glottis, all sounds made using this mechanism are voiceless. The supraglottal constriction, however, can be either one of complete closure, or one of narrow approximation. It follows from this that ejectives can be either plosive, fricative or affricate in nature. The articulation we have just described is a voiceless velar ejective plosive and is transcribed [k']. Note that there is no rule about the position of 'ejective' in the VPM label, but it is good practice

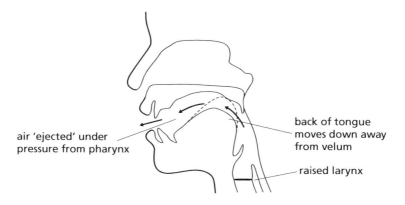

air 'ejected' under
pressure from pharynx

back of tongue
moves down away
from velum

raised larynx

Figure 5.3 The glottalic egressive airstream mechanism: Step 4.

to be systematic. I consider it to be a further manner of articulation and thus use it as part of the manner description, ejective plosive, ejective fricative, etc. The superscript comma in the symbol is indicative of the involvement of the glottal stop gesture, deriving directly from the cursive top of that symbol shape.

Like pulmonic obstruents, ejectives (glottalic obstruents) are **pressure consonants**. That is to say, air is being expelled from the vocal tract under pressure.

Ex 5.1	Based on the VPM label just given for [k'], work out the VPM labels for the following consonants.
1 [p'] 2 [s'] 3 [t͡ʃ'] 4 [ɬ'] 5 [c']	

Ex 5.2   Provide the symbol for each of the following sounds:
1. voiceless dental ejective plosive
2. voiceless alveolar ejective affricate
3. labialized voiceless velar ejective plosive
4. voiceless alveolar ejective lateral affricate
5. voiceless postalveolar ejective plosive

Ejective consonants are widespread and will be found in areas as far apart as the Caucasus, the Americas, Sub-Saharan African and Papua New Guinea. Languages include: Georgian (a Kartvelian language); Dhagestanian languages; Amerindian languages from a number of families including Nez Perce (Penutian, from North America), Tol (spoken in Honduras) and South American Siona (a Tucanoan language from the Ecuador/Colombia border); Afro-Asiatic languages Hausa (spoken in Nigeria) and Amharic (spoken in Ethiopia) and the Niger-Congo language Zulu; the Trans-New Guinea language Hamtai.

Because they do not require the use of lung air at all, one of the best ways to learn to make ejectives is to breathe out completely and then hold your breath and try to say [p], [t] and [k]. If you manage this, you will be making ejective versions of these sounds, [p' t' k']. (Precisely because they do not require lung air, ejective versions of voiceless obstruent consonants are also learnt by speakers who have undergone a laryngectomy.)

Ex 5.3   **Fill in the blanks in the following articulatory description of an ejective consonant.**

There is _____ closure, preventing airflow via the nasal cavities.
The lower lip rises and rests lightly against the upper front _____.
Simultaneously, the _____ close, preventing airflow to and
from the _____. Then, the larynx _____
fractionally, putting momentary pressure on the body of air contained in the speaker's
_____ and causing a small rush of air through the oral cavity which exits
through the narrow constriction between the lower lip and the _____.
There is a narrow jaw aperture throughout. A voiceless _____ ejective
_____ is heard. This sound is represented in transcription by the symbol
_____.

5.2.3 The ingressive glottalic airstream mechanism

Implosives, made using the ingressive glottalic airstream, are found in a smaller number of languages than ejectives, occurring in about 10% – 13% of all languages (Greenberg (1978); Maddieson (2008a)). The sound of an implosive tends to be less familiar to English speakers than the sound of an ejective, although again we do use an implosive articulation paralinguistically. It is often the case that when we want to imitate the sound of liquid glugging from a narrow-necked bottle, we produce a series of voiced uvular implosives: [ɠ ɠ ɠ]!

Again, in the transcription, the curved top of the glottal stop symbol can be identified, although this time, the articulation does not involve complete glottal closure. Nonetheless, this right-pointing hook is added to the upright (or the uppermost end of the writing line) of the related pulmonic plosive symbol in order to represent an implosive value: the voiced bilabial plosive [b] becomes the voiced bilabial implosive [ɓ], [d] becomes [ɗ], [ɟ] becomes [ʄ], [g] becomes [ɠ], and [ɢ] becomes [ʛ].

As with ejectives, the articulatory process can be broken down into a series of steps. For a voiced implosive articulation, these would be:

1. While egressive pulmonic airflow continues, velic closure is formed together with a second complete closure at a more forward place of articulation (a velar closure is represented again in Figure 5.4).

2. Simultaneously, the larynx structure (containing vibrating vocal folds) lowers fractionally, slightly increasing the space in the pharynx ...

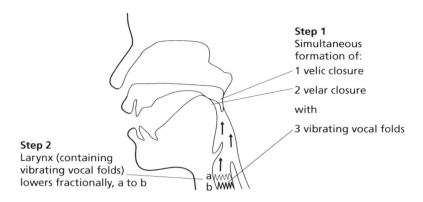

Figure 5.4
The glottalic ingressive airstream mechanism: Steps 1 and 2.

3. ... which *may* cause a fractional drop in intra-oral pressure.

4. Immediately, the oral closure is removed (in Figure 5.4, the back of the tongue would move down, away from the velum) and the intra-oral/ambient air pressure relationship stabilizes again, egressive pulmonic air having continued to flow throughout.

The interesting thing about these sounds is that classic accounts of implosion have always described a drop in intra-oral air pressure such that ambient air is sucked into the vocal tract on the removal of the oral closure in order to equalize the air pressures. However, more recent investigations carried out by Ladefoged and others have shown that this is by no means always the case (Ladefoged and Maddieson (1996)). Quite apart from anything else, for voiced implosives, in the time period between the lowering of the larynx and the removal of the oral closure, pulmonic egressive air continues to flow out of the lungs and into the supraglottal cavities, so any pressure drop will be quite minimal (if it occurs at all). Nonetheless, sounds produced this way still have the distinctive implosive auditory characteristic. Ladefoged and Maddieson suggest that this is a function simply of the larynx movement and its influence on the immediately following vowel sound.

The IPA chart illustrates only voiced implosives because no evidence of voicing contrast has been found in any of the languages known to have implosive consonants. Voiceless ones do occur (such as [ɓ̥] – a voiceless bilabial implosive), but only allophonically. In the case of voiceless implosives, the vocal folds are closed when the larynx lowers. (Reduced air pressure in the pharynx is thus more likely to occur during the articulation of these voiceless variants.)

WALS online mapping shows that implosives are a little less widespread than ejectives (Maddieson (2008a)) with the main concentrations situated in Africa, with languages such as Hausa, Swahili, siSwati, and in South-East Asia (including Tukang Besi), and then more isolated occurrences (Sindhi in India and Chipewyan in North America – one of just a very small number of languages with implosives in this region – and also Yucatec in Central America and Pirahã in South America).

While ejectives are a type of pressure consonant (with air being expelled from the vocal tract under pressure), implosives are **suction consonants**. To make an implosive, air – at least in principle – is drawn (sucked) into the vocal tract.

Ex 5.4	**Based on the VPM label just given for [ɓ], work out the VPM labels for the following consonants:**
1 [ɗ] 2 [ʃʷ] 3 [ɓ] 4 [ɓʲ] 5 [ɖ]	

Ex 5.5	**Provide the symbol for each of the following sounds:**
1.	voiced palatal implosive
2.	voiceless velar implosive
3.	voiced uvular implosive
4.	voiced postalveolar implosive
5.	labialized voiced alveolar implosive

Ex 5.6	**Fill in the blanks in the following articulatory description of an implosive consonant.**

The jaw assumes a medium aperture. The _____ part and _____ assume a rounded position and the velum _____ and forms _____ closure. At the same time, the back of the tongue _____ and forms a firm closure on the _____ palate. The _____ are vibrating for normal voice and the larynx _____ slightly, momentarily reducing air pressure in the pharynx. Immediately, the back of the tongue moves _____ away from the velum and ambient air may be drawn into the oral cavity to equalize the ambient and intra-oral air pressure. A _____ _____ _____ _____ is heard. This sound can be represented in transcription by the symbol _____.

5.3   VELARIC AIRSTREAM MECHANISMS

5.3.1   Air storage, initiation and awareness

The alternative name, **oral airstream mechanism,** makes it clear that in the case of this last variety, the air used is oral air, air held in the mouth. The initiator in this case, however, is velar closure – the back of the tongue sealed against the velum – hence the name we will use here: **velaric airstream mechanism.**

As with the glottalic and pulmonic mechanisms, air can be set in motion in both an egressive and an ingressive direction, but this time it is only the ingressive variant that is used in speech. It follows, therefore, that the sounds made using this mechanism are again going to be suction consonants. The egressive mechanism is used, but not for speech purposes; it is used, instead, for removing foreign bodies from the tip of the tongue. It is also used by oboe, didgeridoo and chanter players as part of the so-called **circular breathing** required to enable the continuous airflow required for performing long, uninterrupted musical phrases, and it is used by people blowing smoke rings.

The ingressive variant, however, is used in speech to produce a group of sounds known as **clicks**. These are very familiar to speakers of English, many of whom make frequent paralinguistic use of clicks to make kissing sounds, express disapproval (we find this sound written in literature as *tut! tut!* or *tsk! tsk!*), express approval (or encourage a horse to move), and imitate the 'clip-clop' sound of horses' hooves. Young speakers, moreover, are familiar with these sounds through **beat-boxing**; there is often quite remarkable insight into how the sounds are made in many of the on-line tutorials and explanations offered by the phonetically-untrained performers on beat-boxing websites. (Of course, you do have to beware – there are also some very misleading accounts!) People are often familiar, too, with songs from the musical *Ipi Tombi* and 'The Click Song' (made famous by the artist Miriam Makeba).

Clicks are the least widespread of all the different consonant types. They are found exclusively in Africa where they occur in all the Khoisan languages and also in a relatively small number of Bantu languages (including Zulu and Xhosa). Although Romanized, the orthographies of languages using click sounds often involve a further application of the ELA to reflect the nature of these consonants - !Xóõ, for example, and Juǀ'hoan are two frequently mentioned in the textbooks. Even <xh> at the start of the name Xhosa indicates (spells) a click.

5.3.2   The ingressive velaric airstream mechanism

5.3.2.1   The basic click-producing mechanism

Like the implosives, the articulation of a click can involve more than one airstream operating simultaneously. (We saw how the ingressive glottalic airstream and the egressive pulmonic one operated in parallel during the production of voiced implosives.) Before discussing this, however, it is important to understand the basic mechanism involved. The basic mechanism can be broken down into five consecutive steps:

1. The back of the tongue rises and forms a firm velar closure at the same time as a more forward complete closure is made somewhere else in the oral cavity (at the lips, for example, or between the tongue tip and/or blade and a point along the dental-to-postalveolar continuum) (Figure 5.5). A small body of air is trapped between these two complete closures and egressive pulmonic airflow is blocked at the velum. (The posterior, velar closure is discussed in more detail in the following sub-section.)

2. A depression forms in the upper surface of the body of the tongue, between the points of closure, giving the surface a concave contour and enlarging the cavity holding the trapped air. The pressure of the trapped air falls and is now lower than the ambient air pressure. These first two steps are outlined in Figure 5.5, representing a dental place of articulation for the click. Steps 3 and 4 can be seen represented in Figure 5.6.

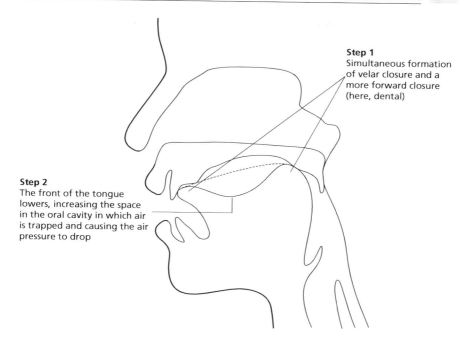

Step 1
Simultaneous formation
of velar closure and a
more forward closure
(here, dental)

Step 2
The front of the tongue
lowers, increasing the space
in the oral cavity in which air
is trapped and causing the air
pressure to drop

Figure 5.5
The velaric ingressive airstream mechanism: Steps 1 and 2.

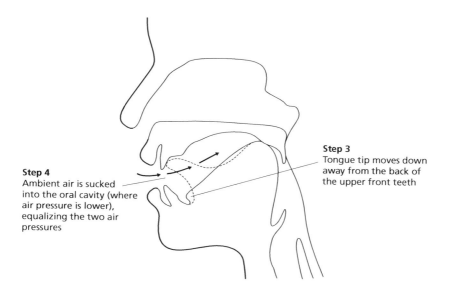

Step 3
Tongue tip moves down
away from the back of
the upper front teeth

Step 4
Ambient air is sucked
into the oral cavity (where
air pressure is lower),
equalizing the two air
pressures

Figure 5.6
The velaric ingressive airstream mechanism: Steps 3 and 4.

3. The frontmost closure is removed, with a percussive sound being heard as the articulators first separate.

4. Ambient air is drawn briefly into the oral cavity, equalizing the ambient and intra-oral air pressures.

5. Almost simultaneously, the back of the tongue moves down away from the velum. (Egressive pulmonic airflow now continues.)

The most forward closure can be one of many subtle variants, but five basic types are provided for on the current IPA chart (see page xiv). Depending on which books you read, you may still come across the old symbols for these sounds. Table 5.1 shows both the old and the new. This book will only use the new ones.

Each symbol here characterizes a particular articulatory gesture made by the lips or the tip and/or blade of the tongue. These can be summarized as follows, the back and body of the tongue behaving as already described:

- *Bilabial:* For bilabial clicks, the lips come together and form a firm closure. The tip of the tongue remains low behind the bottom front teeth. (Completion of this gesture results in what is effectively a kiss, as when you give someone a kiss on the cheek.) The symbol, [ʘ], is known as 'bull's eye'.[1] Basic transcriptions: [k͡ʘ], [g͡ʘ], [ŋ͡ʘ].

- *Dental:* The tip of the tongue rises and forms a firm closure on the back of the upper front teeth. At the same time, the side rims rise and form a firm closure along the inside edges of the upper molars and the edges of the palate. (This is the gesture English speakers use when the want to signal disapproval – the *Tut! Tut!* sound referred to earlier.) The release of the closure is usually accompanied by a certain amount of audible friction and is best described as being rather affricated. Basic transcriptions: [k͡ǀ], [g͡ǀ], [ŋ͡ǀ].

- *(Post)alveolar:* The postalveolar click has an auditorily 'cleaner' or 'clearer' sort of release and is not accompanied by friction in the way in which the dental click is. The point of closure between the tip of the tongue and the roof of

Table 5.1
Click symbols

	Bilabial	Dental	(Post)-alveolar	Alveolar lateral	Palato-alveolar
Old	[ʘ]	[ʇ]	[c]	[ʎ]	
New	[ʘ]	[ǀ]	[!]	[ǁ]	[ǂ]

[1]It is worth noting that although they are listed in the *Handbook of the International Phonetic Association*, symbol names are not routinely used. It also needs to be noted that the phonetic names for many symbols are different from their Unicode names. For example, [ʘ] has the phonetic name 'bull's eye' while its Unicode name is 'Latin letter bilabial click'; less transparent is [ɛ] with the phonetic name 'epsilon' while its Unicode name is 'Latin small letter open e'.

the mouth is often well behind the alveolar ridge and in earlier versions of the IPA chart, this click was described as retroflex or sometimes palatal. (IPA symbols are never accidental and the choice of [!] for this click – which looks like a regular exclamation mark (the actual name is 'exclamation point') – is comprised of the single pipe used for the dental click, with a dot below, as used by classical scholars of Indian languages to represent retroflexion or retraction; the dot is performing the job that would normally be done by the IPA [̠] diacritic, retracting the point of contact of the dental [|] and making it 'post-dental', in fact properly postalveolar in this case.) This sound is sometimes used by English speakers to imitate the clip-clop noise made by horses' hooves; when doing this, speakers usually produce the click with what Eaton (2006) (describing this sound in the Sandawe language spoken in central Tanzania) describes as a 'tongue slap, in which the tongue hits the floor of the mouth', meaning that the click becomes, effectively, a flap articulation (as described in Chapter 4). Basic transcriptions: [k͡!], [g͡!], [ŋ͡!].

- *Alveolar lateral:* For [‖], known as 'double pipe', the tongue tip rises and seals against a point along the dental-postalveolar continuum. At the same time, the side rims rise and seal against the inside edges of the upper molars. After the body of the tongue moves down, the rims of the tongue lower on one side only. The sound made by an alveolar lateral click again has a paralinguistic application in English where speakers use it to encourage a horse to move or (particularly in the case of male speakers) to express approval. Basic transcriptions: [k‖], [g‖],[ŋ‖].

- *Palatoalveolar:* This click is one that some authorities call palatal. The auditory effect of the release always reminds me of bubble-gum popping! There must be postalveolar contact to produce this sound – the blade rises and seals firmly against the very back of the alveolar ridge as the side rims rise and complete the lateral seal. The tip is in contact with the alveolar ridge itself and/or the back of the upper front teeth. As the body of the tongue lowers, the forward closure is pulled back to a (pre-)palatal position before the blade and tip move down away from the roof of the mouth.The symbol is a single pipe with a double bar added and is named, accordingly, 'double-barred pipe'. Basic transcriptions: [k͡ǂ], [g͡ǂ], [ŋ͡ǂ].

There is a lot of variation described in the production of these sounds as they occur in actual languages. This complicates the possibility of giving a completely unambiguous cardinal value from which students can learn the articulation. An additional problem, however, stems from the fact that anatomically speakers of many languages using clicks (all the Khoisan languages, in fact) appear to have a rather different bone structure in the oral cavity from that typically found in Western Europeans, having no alveolar ridge as such, but a smoothly sloping palate, the slope beginning from the back of the upper front teeth (Traill (1985)). Because of this, it may well be necessary in practical terms, for speakers with well-developed alveolar ridges to make rather different accommodations to compensate for this when articulating clicks. For this reason, ear-training is of paramount importance here and I encourage my own students to adjust their articulation until we are jointly satisfied that the correct sound is being produced, worrying less in the case of clicks about the finer points of how this is achieved.

5.3.2.2   Click accompaniments

What we have described so far in respect of this group of sounds is only the manner of articulation. These gestures, each of which occurs at a specific place of articulation (as in the table above) results in a sort of distinctive, percussive sound effect and each is accompanied by one or more other articulatory gestures. One of these gestures is mandatory. The additional simultaneous closure at the back of the mouth (the initiator in the airstream) is usually at the velar place of articulation (as described above). In practice, however, the place ranges from pre-velar to uvular. This second closure is always represented separately within the complete symbol for the sound in question.[2] Accordingly, each basic symbol will always be accompanied by either a [k], [g] or [ŋ], or a [q], [ɢ] or [ɴ]. Without the presence of this second closure, there can be no click sound.

Very rarely, the position of this accompaniment may participate in the production of contrast as in these **near minimal pairs** from !Xóõ: [k‖áã] 'poison' but [q‖áã] 'thigh' or [k̂ǂàã] 'bone' but [q̂ǂâa] 'conceal' (Ladefoged and Maddieson (1996: 266)) and a range of similar near contrasts for ǀGui reported by Nakagawa (1995) including [k̂ǃ'áã] 'to taste like giraffe (meat)' but [q̂ǃ'āã] 'to smell like jackal', and [k̂ǂhaa] 'pan (dry lake bed)' but [q̂ǂhâa] 'lying'. (A 'near minimal pair' refers to two words which differ in only a very small number of sounds – two or three, maybe; in these examples, the only differences lie in the tones and in nasalization of the end of the vowel component.) These combined gestures result, effectively, in what could be called *palatalvelar, alveolarvelar, palataluvular* and *alveolaruvular* clicks, names reflecting the relationships in the double articulations concerned (see double articulations discussed in Chapter 4).

Additionally, so far we have said nothing explicit about voicing. Clicks can be voiced or voiceless. The entire click gesture takes place well in advance of the larynx, which is isolated from the click gesture by the presence of the intervening velar closure, and so the behaviour of the vocal folds is completely independent. However, because there is only one basic symbol per sound-type, the voicing information is added by including in the symbol a transcription of the backmost closure: [k] for

---

[2]There is still a lot of variation in the literature with respect to the transcription of click sounds and in older publications, the posterior closure was not always transcribed for voiceless tokens. Increasingly, however, phoneticians are adopting the good practice established by the late Peter Ladefoged and spelled out in Ladefoged and Maddieson (1996: 260) where they explain *There cannot be a click without an accompaniment of some type and our transcription [...] will always include a way of symbolizing this part of the sound [...] so that most clicks include a velar plosive* k *or* g *or a velar nasal* ŋ *as one of their attributes.* Their transcriptions, often extremely complex in nature, are [...] *an attempt at a systematic approach in accordance with the principles of the International Phonetic Association (1989)* [ibid, page 264].

voiceless clicks (or [q] if this is uvular – see above) and [g] (or [ɢ]) for voiced ones. As in other simultaneous articulations that involve more than one symbol, the [k] or [g] can then be tied to the main symbol using a tie bar diacritic: [k͡ʘ] for voiceless bilabial click, [g͡ʘ] for a voiced bilabial click, [ŋ͡ʘ] for a nasalized voiced bilabial click, and so on. The tie bar is not essential, but it is good practice, especially during the learning process.

At a more advanced level, it is also worth noting here that the click gesture can be glottalized – accompanied not by voicing, but by a concomitant glottal stop. (Glottalized clicks would be symbolized using a superscript glottal stop before or after the main symbol, depending on the timing of the formation and/or release of the two gestures: [ˀk͡ʘ] or [k͡ʘˀ].) Additionally, the click may have breathy voice or creaky voice instead of normal (chest) voice. (In such cases, the appropriate diacritic is added below the voiced accompaniment: breathy voiced [g̤͡ʘ] or [ŋ̤͡ʘ] (see below for nasalized clicks), creaky voiced [g̰͡ʘ] or [ŋ̰͡ʘ].)

The velar or uvular posterior closure also means that each click gesture takes place in advance of the velum. The click gesture is completely isolated from the pharyngeal and nasal cavities by the presence of the velar/uvular closure. This in turn means that the position of the velum itself is also independent of the click gesture – the velum can be closed (as would be the case in the voiced and voiceless bilabial clicks just symbolized) or open. If the velum is open, the pulmonic airstream (which is always operating in parallel with whatever is going on in the mouth, even if it is a voiceless click) can flow freely out through the nasal cavities, just as in any other nasal consonant. This situation gives rise to nasalized clicks. For nasalized clicks, the vocal folds are usually also vibrating and so nasalized clicks tend to be voiced sounds. What is now added to the basic click symbol is not an oral velar stop symbol, but the nasal one, giving for example [ŋ͡ʘ], a nasalized voiced bilabial click. (If the folds are not vibrating, a voiceless nasal will be used instead: [ŋ̥͡ʘ].)

These and other accompaniments are described and illustrated in some detail in Ladefoged and Maddieson (1996: 260–80).

Ex 5.7 **Based on the VPM labels discussed above, work out the VPM labels for the following consonants:**

1 [k͡ʘ] 2 [ŋ͡ǁʷ] 3 [ˀk͡ǂ] 4 [g͡ǃ] 5 [g͡ǁ]

Ex 5.8 **Provide the symbol for each of the following sounds:**

1. voiceless alveolar lateral click
2. labialized voiced dental click
3. nasalized breathy voiced postalveolar click
4. pre-glotallized voiceless dental click
5. voiced palatoalveolar click

Ex 5.9   Fill in the blanks in the following articulatory description of a click consonant.

The jaw assumes a narrow aperture. Simultaneously, the back of the tongue
_____ and seals firmly against _____ and the
_____ of the tongue rises and seals against the back of the upper
front _____. This _____ closure is completed by
the side rims rising and sealing against the inside edges of the upper molars. The main
body of the tongue then _____, increasing the cavity formed inside
the mouth and _____ the air pressure in this enclosed space. At the
same time, the velum lowers, assuming an _____ position and
the _____ vibrate for normal voice. A _____
_____ _____ _____ is heard.
This sound can be represented in transcription by the symbol _____.

Ex 5.10   Non-pulmonic consonants can involve the simultaneous operation of more than one airstream mechanism. Tick the boxes in this table to indicate which mechanisms are involved in the production of each of the sounds symbolized.

Sound	Pulmonic egressive	Glottalic egressive	Glottalic ingressive	Velaric ingressive
1 [k']				
2 [k͡ǁ]				
3 [ɠ]				
4 [t̪θ']				
5 [ɦ]				
6 [ɠ͡ǃ]				
7 [ɗ]				
8 [ŋ͡ʘ]				
9 [ʃ']				
10 [ɓ]				

Ex 5.11   Field Notebook: Phonetics in One Word

Entry 5 Use the theory you have just learned in order to continue writing your Field Notebook, applying your knowledge to the detailed phonetic description of the word *completes*.
Go to www.routledge.com/cw/ashby for instructions and feedback.

5.4 SUMMARY

- This chapter has looked in detail at the various airstream mechanisms used in speech production – the universal pulmonic egressive mechanism and also the rarer glottalic mechanisms (egressive used in the production of ejectives and ingressive used in the production of implosives) and the velaric ingressive mechanism (used in the production of clicks).

- We saw how these mechanisms increase the number of consonantal sound types or manners.

- A summary was made of some of the most common click 'accompaniments' which give rise to voicing contrasts and different voice qualities as well as the possibility of glottalization.

- The relationship between the phonetic concept of double articulation and the way in which ejectives, implosives and clicks are produced was explored.

 Ear-training

Once you have studied this chapter carefully, continue the development of your practical skills by attempting the ear-training exercises for this chapter, available as recordings at www.routledge.com/cw/ashby.

FURTHER READING

Airstream mechanisms are covered at a basic level in a variety of volumes, including Chapter 6 in Ashby (2005), Chapter 7 in Ashby & Maidment (2005), Chapter 10 in Ogden (2009), and together with a discussion of phonation, in Chapter 6 of Ladefoged (2001).

Slightly more advanced discussion of non-pulmonic consonants can be found in Chapter 6 of Laver (1994). See clicks in Chapter 8, and ejectives and implosives in Chapter 3, of Ladefoged & Maddieson (1996), ejectives and implosives in Chapter 13 in Ladefoged (2005), and clicks in Chapter 14 of Ladefoged (2005).

Describing vowels

This chapter discusses the way in which phoneticians describe vowel sounds, introducing the Cardinal Vowels and outlining the principal parameters of vowel quality variation. It compares vowels and consonants and establishes the vowel labelling system employed by phoneticians. Representations of vowels are explored, including waveforms and spectrographic images as well as impressionistic records (vowel diagrams, including the IPA Chart vowel diagram, and the use of diacritics in the phonetic transcription of vowels).

6.1 BASIC PARAMETERS OF VOWEL DESCRIPTION

6.1.1 The vowel-consonant relationship

Knowledge accumulated so far about the parts of the tongue (Chapter 2), relationships between active and passive articulators (Chapter 3), and the scale of strictures (Chapter 4) means we already know quite a lot about vowels.

Vowels are made well back in the vocal tract, using only the body of the tongue – the front, centre and back (see Figure 3.4 on p. 34). In terms of place of articulation, therefore, they are located between palatal and velar. In addition to this, they are located at the lowest end of the scale of strictures, being sounds produced with wide or open approximation between the active and passive articulators, which makes them members of the sonorant category of speech sounds.

Chapter 4 focused on different manners of consonant articulation and asked you to think about what you could feel when you articulated particular consonant sounds. If we now compare what was felt for consonant sounds with what we feel when prolonging an [ɑ]-like sound – say a long, drawn-out *Ah!* – we start to identify the rather different nature of vowel articulation. If I asked you to describe [ɑ] in the way in which it was possible to describe [m] or [l] or [d], you would find it impossible. You can feel that the jaw aperture is quite wide (a feeling confirmed by looking in the mirror) but after that, it is difficult to be precise. You may have the impression (because you can't really feel it at all) that the tongue seems low in the mouth. But that is only an impression because there is really no tactile feedback of the sort available for bilabials like [m] or for the alveolar stop consonants like [n], [l], [d] or [t]. Even if you sustain the sound, making a very long [ɑː] (note the addition of the 'longer than' or *length* diacritic [ː] to show the relatively longer duration), you still cannot feel anything. And not only is there no tactile information, there is no kinaesthetic feedback either because nothing moves.

This problem with vowel description had long been recognized, but it was Daniel Jones who a century ago proposed the working solution that we still employ today. Jones instituted an auditorily-based descriptive system for vowels, devising what came to be known as the **Cardinal Vowels**.

6.1.2   The Cardinal Vowels

6.1.2.1   What are they?

As a phonetician, Jones knew about the sonorant nature of vowels and about the vowel articulatory space. He also knew that the extreme flexibility of the tongue meant that between palatal and velar any point on the surface was capable of rising to produce an almost infinite number of different constrictions, each with its own unique resonance. His goal was to design a descriptive system that was subtle enough to account for this wealth of variation – something that could not be achieved using the widely spaced places of articulation that were adequate for describing consonants.

Cardinal Vowels are an auditory measuring stick. Just as all the different consonants in the IPA consonant matrix are cardinal or fixed values which enable us to describe similar sounds used in real languages, so too are the Cardinal Vowels. Phoneticians learn the values and then learn to use them to measure, by ear, the values of real vowel sounds found in actual languages. The Cardinal Vowels are not the vowels of a particular language. Coincidentally, though, languages are found that have one or more vowels that are a pretty close match to an absolute cardinal value. But this *is* simply coincidence and that must not be forgotten. The Cardinal Vowels are an abstract measuring system – nothing more and nothing less.

6.1.2.2   How are they produced?

Unfortunately, although the Cardinal Vowels work extremely well, they are open to criticism. The first problem is that although they are presented as an auditorily-based system, their description depends heavily on articulatory facts and terminology.

Jones's system (which, for the greater part, *is* auditorily based) relies on two articulatorily defined hinge-points. He began by raising the front of the tongue (which remains the highest point of the tongue throughout the articulation) as close as possible towards the hard palate without producing audible friction. Further narrowing of this constriction produces the palatal fricative [j]. This defined Cardinal Vowel 1 (CV1), marking the most front and close extremes of the vowel articulatory space.

At the opposite extreme, Jones delineated the most back, open vowel value by positioning the back of the tongue as far away as possible from the velum. This vowel has a rather pharyngeal resonance. If the back of the tongue is any lower or more retracted in the mouth, the pharyngeal fricative [ʕ] is produced. This most back, open value is known as Cardinal Vowel 5 (CV5) and the back of the tongue (although low in the mouth) is the highest point during its production.

The intermediate points between these two articulatorily defined extremes were determined strictly by ear and resulted in a set of eight cardinal values: 1 [i], 2 [e], 3 [ɛ], 4 [a], 5 [ɑ], 6 [ɔ], 7 [o] and 8 [u]. Jones had a particularly good ear (Collins and Mees (1999: 4)) and he adjusted his tongue in such a way as to produce auditorily equidistant values between these two hinge-points, three values achieved through progressive lowering of the front of the tongue from the most close stricture (CV1, which he transcribed [i]) to the most open (CV4, transcribed [a]) and a further three through progressive raising of the back of the tongue from the most open stricture (CV5, transcribed [ɑ]) to the most close (CV8, transcribed [u]).

Irrationally (although almost certainly influenced by close collaboration with the French phonetician Paul Passy – Jones's friend and mentor – and by his knowledge of the vowel systems of other western European languages, none of which have non-open back unrounded vowels), the last three values are produced with rounded lips, the rounding becoming tighter as the jaw aperture closes, from the open rounding of CV6, [ɔ], to the quite tight rounding of CV8, [u]. This arbitrary switch in lip position from unrounded to rounded in the back vowel series is the second point of criticism – in a truly scientific scale, the lip-position would remain unchanged throughout.

6.1.2.3   Extending the scale

These eight values were already extremely useful (being sufficient, for example, to enable full phonetic descriptions of the vowels of many languages from all over the world – Spanish, Italian, Modern Greek, Hausa, Bengali, Quechua, and so on), but they were inadequate for dealing comprehensively with very many other vowel systems (even English, French, German and Dutch vowels were not fully covered, for example).

To overcome this, Jones's next step was to double the size of the system by retaining the eight tongue positions and switching the contribution made by the lips. Unrounded vowels of this first series became rounded and the rounded vowels became unrounded. This generated CVs 9 to 16, the **secondary Cardinal Vowels** (sCVs). Table 6.1 summarizes these tongue:lip relationships. CVs 1-8 were now termed **primary Cardinal Vowels** (pCVs). The values were then plotted on a 'map' of the auditory vowel space that eventually became the vowel quadrilateral that we use today (see Figure 6.1).

Table 6.1
Summary of tongue:lip relationships in the Cardinal Vowels

	Unrounded lips	Rounded lips
Front of tongue	pCV1 – 5	sCV1 – 5 (= CVs 9 – 13)
Back of tongue	sCV6 – 8 (= CVs 14 – 16)	pCV6 – 8

(Note that in this book, I will not refer to CV15 or CV11, etc. It is much simpler and clearer to regard the numbers 1 to 8 as identifying the eight tongue positions and then use 'primary' or 'secondary' to identify the lip position. This gives us: pCV1 [i] and sCV1 [y], pCV2 [e] and sCV2 [ø], etc.)

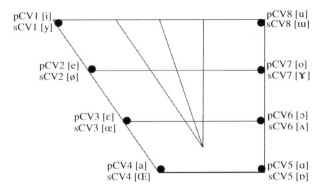

Figure 6.1
A vowel quadrilateral showing the Cardinal Vowels.

6.2   REPRESENTING VOWELS

6.2.1   Diagrammatic representation—reading a vowel quadrilateral

The vowel diagram (vowel quadrilateral) is for vowels what the vocal tract diagram is for consonants. It allows us to represent a sound in diagram form.

What the four-sided ('quadrilateral') figure shows us is a schematization of two dimensions of tongue movement (see Figure 6.2), demarcating the boundaries of the vowel articulatory space within the oral cavity. The slanted left-hand line marks vertical displacement of the front of the tongue, showing us different degrees of open approximation. The top line, which we call **close** (as in 'near to'), represents a position just wider than the degree of stricture required to generate friction. The jaw aperture is **narrow** and to reach this height, close, the front of the tongue is bunched up in the sort of position that also associates with the approximant consonant [j]

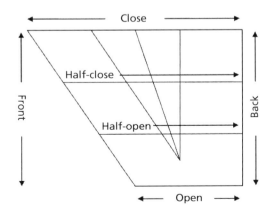

Figure 6.2
The dimensions of the vowel diagram.

(much like the sound at the beginning of English *yet*). For front vowel values, the tongue retains an arched, convex posture, with the front always the highest part, but successive increases in jaw aperture take it further and further away from the hard palate, through heights Jones called **half-close** and **half-open** (articulated with **medium** jaw aperture) to the fully **open** value of [a] (where the jaw aperture is **wide**). Effectively, then, although vowels are produced with open approximation, the adjustments of the tongue are so subtle that it is necessary to break this stricture down into further subdivisions. (A synonym for close that will be found in some phonetics texts and which is almost always used by phonologists is **high** and the equivalent synonym for open is **low**.)

The right-hand line, drawn at right-angles to the horizontals, plots vertical displacement of the back of the tongue. This is shorter than the left-hand line, reflecting the fact that the back of the tongue has a smaller distance through which to move, being nearer to the angle of the jaw. Again, the line intersects with the height lines, allowing us to measure the extent of the vertical displacement in relation to the roof of the mouth, in this case in relation to the soft-palate or velum. Here, the back of the tongue will always be the highest point – the centre and front remaining lower than the back in all cases.

From left to right at any height, therefore, we can identify successive points along the upper surface of the body of the tongue, from front, through centre, to back. The dot placed on the diagram shows that point and shows how high up in the mouth that particular point has risen.

The four peripheral lines thus mark the boundaries of the vowel articulatory space. The relation of this to the oral cavity is schematically represented in Figure 6.3, showing just how small the vowel articulatory area is.

The third dimension of vowel description, the lip position, is not transparent in the same way. Lip position is understood from recognizing the symbol and knowing

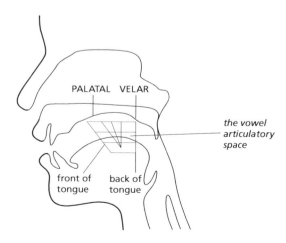

Figure 6.3
Schematization of the vowel articulatory space.

whether this represents a rounded or an unrounded value. For example, the vowel diagram on the IPA chart tells us that *Where symbols appear in pairs, the one to the right represents a rounded vowel.* On the chart, we can see pairs like [i y] and [ɤ o]. Solitary symbols can all be interpreted in the light of a general tendency for lip-rounding to associate with back vowels (especially the non-open ones) and unrounded lips with central and front vowels. On the IPA diagram, therefore, you can guess correctly that [ʊ] is a rounded vowel, while central [ɐ] and [ə] and front [æ] are all unrounded.

In spite of the use of articulatory terminology to describe and label vowels, the lack of easily verifiable precise articulatory correlates means we hardly ever draw vocal tract diagrams for vowels. We can never be absolutely sure about tongue posture. Plotting them as auditory values on a vowel diagram avoids having to guess at this. The one certain articulatory truth, however, is that there is a systematic correlation between the auditory effect or **vowel quality** and the shaping of the vocal tract. Identifying the highest point of the tongue is the single simplest way of describing what this shaping is.

6.2.2 What quality means

Vowel quality refers to the nature of the sound that we hear. It is the name given to the combined auditory effect of the three principal parameters of variation – the unique Backness-Openness-Rounding combination. For example, if you describe a value as being back, close and rounded, I would know that this was the sound [u]. These combinations form the basis of the vowel labelling system described below.

6.2.3 Vowel labelling

Just like consonants, vowels can be represented by means of labels and like consonant labels, vowel labels have three components. In the case of vowels these refer to the **backness** (pinpointing the active part of the tongue) using the basic labels back, central and front, the **openness** of the vowel (describing how near to the palate the active part of the tongue rises) using the labels close, half-close, half-open and open, and lip **rounding** (whether the lips are spread, neutral or rounded). For consonants, we spoke of VPM labels. There is no agreed abbreviation of this kind for vowels, but my habit is always to speak of **BOR labels** (analogous to the VPM labels for consonants) and that is what I will do here.

Typically, then, we can label vowels using the articulatory terminology summarized in the diagram in Figure 6.2. The BOR label for [i] is front close spread and for [ɔ], back half-open rounded. We will see later that these labels can be modified to pinpoint precise positions of vowel values occurring in non-Cardinal positions.

Ex 6.1   **Using the labels for [i] and [ɔ] as a model, write BOR labels for the remaining Cardinal Vowels.**

6.2.4   Transcribing vowels

Like transcribing consonants, we transcribe vowels using the symbols of the IPA Chart. This offers us not only the 16 peripheral vowel values of the Cardinal Vowel system, but also additional, intermediate values that reduce the need for multiple diacritics. The IPA vowel diagram together with some of the most commonly used diacritics for vowel transcription are discussed in detail below (Section 6.3).

6.2.5   Acoustic representations of vowels (waveforms and spectrograms)

6.2.5.1   Interpreting vowel waveforms

To be able to understand more about the relation between what we hear and describe when doing impressionistic phonetics and what we see in a spectrogram when doing acoustic phonetics, we need to know a little bit about waveforms. As we saw in Chapter 4, speech waveforms are of two kinds: periodic and aperiodic (the latter being sustained in the case of fricatives or transient as in the case of plosives). Vowel waveforms are periodic. Periodic waveforms can be one of two types: **simple** (also known as **sinewaves**) or **complex**. Complex waves are the sum of a number of sinewaves which means they consist of a number of different components and are capable of being broken down into these components. All periodic waveforms in speech are complex waveforms.

To appreciate complex waves, we need to know something about their sinewave components. Sinewaves can vary in two dimensions: frequency (which we have already seen means how many times they repeat each second) and **amplitude** (which means how exaggerated the vertical displacement is). These differences are illustrated and explained in Figure 6.4.

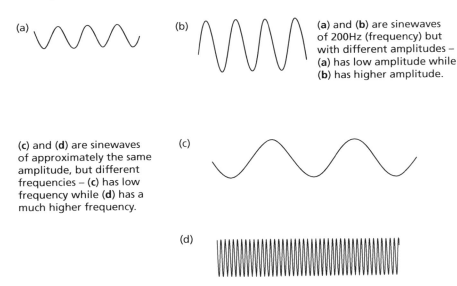

(a) and (b) are sinewaves of 200Hz (frequency) but with different amplitudes – (a) has low amplitude while (b) has higher amplitude.

(c) and (d) are sinewaves of approximately the same amplitude, but different frequencies – (c) has low frequency while (d) has a much higher frequency.

Figure 6.4
Sinewaves of different amplitudes and frequencies.

It is waves such as these in Figure 6.4 that combine to form complex waves. How this comes about can be seen in the very simple example in Figure 6.5. The figure shows three sinewaves, one with a frequency of 100Hz, one of 200Hz and one of 300Hz. The vertical displacement, reflecting the amplitude, is different in each. The 100Hz wave has the greatest amplitude and the 200Hz wave, the smallest. The dotted lines at points A and B (which could be placed anywhere along the time line for the purpose of this illustration) represent two points where you can add up the amplitude measurements in the sinewave components and find that the total is that of the amplitude at that same point in the resultant complex wave – the complex wave is quite literally the sum

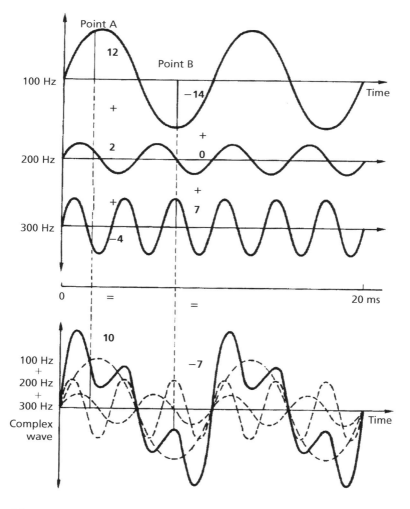

Figure 6.5

Constructing a complex wave. *Source*: Ladefoged, P. (1962) *Elements of Acoustic Phonetics*. Chicago: Chicago University Press.

of the three sinewaves. I made these measurements in millimetres on my computer screen – you try the same thing in your printed copy. My measurements demonstrate that at Point A, on my screen, the waves have amplitude values of '12', '2' and '–4' (with positive values above the zero line and negative values when the wave dips below it). Adding these together produces '10' which is the value at the corresponding point in the complex wave. At point B, I added the values '–14', 'zero' and '7', giving a total of –7 which again matches the corresponding point in the complex wave.[1]

Adding the values of each simple wave together at any particular point in time gives, eventually, the complex wave shape shown on the fourth line.

6.2.5.2   Source-filter theory

Returning to speech and vowel representation, vowel waveforms are periodic (just like those we saw for sonorant consonants – the nasals and approximants). Just as with those earlier waveforms in Chapter 4, each cycle (repeat of a complete pattern of undulations) corresponds to a complete cycle in the larynx waveform (Lx) that we saw in Chapter 2. We will eventually see that the start of each cycle (the largest peak in the speech waveform and the top of the 'v' in the larynx waveform) appears as a vertical striation on a spectrogram (see voiced [z] in Figure 4.10, for example). These striations tell us that the sound is voiced. This alignment is demonstrated in Figure 6.6.

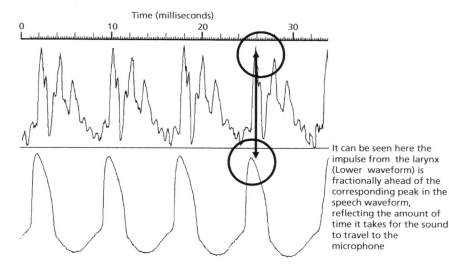

It can be seen here the impulse from the larynx (Lower waveform) is fractionally ahead of the corresponding peak in the speech waveform, reflecting the amount of time it takes for the sound to travel to the microphone

Figure 6.6
Speech and larynx waveform aligned. *Source*: Ashby and Maidment (2005).

[1] You can create waves like this for yourself using a freely available on-line resource called ESYNTH (written by Mark Huckvale) at http://www.phon.ucl.ac.uk/resource/sfs/esynth.htm, which enables you to build your own complex waveforms directly from sinewaves and play out the sound to hear the different qualities you can create.

To understand why the speech waveform is different from the larynx waveform we need to digress and consider what is known as the **source-filter theory**, an acoustic theory of speech production. As the name implies, there are two principal components involved: the sound source is one (and in this case, the source is voice – the name given to the tone produced by vocal fold vibration – a pulsating flow of air), and the other is what happens to it as it passes through the vocal tract (the tract acting as a kind of filter).

Although they are not exactly the same, musical instruments are an analogy often used for what is going on here. Take a guitar, for instance – a traditional Spanish or acoustic guitar, a hollow box with strings on. If you pluck a string, you can sometimes just see it vibrating – if you watch it, you will find that it goes a bit blurred or out of focus. (The strings are analogous to the vocal folds.) But you can also hear the effect of this vibratory movement and the reason for that is because the vibrations are being passed to the hollow box, the body of the guitar, which (together with the volume of air inside it) also starts to vibrate. It is these vibrations we then hear. If you just tied the guitar string tightly between two pegs in your garden, you would barely hear it all if you plucked it. The vibrating string still causes similar vibrations in the molecules of air around it, but they are too small to hear unless there is what is called a **resonator** involved as well. In the case of the guitar, its hollow body is the resonator. (The body containing air is analogous to the vocal tract.)

Another point to make here is that different resonators respond differently to the sound source. You can check this out for yourself by lining up a row of different containers (a number of different drinking glasses, for example) and then tapping them all once with your pencil. Each will sound different. This is because each has its own preferred resonance frequency (rate of vibration) and so it vibrates differently when the pencil hits it. Just as with a guitar, we are hearing the vibrations not of the shock itself, but of the container filtering (and amplifying) that sound source. We can hear very easily that each different resonator filters the source differently.

The vocal tract, then, is like a whole series of individually shaped resonators coupled together into a long tube. Each section of this tube will have a preferred way of vibrating and so each will modify or 'filter' in a different way the sound that enters it, enhancing or suppressing different components of the wave depending on how close they come to its own preferred resonance frequency. The undulating waveform of the pulsating airstream that goes in at the beginning will have a very different shape by the time it leaves the tract and radiates out, travelling through the air, towards the listener at the end of its journey. What is more, every time we adjust the positions of the articulators to make a different speech sound, the source passes through a new and unique series of filters. Accordingly, the waveform of every different speech sound has a unique and different shape and makes a unique and different impression on the listener's ear. The different waveforms typical of the vowels [i], [ɑ] and [u] can be seen in Figure 6.7.

Another way of representing this information is through **amplitude/frequency spectra (a/f spectra)**. The difference between these spectra (shown in Figure 6.8) and the waveforms in Figure 6.7 is that whereas the waveforms also include a time dimension (moving from left to right of the image marks the passing of real time, measured usually in milliseconds, ms), an a/f spectrum is like a still photo, capturing the individual structure of the wave at any one point in time.

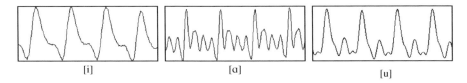

Figure 6.7
Speech waveforms of [i], [ɑ] and [u].

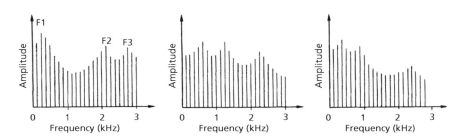

Figure 6.8
Spectra of [i], [ɑ] and [u] (with formants 1-3 labelled for [i]). *Source*: Clark & Yallop 1990.

In each spectrum, you can see a different alignment of prominences – energy peaks at specific frequencies. These represent the strongest ('loudest') components in the signal, those which have the greatest amplitude. When the vocal tract is in the position required for [i], for example, we can see that it resonates particularly well at around 250Hz, 2,200Hz and 2,800Hz. By comparison, when it gets into the shape for saying [ɑ], the predominant frequencies are at approximately 700Hz and 1,200Hz with another occurring at around 2,400Hz. The spectrum, then, is giving us information about frequency (rate of vibration) and amplitude (the size of the vibration, contributing to its loudness). The peaks constitute the identifying characteristics of vowels and are known as **formants**. Each different vowel sound has a different and unique arrangement of formants.

6.2.5.3 Interpreting spectrograms

It is the peaks of these spectra, representing the dominant components of the waveform, that can be seen when we look at the spectrogram of a vowel as in Figure 6.9. In a spectrogram – specifically a **wideband spectrogram** – it is as if each a/f spectrum has been turned through 90° and the peaks or formants now appear as dark horizontal bands, with F1 at the bottom. But there is one major and very important difference here: the a/f spectrum is static – a snapshot of the sound at a point in time – but the spectrogram is dynamic, capturing again the time dimension that is also present in the speech waveform, such that we can see each spectral peak now has duration in time which corresponds to the duration of the vowel. Just as each vowel has its own identifiable a/f spectrum, it follows that each will have a correspondingly unique spectrographic image. With practice, you can learn

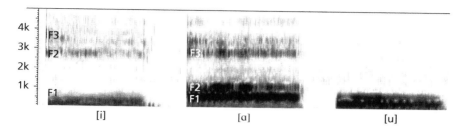

Figure 6.9
Spectrograms of [i], [ɑ] and [u] with formants 1-3 labelled for [i] and [ɑ].

to read these. The formants, then, which are numbered from left to right in the spectrum, now appear as bands of energy, sustained through time and numbered from bottom to top in the spectrogram. The precise amplitude value is lost but this is retained impressionistically in the relative darkness of the formant – the stronger the amplitude, the darker the image. Of course, every time we pronounce a vowel, that in itself is a unique event and there will always be slight variations, but the variations tend to fall within an identifiable range and the vowel is still recognized by the listener, regardless of who says it or when.

Ex 6.2 **Describe the waveforms represented by each of the following schematic a/f spectra. Say whether the wave is simple or complex. If it is complex, describe the components in terms of their frequency and relative amplitude.**

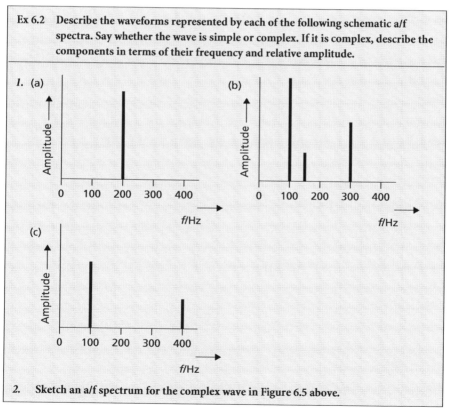

2. **Sketch an a/f spectrum for the complex wave in Figure 6.5 above.**

6.3   THE IPA CHART VOWEL DIAGRAM

6.3.1   Terminology and basic symbols

The IPA chart uses slightly different terminology to refer to the height lines in the vowel diagram from the terminology originally used by Daniel Jones. Half-close becomes **close-mid** and half-open becomes **open-mid**. These are synonyms and they are not problematic. Both sets of terms are in current use.

Vowel values plotted on the IPA vowel diagram are based on the Cardinal Vowel system, but rationalized to remove the arbitrary switch of lip position that we saw occurring just over half way through each of the two Cardinal Vowel series. An explanation of how to read the IPA vowel diagram was given in Section 6.2.1.

> **Ex 6.3   Look at the following fairly broad phonetic transcriptions of the typical MRP pronunciation of English words. Compare the vowel symbol with the IPA chart vowel diagram and try to work out preliminary BOR labels for the MRP vowels.**
>
> 1 *seat* [siːt]   2 *four* [fɔː]   3 *two, too* [tuː]
> 4 *calm* [kɑːm]   5 *third* [θɜːd]

6.3.2   Diacritics

The additional symbols on the IPA chart vowel diagram ([æ], [ɪ], and so on) are useful in that they avoid the need to apply diacritics to modify Cardinal Vowel values. They help to keep the transcription simple and clear. Sometimes, however, we have a real choice between using diacritically modified Cardinal Vowels or the straightforward IPA symbol. In such cases, when you are dealing with pure phonetic values and you are not constrained by the need to reflect the vowel system of a particular language, the best practice is always to go for the simplest option.

Sometimes, there is more than one choice. For a vowel sound that is half way between pCV2 [e] and pCV3 [ɛ], for example, we can select either of those symbol shapes and adjust them by the application of a diacritic. We can select [e] and make the value 'more open than' pCV2 by applying the 'lowered' diacritic, [ˌ], to give [e̞]. Alternatively, we could start from pCV3, [ɛ], and raise this by adding the raised diacritic [ˌ], making it 'more close than' pCV3, [ɛ̝]. What this means in terms of articulation is that the vowel is made using the front of the tongue as the active articulator and that this rises to a height mid-way between half-open and half-close. In terms of labelling, we could say a *front raised half-open spread* vowel ([ɛ̝]) or a *front lowered half-close spread* vowel ([e̞]). Alternatively again, we can call it a front mid spread vowel. However detailed the expression, there is still a certain lack of precision in these labels just as there is sometimes a lack of precision in consonantal VPM labels, but accompanied by a vowel diagram representing the intended value and/or a brief descriptive statement which serves to further define the symbolization, this is rarely a problem in practice.

To represent [ɪ], it would be possible to start from the nearest Cardinal reference point, pCV2, [e], and centralize this using another very common diacritic, the **centralization diaeresis**, [¨], giving [ë], and also raise it a little, [ë̝], giving a value that is made by means of raising a part of the tongue nearer to the centre than the front (the active articulator) to a height that is just above half-close and using unrounded lips. (The nearer the unrounded value is towards the centre of the vowel articulatory space, the less spread and more neutral it tends to be.) As far as giving a BOR label to such a value is concerned, we could say something like a *centralized front raised half-close unrounded* vowel. A more discursive version this time would be *centralized from fully front, raised from half-close, unrounded* vowel. However, once you understand how to interpret the more cryptic version of the labels, the prepositional additions are unnecessary and my preference, again, is to keep the label itself simple.

Right in the middle of the IPA chart vowel diagram, is the symbol [ə]. This is the most distant value from any Cardinal reference point and if we wanted to represent it using a Cardinal Vowel symbol, modified by the addition of diacritics, it is difficult even to know which value would be the most appropriate one to start from. There is no obvious solution to the question of how to represent [ə] in this way. For this sound (the first sound in the word *about* for most English speakers), we generally use the IPA [ə] symbol. (This symbol is often referred to by its name, **schwa**.) This vowel is a *central mid neutral* vowel.

These three diacritics, centralizing, raising and lowering, are probably the most widely used **vowel quality** modifiers and in some languages they are the only ones you would ever need. They can be used at the same time as the length mark we used earlier, [ː].

Ex 6.4   **Using the descriptions above as your model, interpret the following narrow phonetic transcriptions of the MRP English long simple vowels with regard to their BOR characteristics. (If you are in doubt about any of the diacritics used here, check them against the diacritics illustrated on the IPA chart.)**

1 [ï̞ː]   2 [əː]   3 [ɑ̈ː]   4 [ÿː]   5 [ɔ̞ː]

6.3.3   Plotting vowels on the vowel diagram

Just as they can read and produce the sounds represented by symbols of the sort in the exercises above, so phoneticians can transfer these symbols to vowel diagrams, plotting on the diagram the quality represented.

pCV3 [ɛ], shown in Figure 6.10, is a front half-open/open-mid unrounded vowel. This BOR label tells us exactly where to place it on a vowel diagram – at the intersection of the front line and the half-open/open-mid line, named in Figure 6.2. What the dot tells us is that *this vowel sounds as if it is being made with this part of the tongue* (for [ɛ] that would be the *front of the tongue*) *in the highest position* (and for [ɛ] that would be at the *half-open height*) – so, [ɛ] sounds as if it is being made with the front of the tongue raised to a half-open height.

If, however, the centralization diacritic is added, or the retracted diacritic, giving [ɛ̈] or [ɛ̠], the dot used to plot the resonance would need to be moved slightly to the

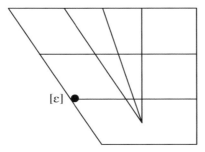

Figure 6.10 Vowel diagram showing resonance of [ɛ].

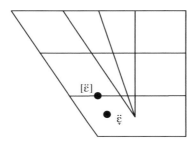

Figure 6.11 Vowel diagram showing the resonances of [ë] and [ë̞].

right (although still on the half-open line). If a more open diacritic was then added to this new value, the dot would need to be positioned below the half-open line. You can see the effect of the addition of these diacritics in Figure 6.11.

We can also make use of diacritics to suggest different degrees of centralization. [ë] and [ë̞], for example, in Figure 6.11 are about mid-way between fully front and central, but if the value was nearer to front than central, we could use the retracted diacritic to show this, as in Figure 6.12, and reserve the centralization diacritic for a value that is more central still. There is no established way of demonstrating these small distinctions. Phoneticians apply the diacritics as they see best and explain how they are using them in order to overcome any ambiguity. Each case is treated individually.

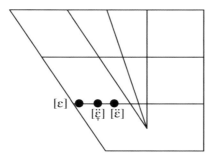

Figure 6.12 Using diacritics to suggest degrees of centralisation.

Ex 6.5 **Using these examples as a model, try to plot the resonances given in Exercise 6.4 on a vowel diagram. (Make sure you draw a big enough diagram to allow plenty of space for plotting the values clearly – place a dot and write the symbol next to it.)**

Ex 6.6 **Using what you learnt in Exercise 6.3 and what you have now read above, interpret the following transcriptions with regard to their BOR characteristics. (If you are in doubt about any of the diacritics used here, check them against the diacritics illustrated on the IPA chart.)**

1 [ə̃] 2 [ɤ] 3 [ÿ] 4 [e̠] 5 [ɔ̥]

Ex 6.7 **Write BOR descriptive labels for the MRP short simple vowel values plotted on the following diagram. (The lip positions are indicated.)**

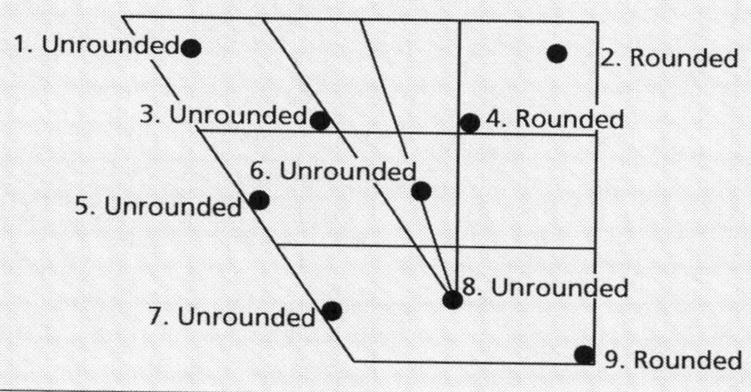

Ex 6.8 **Transcribe the values that you have identified in Exercise 6.7.**

6.4 LEARNING AND REMEMBERING THE SOUNDS

Students of phonetics are traditionally taught the Cardinal Vowel measuring system in ear-training classes where they learn to recognize the models provided by the teacher and, eventually, to produce these for themselves. Some readers of this book will be studying in such a learning environment. Others will be relying on access to recorded materials. However you are learning them, it can often be useful to enlist the help of real language examples with particularly close-to-cardinal values. Such examples are summarized in Table 6.2. (Obviously, not everyone knows all of these languages, but sometimes such mnemonics are useful.)

Table 6.2
A Cardinal Vowel guide

Number	Symbol	Language data
pCV1	[i]	Near French *si* (if); much more tense and narrow than the vowel in English *seed*.
pCV2	[e]	Near French *thé* (tea); near the Scottish English pronunciation of *day*.
pCV3	[ɛ]	Near French *mettre* (to put), *maître* (master); near Dutch *bed* (bed).
pCV4	[a]	Near Conservative Parisian French *patte* (paw); near Dutch *kater* (hangover).
pCV5	[ɑ]	Near Conservative Parisian French *pas* (not).
pCV6	[ɔ]	Near French *porte* (door); near North Yorkshire *four*; near Scottish English *hot*.
pCV7	[o]	Near French *beau* (beautiful); near Scottish English *coat*.
pCV8	[u]	Near French *tout* (all).
sCV1	[y]	Near French *tu* (you), *lune* (moon); German *Füße* (feet).
sCV2	[ø]	Near French *peu* (afraid).
sCV3	[æ]	Near French *oeuf* (egg), *veuve* (widowed).
sCV4	[ɶ]	
sCV5	[ɒ]	Near Standard British English *hot*.
sCV6	[ʌ]	Near the Vietnamese word for *favour*, [ʌŋ].[1] Otherwise, comparable to a very old-fashioned variety of the vowel in Standard British English *cup*.
sCV7	[ɤ]	Near the Vietnamese word for *silk* [tɤ]. A somewhat centralized version occurs in the Thai word for *silver*, [ŋɤn].
sCV8	[ɯ]	Near the first vowel in Korean [ɯmçik] meaning *food and drink*;[2] a more centralized version is heard as the first vowel in older speakers of Japanese *Fuji* (younger speakers tend to have lip-rounding).

1 The reader should note that in the Vietnamese and Thai examples that are used here, the tones have been omitted in order to keep the transcriptions clear and simple.
2 Grateful thanks are due to Professor Kim, Professor of Korean Language, of Dongguk University, Korea, for this example.

Ex 6.9 **Turkish has eight vowels which can be represented phonetically as:**
[i u e ʌ o y ø ɯ]. The vowels participate in six sub-groups:

(i) front vowels
(ii) back vowels
(iii) close vowels
(iv) non-close vowels
(v) rounded vowels
(vi) unrounded vowels

Sort the vowels into these six sub-groups. (You should end up with four values in each; values may appear in more than one group.)

> **Ex 6.10   Field Notebook: Phonetics in One Word**
>
> **Entry 6** Use the theory you have just learned in order to continue writing your Field Notebook, applying your knowledge to the detailed phonetic description of the word *completes*.
>
> Go to www.routledge.com/cw/ashby for instructions and feedback.

6.5   SUMMARY

- This chapter has outlined the phonetic nature of vowels, comparing them with consonants.

- It has explained and described the Cardinal Vowel system, identifying the three basic parameters of vowel quality variation: the active part of the tongue (front-back), how high in the mouth this rises (open-close) and the accompanying lip position (rounded-unrounded).

- Representation of vowels has been explored in some detail, including the study of waveforms and spectrograms.

- The vowel diagram has also been studied to understand the operation of the back-central-front and open-mid-close parameters and how actual vowel qualities are plotted in this quadrilateral space.

- The chapter explored vowel transcription including the effects of a small range of diacritics and the conversion between vowel labels, plots (diagrammatic representations) and transcriptions.

 Ear-training

Once you have studied this chapter carefully, continue the development of your practical skills by attempting the ear-training exercises for this chapter, available as recordings at www.routledge.com/cw/ashby.

FURTHER READING

Extending the study of manner of articulation, basic reading on vowel description can be found in Chapters 2 and 4 of Ashby (2005), Chapter 4 of Cruttenden (2008), and Chapter 2 of Lodge (2009).

Chapter 4 in Ladefoged (2001) deals with vowels, focusing specifically on English vowels. Combine this with your reading about acoustics and Chapter 5 of Ashby & Maidment (2005) provides a good, basic introduction, as does Chapter 8 in Ladefoged (2001). At a more advanced level, Chapter 6 of Hayward (2000) offers an excellent account of vowel acoustics.

If you are interested in an overview of the physics of speech, in addition to the introductory chapter of Chapter 9 in Lodge (2009), there are several small, very readable volumes on the subject, including Ladefoged (1962), Denes & Pinson (1993) and Malmberg (1963).

Further parameters of
variation in vowels

Chapter 7 extends the description of vowel variation, describing other common and less common differences which operate independently of the basic vowel qualities described in Chapter 6. Referring to a range of languages (including English), the chapter explores vowel duration (long vs short) and clipping processes affecting this; direction of airflow (oral vs nasalized); complexity, including monophthong/diphthong/triphthong, prominence, smoothing and compression, diphthongization and breaking; tongue root and tip gestures ([ATR], r-colouring); fricativization and the effects of phonation types (fricative vowels, voiced and voiceless, breathy, creaky).

7.1   QUANTITY

7.1.1   Long vs short

We have just looked at vowel quality – the different combinations of backness, openness and lip position that create noticeably different vocalic resonances. Languages can also choose how long they want a particular sound to last. This measurable duration of a vowel sound is known as **vowel quantity**.

Although a fascinating topic in its own right, this section is not primarily concerned with the intrinsic duration of vowels. There is a considerable literature demonstrating, for example, that across languages the intrinsic duration of vowels correlates well with tongue height (closer vowels tend to be shorter than open vowels, for example). There is also little doubt that the phonetic environment also plays a part. How far the tongue is required to travel in order to establish the position required for a following consonant unavoidably affects vowel length – the greater the distance, the longer the vowel. For example, all vowels tend to be shorter when followed by a labial consonant because the tongue is not involved at all in the articulation of that consonant. However, if there is a back vowel such as [u] followed by an apical consonant such as [d], that vowel will be proportionally longer than if it was followed by a dorsal consonant such as [g]. An excellent and clear summary of some of the early studies of intrinsic vowel duration across languages is given in Lehiste (1970).

For the purpose of everyday speech, duration in vowels is always relative. Human beings are not capable of producing vowels with absolute durations. So, in English, the vowels in *bee* and *fall* are normally longer than the vowels in *it* or *left*.

We show this in the transcription by adding the length diacritic ([ː]) to the longer ones, giving [biː, fɔːɫ] but we omit this when transcribing the shorter ones, giving [ɪt, left].[1]

Some languages use the duration of a vowel to change meaning. When a particular vowel quality is sustained for a short time, a particular meaning is understood, but when (more or less) the same quality is used with a longer duration, the meaning changes. Although usually in English this is not the case, the longer vowels have different qualities from the shorter vowels, MRP English provides three exceptions to this generalization which do result in potential contrasts:

[iː] and [i] in:

> *car key* (as opposed to *door key*) vs *khaki* (['kɑː kiː] vs ['kɑːki]) *marquee* vs *Marky* (although this also involves a change of stress position: [mɑːˈkiː] vs ['mɑːki]), etc.

> On an anecdotal level, while I was writing this chapter, my husband picked up my mug of tea – I responded *(that's) **my** tea* ['maɪ tiː] (as opposed to *(that's) mighty* ['maɪti]).

[uː] and [u] in:

> *too open* vs *to open* ([tuː 'əʊpən] vs [tu 'əʊpən])

> *two Americans* vs *to Americans* [tuː əˈmerɪkənz] vs [tu əˈmerɪkənz]), etc.

[əː] and [ə] in:

> *foreword* vs *forward* (['fɔːwəːd] vs ['fɔːwəd]) or *fur lining* vs *for lining* ([fəː 'laɪnɪŋ] vs [fə 'laɪnɪŋ]) etc.

Contrasts such as these are one of the reasons why many phoneticians prefer to mark length overtly in the phonemic transcription of English instead of introducing additional different symbol shapes to distinguish what are really long vs short pairs. Different shapes (such as are unfortunately used, in addition to marking length) for the third contrast, transcribed phonemically using /ɜː/ and /ə/, obscure the fact that the quality of the vowels is actually the same. /ɜː/ – note the slant, phonemic brackets here – is the usual phonemic representation of [əː], and /ə/ of [ə] (see, for example, Wells (2008) and Cruttenden (2008)).

Examples like these help us to understand how some languages choose to operate a length contrast for most or all of their different vowel qualities. In Thai, for example, [krìt] and [krìːt], both spoken on a low tone (which is indicated in transcription by the downward pointing line over the vowel), mean 'dagger' and 'to cut' respectively. By sustaining the vowel for a longer duration, the meaning is changed. Likewise in [sùt] and [sùːt] meaning respectively 'last/rearmost' and 'to inhale' (Tsingsabadh and Abramson (1999)). Contrasts of this kind allow us to talk about **long** and **short** vowels (although because these lengths are always relative, it would be better to talk about **longer** and **short(er)**).

---

[1] Do not worry about the different symbols used for the l-sound here. We will come back to these later.

Two contrastive degrees of length are usually the maximum, but there are a very small number of languages reported, including Estonian and Mixe (spoken in Mexico), in which three degrees are recorded. However, the status of vowel length in the two languages is arguably different. In Mixe, there is little doubt that vowel length alone, in any position in the word, brings about a change of meaning, for example, [pe] 'climb (n)', [peˑt] 'broom', [peːt] 'Peter' (Hoogshagen (1959)). In Estonian, however, the length of the vowel is determined largely by the structure of the word and vowel length itself (short, longer and longest) is contrastive only in the first syllable (Lehiste (1970: 158)).

Ex 7.1   **Different accents of English pronounce vowels in rather different ways both with regard to quality and to quantity. For your pronunciation, try to decide whether the vowels in the following pairs of words are the same in length or whether one is longer than the other.**

1 hit, heat	2 should, shooed	3 sod, sword	4 Pam, palm	5 bun, burn
6 fizz, fees	7 blood, blurred	8 wok, walk	9 foot, food	10 hat, heart

---

7.1.2   Clipping

7.1.2.1   *Phonological vs phonetic length differences*

Length in the contrastive sense – the sort just explored above – is controlled by the speaker and has phonological status as we saw in the examples from Thai and MRP English. However, there are also purely phonetic processes at work that affect the duration of a vowel. One such process is called **clipping**.

Two forms of clipping occur in English and these processes affect the duration of all vowels, long and short alike. Essentially, in particular phonetic environments, the duration of a given vowel is shorter than it would be if it was the **norm allophone** (the usual way of realizing a phoneme, by which all other variants are judged). In English, this is caused either when a syllable is terminated by a voiceless consonant (also called a **fortis** consonant, see below) or when a stressed vowel is followed by multiple unstressed syllables within the same rhythm unit (often referred to as a **rhythmic foot**). These two contexts give rise to what are called **pre-fortis clipping** and **rhythmic clipping** respectively.

7.1.2.2   *Pre-fortis clipping*

The terms fortis and **lenis** are discussed in more detail in Chapter 8. For our present purposes, it is sufficient to know that *fortis* is another name for the group of consonants we have so far referred to as voiceless and *lenis* for the group we have referred to as voiced. This means that the voiceless consonants in English (all obstruents: the plosives /p t k/, the fricatives /f θ s ʃ/ and the affricate /tʃ/) are also known as fortis consonants.

When vowels in English occur in open syllables (syllables with the structure CV) or in ones closed by a lenis consonant (any of the so-called voiced obstruents or any of the sonorant consonants), they are usually pronounced with their 'norm' duration – that is to say, all vowels have their full length whether they are members

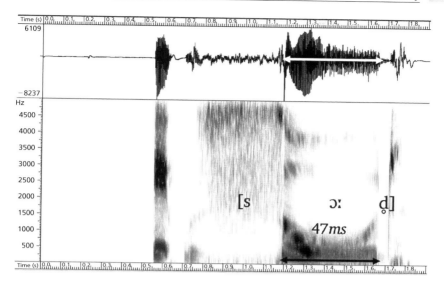

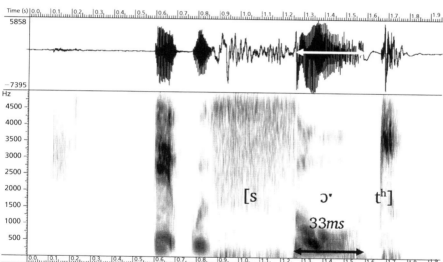

Figure 7.1
Annotated spectrograms of *It was sword* (above) and *It was sort* (below) (Speaker PA 150109).

of the longer or shorter vowel groups. However, when a vowel occurs in a syllable closed by a fortis consonant, the vowel becomes appreciably shorter in duration. This difference can be measured in either speech waveforms or spectrograms as in Figure 7.1.[2] What you can see there are images of two recordings of me comparing

[2] English voiceless (fortis) and voiced (lenis) consonants have all sorts of phonetic characteristics which will be discussed in more depth in Chapter 8. Two of these, 'devoicing' of voiced/lenis [d] (giving [d̥]) and what is called 'aspiration' of voiceless/fortis [t] (giving [tʰ]) are included in the narrow phonetic transcription of the final consonants in the spectrograms here because they are clearly visible.

(1) The vowel is fully long in this open syllable, e.g. *Oh!*

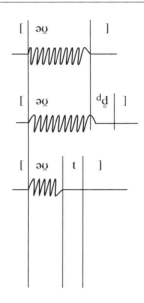

(2) To all intents and purposes, the vowel is also fully long when the syllable is closed by a lenis consonant, *ode* — although note that the consonant itself has lost most of its voicing (this is typical behaviour for a lenis obstruent in final position).

(3) When the syllable is closed by a fortis consonant, *oat*, the vowel is appreciably shorter in duration — we call this effect **pre-fortis clipping**.

Figure 7.2
Voicing diagrams demonstrating pre-fortis clipping of [əʊ].

the words *sword* and *sort*. Not only can I hear that the words *sword* and *sort* are different in duration, I can also see and measure this. These were just two versions picked at random from half a dozen recordings. The vowel in *sword* measures 47 milliseconds (ms) while the 'same' vowel in *sort* measures only 33. In *sort* the syllable is closed by a fortis consonant and the vowel has undergone pre-fortis clipping, its length here reduced by 14 ms. This effect can be suggested in transcription by using **half-long** [ˑ] instead of the fully long [ː]. It can be represented schematically by drawing impressionistic voicing diagrams of the sort shown in Figure 7.2.

Ex 7.2	In which of the following English words will pre-fortis clipping occur?			
1 ease	2 cough	3 lapsed	4 cars	5 soothe
6 walk	7 breath	8 debt	9 raised	10 scar

7.1.2.3   Rhythmic clipping

The length of a vowel is also affected by how many unstressed syllables follow. English is what we call a **stress-timed** language, meaning that we perceive the time between rhythmic beats or stresses when we are speaking to be roughly equal; each stress seems like the tick on a metronome.[3] So, in comparable contexts, the stressed [æ]-vowel in *man* is fully long, but relatively, the same vowel in *manage* is a little bit shorter while

---

[3] For more information on stress-timing, see Chapter 10.

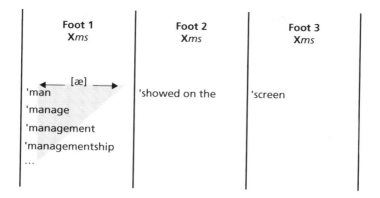

Figure 7.3
Diagram demonstrating reduced time available for the stressed vowel in Foot 1 as the number of syllables within the foot increases.

the same vowel in *managementship* is shortest of all. This is illustrated schematically in Figure 7.3. This figure shows three rhythmic feet of equal duration. In the first, the number of syllables increases by one in each utterance. The amount of time available for the stressed vowel [æ] decreases accordingly because all the additional syllables have to be articulated within the same time frame, *Xms*. Unfortunately, transcribing this amount of minute variation is tricky. There is no clear-cut solution, although the IPA does provide an **extra short** diacritic, [˘], for anything that is of exceptionally short duration. (Note that this is never a question of a specific number of milliseconds, because the perception of length is always relative, comparative.)

Interestingly, given a suitable context, because of the operation of these clipping processes it is possible to have so-called long vowels that are the same length as so-called short vowels in connected speech in English. For example, if we coined a word such as *ownershipfulness* and insert this into the same carrier frame as in the example in Figure 7.3, there is much, much less time to devote to the long vowel [əʊ] than there is to say the short vowel [æ] because we have to articulate five syllables in *ownershipfulness* in the time accorded to just one in *man* or four in *managementship*. In real terms, then, so-called 'long' [əʊ] could even become measurably shorter than so-called 'short' [æ].

Ex 7.3	**Identify the vowels that are likely to undergo clipping in the following English utterances (pre-fortis and/or rhythmic):**
1.	Many hands make light work.
2.	A bird in the hand is worth two in the bush.
3.	A stitch in time saves nine.
4.	Many a slip twixt cup and lip.
5.	A rolling stone gathers no moss.

7.2　COMPLEXITY

7.2.1　Intentional or phonological complexity

A very common source of variation and contrast (occurring in at least 33 per cent of the world's languages according to Lindau *et al.* (1985)) is **complexity**. Listening for the Consonant-Vowel structure of utterances in Chapter 1, we encountered a type of complex or gliding/changing vowel quality that we called a diphthong, a vowel that changes quality in the space of a single syllable. It can be considered as a vowel with two different targets. Vowels whose quality remains relatively constant are known as monophthongs. These differences can be seen in the spectrograms in Figure 7.4 where formants remain steady for the monophthongal vowels in *see-saw* but change in value during the diphthongs in *say so*.

English is one of many languages to make use of diphthongs. But, do not be misled by the spelling of vowels in English. The spelling has been relatively unchanged

(a) *see-saw*

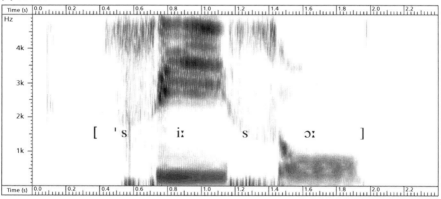

(b) *say-so*

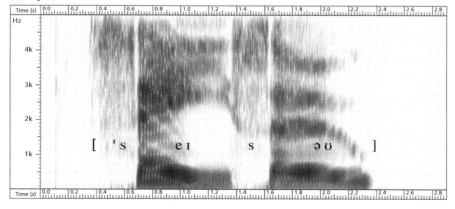

Figure 7.4
Monophthongs and diphthongs: spectrograms of *see-saw* [siː sɔː] and *say so* [seɪ səʊ] (speaker PA).

for over two hundred years, even though during that time the pronunciation has continued to evolve. If you are interested in the historical development of these sounds, you can refer to volumes such as Baugh and Cable (2002) or Freeborn (2006) for accounts of these changes. For example, today the vowel in MRP English *thief* is a monophthong, although we still use two vowel letters in the spelling. On the other hand, the vowel in the first syllable of *holy* is a diphthong in many accents, but it is spelled with just one alphabetic letter.

Ex 7.4	In your pronunciation, which of the following words have a monophthong and which have a diphthong?			
1 day	2 please	3 saw	4 seize	5 boat
6 friend	7 die	8 rhyme	9 laughed	10 sleeve

Ex 7.5 Provide narrow phonetic transcriptions for the MRP English closing diphthongs plotted on the following vowel diagrams. (Closing diphthongs are those starting from a particular quality and gliding to a closer quality in terms of openness.)

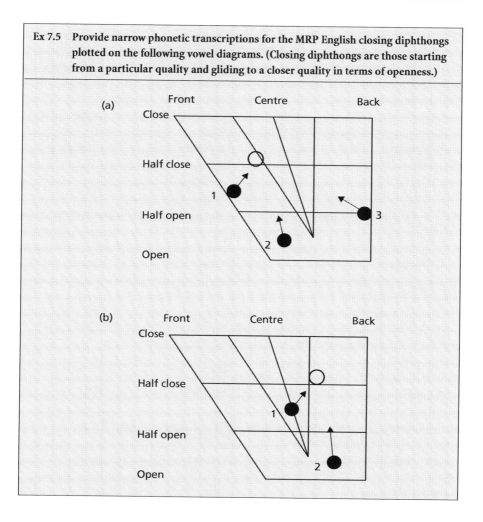

Table 7.1
MRP English triphthongs

Broad phonetic representation	Keyword
[laɪə]	liar/lyre
[leɪə]	layer
[lɔɪə]	lawyer
[ləʊə]	lower
[laʊə]	(f)lour

In addition to a total of eight diphthongal values (including the **centring diphthongs** which glide from a more peripheral quality to schwa, [ɪə, ʊə eə]), English also has a series of five **triphthongs** (or diphthongs + schwa as they are sometimes called). These occur in words such as shown in Table 7.1.

Added to the regular vowel phoneme list for English, these would give an inventory of at least 27 vowels. However, these sounds present a perceptual problem which calls into question their status as separate phonemes. They are often the cause of disagreement between speakers as to how many syllables are involved. Are they, in fact, a sequence of two separate vowels and therefore two syllables or are they single syllabic nuclei? How many syllables are there in the word *higher* and is this the same as the number occurring in *hire*? Are we dealing with one vowel or two?

Bi-directional glides of this kind are much less common than the uni-directional diphthongs. Triphthongs are also subject to simplification as a function of a process called **smoothing** (described below) by which a triphthong can become a diphthong or even a simple monophthongal vowel.

7.2.2 Prominence

In any vocalic glide, one element is the prominent one, said to be the syllabic component. (Sometimes people speak of the stressed component.) Languages can vary as to which element this is, especially in triphthongs.

In English, in the norm allophone of all eight diphthongs it is the first element of the glide that stands out and the sounds are thus described as having **falling prominence**. Early on, in Chapter 1, the one-vowel:one-syllable relationship was established. It follows, then, that since diphthongs are just 'one vowel' in the syllabic sense, even if there is an overlap or partial overlap of quality, each part cannot be the equivalent of any one of the simple vowels with which it appears to identify. If that was the case, every time we heard a diphthong, we would have the impression of there being two syllables, as in the onomatopoeically named donkey in A.A. Milne's *Winnie-the-Pooh* stories, Eeyore ['iː ɔː]. But that is not the case – when we hear a diphthong, it generally gives us the impression of only one syllable.

This impression is due to a number of factors including the width of the glide, accuracy of target articulation, speed of glide, and so forth and these vary from language to language. In English, interpretation of two successive vowels as a diphthong, a monosyllabic unit, is in part because of the relative prominence of the two components. This is because although the first target is fully articulated, the tongue position may even be sustained for a moment (if you look carefully at the spectrograms of English diphthongs, you can sometimes see this brief pause at the beginning where the formants remain steady, parallel), but immediately after, the part of the tongue which is active in the production of the second component starts to rise and a glide is heard as the audible quality starts to change. However, in colloquial English speech, it is rarely the case that the tongue will move all the way to the position required for the second value. This makes English diphthongs characteristically bi-partite sounds with a target+off-glide pattern. (By comparison, diphthongs in German, for example, are described as tri-partite. The glide is usually completed in such a way that both targets are fully articulated, giving a target + glide + target pattern. Here the duration of the components plays a more important role in their perception as monosyllabic. The combined duration will be less than two adjacent short vowels.)

Auditorily, one of the effects of the English pattern is to make the starting quality more prominent. Accordingly, the norm allophone of all English diphthongs is a pronunciation with falling prominence. This is shown in transcription by adding a **non-syllabic** diacritic beneath the second symbol in the norm allophone of each vowel, for example MRP English [eɪ], which begins gliding from a value almost identical with the short simple vowel [e] of *bed*, becomes [eɪ̯]. This effect, rather like a musical *diminuendo*, is portrayed impressionistically in the diagram in Figure 7.5.

Rising prominence is rarer and it is often the case that this is analysed as consisting of an approximant (of the semi-vowel variety) plus a vowel rather than as a simple vowel glide. This decision is often motivated by economy. Words like *wet* and *yet* in English could be argued to start with diphthongs with rising prominence, [ʊe] and [ɪe]. However, if we took this view, it would be extremely uneconomical in linguistic terms, almost tripling the number of vowels in the language (including adding a whole series of new triphthongs) since [w] and [j] can occur before almost all the existing vowels. This kind of debate occurs when deciding how to treat such sequences in many languages, not just English.

Similar prominence-related issues arise in triphthongs. In English, the first element is again the dominant one, the second is the non-syllabic or weak element and prominence increases again for the final schwa (as shown in the phonetic

Figure 7.5
Impressionistic representation of the auditory effect of falling prominence.

transcriptions [eɪ̯ə, aɪ̯ə, ɔɪ̯ə, əʊ̯ə, ɑʊ̯ə]). This prominence relationship often interferes with perception and the three-quality glides are then perceived by listeners as being two syllables instead of one (as mentioned above), a target + off-glide, followed by a further separate target. Prominence relationships will also be seen to play an important role in the phonetic process known as smoothing.

Before looking at smoothing in more detail, however, one final point to discuss on the topic of prominence is the possibility of **prominence shift**. This happens in English in relation to two of the centring diphthongs (diphthongs gliding towards central schwa), the phonemes /ɪə/ and /ʊə/. As already explained, in common with all other diphthongs in English, these segments have a norm allophone with falling prominence, [ɪə̯] and [ʊə̯]. These will be used respectively in words such as *fear* and *revere,* and *tour* and *skewer.* However, each of these phonemes has a second major allophone which differs from the norm in that the prominence moves from the first to the second element. This is called prominence shift and it occurs when the vowel is used in an unstressed syllable immediately following a stressed syllable. The allophones are [ɪ̯ə] and [ʊ̯ə] respectively and can be heard in the second syllable of words such as: *happier* and *jaguar,* ['hæpɪ̯ə] and ['dʒægjʊ̯ə]. These two new allophones have **rising prominence**. Wells, in the LPD, has re-transcribed these variants to reflect the difficulty we now have of knowing whether the first quality is still [ɪ] and [ʊ] or whether it is [iː] and [uː] when another vowel follows immediately. Reflecting this loss of contrast, Wells uses **schwi** (the so-called 'happy-vowel') and **schwu** (weak-u), replacing [ɪ] and [ʊ] and giving ['hæpiə] and ['dʒægjuə]. This change, this shift of prominence, also makes people question whether the words are two or three syllables long. What about a word like *wearier* – has this two syllables or three? And *inferior* or *curious*? How many syllables in these words? This is something to think about.

Ex 7.6	There is no single right or wrong answer to this question because individual perception can differ, but it is still worth trying to decide how many syllables you personally think there are in each of the following words. Most can be pronounced using a triphthong.

1 *hire*	2 *flower growers*	3 *(re-)wire*	4 *(en)quire*	5 *higher*
6 *player*	7 *curious*	8 *mower*	9 *flour*	10 *choir*

Ask other people – do they agree with you?

7.2.3   Smoothing and compression

7.2.3.1   *Smoothing*

Smoothing is the technical term used to refer to the simplification of complex vowels into simpler or simple vowels by means of which triphthongs become diphthongs and diphthongs become monophthongs. This is another process that features in English speech. Not all complex vowels in a system need be equally affected by this process, but one of the most radically affected in English is the potential triphthong [ɑʊ̯ə] as in *hour/our, flower,* etc., transcribed phonemically as /aʊə/. Current pronunciation of this vowel frequently overlaps another vowel in the MRP system, the long simple /ɑː/ phoneme.

This overlap comes about through a two tier smoothing process. Smoothing involves the deletion of the non-prominent or non-syllabic glide element. In the case of MRP triphthongs, this is the middle element. [aʊə], for example, would lose the medial [ʊ] value. This in turn creates a new diphthong which, in keeping with the norm for MRP English diphthongs, has falling prominence, [aə], schwa now assuming the off-glide role. This new sound in turn undergoes the same smoothing process and, the weak element removed, it eventually overlaps the existing long simple vowel [ɑː].

In years to come, it is possible that continued application and consolidation of this process will result in a rather differently formed vowel system in MRP English, but that is unlikely to happen with any great speed.

Ex 7.7   **What do you think could be the end product if the following triphthongs undergo smoothing? (Try this exercise out before you read any further ahead.)**

  [aɪə]
  [əʊə]

As you adapt the symbols, consider whether there is likely to be any resultant overlap with existing vowel qualities and whether any new vowels are likely to be created?

If we summarize the effects of multiple applications of smoothing on the triphthongs listed in Table 7.1, we find the patterns documented in Table 7.2. What the information in Table 7.2 demonstrates is that while a couple of the smoothing processes could, in the long term, result not only in the loss of triphthongs but

Table 7.2

Smoothing in MRP English triphthongs

Existing triphthong	Smoothed once (potential new diphthong)	Smoothed again (potential new monophthong)	Eventual (new) phoneme
/aɪə/ = [ɑ̈ɪ̯ə][1]	[ɑ̈ə]	[ɑ̈ː]	/ɑː/ (new)
/eɪə/ = [ɛ̞ɪ̯ə]	[ɛ̞ə][2]	[ɛː]	/ɛː/ (new)
/ɔɪə/ = [ɔɪ̯ə]	[ɔə]	[ɔː][3]	/ɔː/
/aʊə/= [ɑ̈ʊ̯ə]	[ɑ̈ə]	[ɑ̈ː][4]	/ɑː/
/əʊə/= [əʊ̯ə]	([ə̜̈ə])[5]	[əː]	/ɜː/

Notes:
1 For explanation of the phonetic representations of these phonemes, see Cruttenden (2008).
2 Merger with the existing /eə/ diphthong takes place at this first stage of the smoothing process.
3 Merger with an existing phoneme takes place at the second stage of the smoothing process.
4 As note 3 above.
5 Merger with the existing phoneme /ɜː/ takes place at this point, smoothing resulting in adjacent identical vowel qualities, creating a long simple vowel

also the addition of a couple of new simple vowel phonemes to the MRP vowel system, the majority actually result in mergers with existing phonemes, reducing the number of contrasts operated by the language.

Another language making routine use of monosyllabic triphthongs is Modern Standard Chinese where we find, for example, [çiau˥] 'to disappear', [ʃuai˥] 'to fall down', [çiou˥] 'to rest', [xuei˥] 'ash'. (Lee and Zee 2003, [˥] denoting that all words are pronounced using a high level tone.)

7.2.3.2   Compression

The process known as **compression** often reduces the number of syllables in a particular word or phrase. Compression is effected by either deleting a vowel altogether (**vowel elision**), or by changing the class of the sound (**class change**, such that what was a syllabic segment, a vowel, becomes a related consonantal glide, a semi-vowel) or by collapsing two vowels into one in a form of **coalescence** (meaning two adjacent sounds come together to form one different but related sound). In MRP English, compression typically affects diphthongs with rising prominence and triphthongs. Compression is usually used in faster, more informal or casual speech.

In the case of diphthongs with rising prominence, such as the last part of *emollient* or *arduous*, [ɪˈmɒli̯ənt] and [ˈɑːdʒu̯əs], syllabification for many speakers will be [ɪ ˈmɒl i ənt] and [ˈɑːdʒ u əs] (the space marking the syllable boundary, following LPD convention). In faster speech, the isolated weak vowels schwi and schwu change to approximants, creating consonantal sequences as in [ɪˈmɒljənt] and [ˈɑːdʒwəs]. Once this happens, people again stop disagreeing on how many syllables are involved and agree on the lower number, [ɪ ˈmɒl jənt] with three syllables and [ˈɑːdʒ wəs] with two.

In English words such as *flower* and *fire*, many people feel there are two syllables. Smoothing reduces this to one by creating either a diphthong with falling prominence or a long simple vowel, and people then agree there is just one syllable. Effectively, a form of compression has occurred, reducing the number of syllables through class change (a vowel becoming a consonant), or elision. Although such compression frequently results in a form which merges with an existing segment (such as when [iː] or [uː] plus [ə] merge into [ɪə] or [ʊə] in words such as *foreseeable* and *(dis)agreeable* or *(un)do-able* and *renewable*), such compression also occasionally results in the creation of a new phonetic diphthong, such as *ruinous* where [uː] plus [ɪ] merges to [ʊɪ].

A final form of compression is a type of coalescence whereby two vowels combine together to form one different but related vowel in connected speech. A good example of this is found in Spanish. Spanish has a very straightforward vowel system by comparison with English, just five simple vowel qualities, usually transcribed /i e a o u/. Sometimes, when these vowels occur next to each other in the speech continuum – in collocations such as *una hollandesa* (<h> in Spanish is silent) [una olandesa] 'a Dutchwoman', or within words such as *alcohol* literally [alko ol] 'acohhol' – compression occurs. When like vowels are adjacent, one is effectively deleted (the process is known as **geminate simplification**, meaning 'twins' are reduced to a singleton), so *alcohol* is pronounced [alˈkol]. But when unlike vowels are involved, a diphthong (with rising prominence) is formed, so [a̯o] in the first example, [un̯aolan'desa]. Interestingly, when a close vowel is involved, [i] or [u], this becomes non-syllabic, changing to [j] or [w]. If the close vowels occur second in the string, as in *aun* [a un] 'yet', a diphthong with falling prominence is heard, transcribed in the Spanish tradition as [awn] (for [au̯n]), but if the close vowel comes first, then the phonetic effect is of a diphthong with rising prominence as in *su hermano* [su ɛr 'ma no], giving [su̯ɛr'mano] (transcribed in the Spanish tradition as [swɛr'mano]). (Note that although people are using and applying the IPA alphabet, different languages often develop different preferences and conventions for how to represent things; the use of the semi-vowels [j w] here leaves the reader in no doubt as to the syllabic status of the vowel itself in the transcribed form as no diacritics are needed to determine the relative prominence of the segments.) Across a word boundary, Spanish phonology calls this process **syneresis**; within words, it is termed **synalepha** – both are instances of compression.

7.2.4 Diphthongization and breaking

7.2.4.1 Diphthongization

The previous section described processes which reduced the complexity of vocalic sequences. Certain other processes increase complexity. Diphthongization, for example, is a process by which a simple vowel becomes a diphthong.

Diphthongization is a process which currently affects two of the MRP English long vowel phonemes, /iː/ and /uː/. When used in utterance final position, such as *I'd like <u>tea</u>* or *Give me <u>two</u>*, these vowels display a tendency to glide. The glide begins at a position nearer to the qualities [ɪ] and [ʊ], as if there has been some form of **articulatory undershoot**, and then immediately glides to the intended target at the [ï] and [ü] positions respectively, as in the vowel diagram in Figure 7.6, creating two diphthongs with rising prominence, respectively [ɪ̯ï] and [ʊ̯ü].

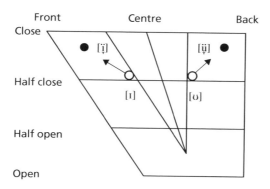

Figure 7.6

Vowel diagram showing the resonances of the diphthongal allophones of **MRP English** /iː/ and /uː/ (pronounced [ɪ̯ï] and [ʊ̯ü])]).

Diphthongization also affects a number of Dutch vowels which, in the standard northern accent ABN (Algemeen Beschaafd Nederlands) are often still represented as simple vowel phonemes (like English /iː/ and /uː/). These are the vowels /eː/, /øː/ and /oː/. Especially in the north, the pronunciation of these vowels is fairly consistently diphthongal. This is confirmed in a number of studies, including Jacobi *et al.* (2007). It is interesting to note, however, that the glide has been developing for a long time. (Mees and Collins (1983), for example, record the Randstad[4] pronunciations [ei̯, ou̯, öÿ] – my transcriptions based on their vowel diagram – as *potential diphthongs* (ibid., p. 68)).

7.2.4.2   Breaking

A special form of diphthongization which occurs in pre-lateral positions in MRP English is called **breaking**. Like smoothing, this is not a new phenomenon. Indeed, a clear account of earlier incidences of this can be found in Lutz (1994) in a discussion of the vocalization of post-vocalic /r/ in the sixteenth and seventeenth centuries.

Breaking is the insertion of a central-vowel glide after certain vowels in syllables closed by /l/ or /r/. Historically, the MRP English centring diphthongs were a product of this process which occurred before syllable-final /r/; when the /r/ itself was dropped, this left diphthongs such as /ɪə/, /eə/ and /ʊə/. The exact same process is current today in GAm, where a schwa-glide may occur between /ɪ/, /e/ or /æ/ and syllable final /r/, giving alternative pronunciations such as [fɪr] or [fɪər] for *fear,* or [(h)wer, (h)wær] or [(h)weər, (h)wæər] for *where*, etc. The vowels essentially become diphthongs: [ɪə], and [eə] or [æə]. This is termed **pre-r breaking.**

In MRP English, this same process can be heard before syllable final /l/, termed **pre-l breaking**, and affects especially the close front vowel /iː/ and closing diphthongs gliding to [ɪ], /eɪ, aɪ, ɔɪ/. Not all speakers do this and those who do may not do it on every occasion. The resultant variants are alternative pronunciations, just as was noted for the pre-r breaking forms in GAm. However, when pre-l breaking does occur, it results in a further diphthongal allophone of /iː/ as in *feel* pronounced [fiːəɫ] (which often merges with /ɪə/ to give [fɪəɫ]) and in triphthongal allophones of the diphthongs in words such as *ale* [eɪ̯əɫ], *aisle/I'll* [aɪ̯əɫ] and *oil* [ɔɪ̯əɫ].

Some speakers with a GAm accent also have pre-l breaking, but after close back vowels rather than close front ones. Accordingly, /uː, oʊ, aʊ/ are all affected, giving rise to pronunciations such as *fool* [fuːəɫ], *foal* [foʊ̯əɫ] and *foul* [faʊ̯əɫ].

7.3   OTHER TONGUE GESTURES

7.3.1   Advanced tongue root

The root of the tongue is not a primary articulator in vowel production, but like the lips, the tongue root can be adjusted independently of the tongue body movements. Some languages, especially West African languages, exploit this possibility to create further vowel contrasts. Although not particularly flexible, the tongue root can be advanced (drawn forward) or retracted (drawn back). The effect is to widen

---

[4]The Randstad refers to the joint conurbation of Amsterdam, Rotterdam, The Hague and Utrecht.

or narrow the space in the pharynx. The IPA provides diacritics with which these gestures can be noted in transcription: [i̘] a close front vowel with **advanced tongue root** [ATR] and [i̙] a close front vowel with retracted tongue root.

Igbo (a Niger-Kordofanian language spoken in Nigeria), for example, has two sets of vowels, one *with* the gesture ([i̘ e̘ o̘ u̘] are all [+ATR]) and a corresponding set *without* ([i̙ a̙ o̙ u̙] are all [−ATR]). We find pairs of words such as [i̘si̘] 'head' and [i̙si̙] 'tell' which are distinguished by the tongue root gesture. (That both vowels in each word are the same is not entirely a coincidence: a vowel harmony system operates in Igbo that permits vowels from only one of the two sub-sets to be used in any non-compound word, so vowels would either be all [+ATR] as in the first example or all [−ATR] as in the second.)

In phonology, specifically feature theory, this is the gesture that lies behind the feature [ATR] (advanced tongue root).

7.3.2   r-coloured vowels

So-called r-coloured or **rhotic** vowels are usually (although not necessarily) accompanied by some degree of retroflexion or retraction of the tongue tip and/ or bunching up of the tongue body. These gestures accompany the main vowel articulation throughout as in production of American [ɜ˞] in *bird*.

Simultaneously, there can also be some retraction of the tongue root which brings about a narrowing in the pharynx. r-coloured vowels are also characteristic of a number of varieties of Chinese (Sinitic languages), including Modern Standard Chinese (the Beijing dialect of Mandarin, see below). Overall, however, they are quite rare, occurring in less than one percent of languages (Maddieson 1984).

Acoustically, such vowels are characterized by a low third formant − similar to the low dip in F3 that distinguishes realizations of English /r/ from English /l/. It is this particular acoustic characteristic that determines such vowels, rather than their actual articulation (which is less than homogeneous).

7.4   FURTHER PARAMETERS OF VARIATION

7.4.1   Friction

Vowels are sonorants − sounds in which the norm realization permits free passage of the airstream, centrally through the oral cavity such that there is no audible friction. Exceptionally, however, some languages, including Swedish and Modern Standard Chinese, add friction to certain vowels. This is achieved in various different ways. In Swedish, for example, palatal or labial friction may be added (allophonically) to long close vowels, giving [i̝j], [y̝ɥ], [u̝β] and [ʉ̝β]. Standard Chinese rhotacizes, with friction, the mid central neutral vowel [ə˞], whenever this occurs in an open syllable.

7.4.2   Phonation variants

All sonorants can be made without voice. [h], the so-called voiceless glottal fricative, is effectively a voiceless vowel. You can check this out yourself by whispering expressions such as *hee-hee-hee*, *ha-ha-ha* and *ho-ho-ho*. You will hear three different h-sounds – one like [i], one like [ɑ] and one like [əʊ] (essentially [i̥ i̥ i̥], [ɑ̥ ɑ̥ ɑ̥], [ə̥ʊ ə̥ʊ ə̥ʊ]). This audible, voiceless, fricative quality is a direct function of the shape of the vocal tract, causing this type of friction to be called **cavity friction**. It is a function of the total cavity shape rather than of turbulence generated by a narrow constriction at one specific place of articulation (as in palatal [ç] or alveolar [s], etc.). This is also the explanation behind the fact that feature theory treats [h] not as an obstruent, but as a sonorant. (All the other fricatives were members of the non-sonorant or obstruent group.)

Voiceless vowels are rare, however, and Maddieson (1984) cites only two languages as making use of contrastive voiceless vowels: Ik (a Nilo-Saharan language spoken in Uganda) and Dafla (a Sino-Tibetan language spoken in Assam, India). More often, voiceless vowels are allophones of voiced ones. This happens in Japanese, for example, when vowels occur between voiceless obstruents, such as [ki̥ʃi] 'shore' and [ku̥ʃi] 'comb'. Partial devoicing of vowels also occurs in English when a long VOT (see 8.1.3 below) follows the release of syllable initial voiceless plosives.

Audible friction is also a characteristic of breathy voiced vowels (for example, Gujarati [baɾ] 'twelve' but [ba̤ɾ] 'outside'). Creaky voice, too, is also used by a small number of languages to bring about additional vowel contrasts, as in Sedang (an Austro-Asiatic language spoken in Vietnam and Laos) and Southern Nambiquara (spoken in Brazil).

Ex 7.8   Field Notebook: Phonetics in One Word

Entry 7 Use the theory you have just learned in order to continue writing your Field Notebook, applying your knowledge to the detailed phonetic description of the word *completes*.

Go to www.routledge.com/cw/ashby for instructions and feedback.

7.5   SUMMARY

- The chapter took the study of vowels beyond the basic quality values presented in Chapter 6, identifying additional parameters of variation, including suprasegmental characteristics.

- Vowel duration was discussed, including some of the environmental influences affecting this (clipping processes, for example).

- Oral vs nasalized vowels were explored.

- The concept of complexity was introduced (monophthongs, diphthongs and triphthongs) and some of the processes impacting on complexity (smoothing, compression, diphthongization, breaking).

- Lastly, the contribution of the tongue root and tongue tip gestures ([ATR] and r-colouring), fricativization of vowels and phonation differences were introduced and illustrated.

Ear-training

Once you have studied this chapter carefully, continue the development of your practical skills by attempting the ear-training exercises for this chapter, available as recordings at www.routledge.com/cw/ashby.

FURTHER READING

As well as the suggestions for further reading about vowels and about the physics of speech provided at the end of the previous chapter, you can find even more useful and interesting information in Chapter 9 of Ladefoged (2001), Chapter 15 of Ladefoged (2005), and Chapter 9 of Ladefoged & Maddieson (1996). For those requiring in-depth information about English vowels, Chapter 8 of Cruttenden (2008) is recommended, while a summary can be found in Chapter 5 of Ogden (2009).

Further parameters of variation in consonants

Chapter 8 extends the descriptive framework for consonants, exploring ways in which languages achieve further variety and contrast in the articulation of consonant sounds. The chapter describes more contributions made by the vocal folds (voicing and devoicing and the fortis/lenis dichotomy; voice onset time and aspiration; glottalization), variations on place of articulation (primary and secondary articulations, including palatalization, velarization and pharyngealization), and manner variation (lenition, variations affecting plosives, and grooved fricatives).

8.1 FURTHER CONTRIBUTIONS BY THE VOCAL FOLDS

8.1.1 Fortis and lenis consonants

Vocal fold behaviour can affect not only the steady state of a consonant stricture but also the approach to that position and the period immediately following it. We began to see some of the effects of this behaviour in Chapter 7 where the terms fortis and lenis were introduced. Fortis and lenis are variously defined in the literature, equated with differences of respiratory energy, articulatory (muscular) energy, and duration. The literal meanings, 'strong' and 'weak' respectively, imply that voiceless sounds are strong sounds and voiced ones weak.

On one level, there is some truth in this. Voiceless consonants (other than [ʔ]) are produced with open vocal folds, permitting free flow of egressive pulmonic air. Compared with the correspondingly reduced air flow (pulses of air) which occurs when the vocal folds are vibrating, this voiceless flow is 'strong'. The amount of air passing through the vocal tract in a corresponding time-span during production of normal voice is rather less. To that extent the voiced, lenis sounds can be thought of as 'weaker'. However, this is coincidental. Alterations in airflow are not the direct effect of applying increased or decreased articulatory energy, and there is – as yet – no single, empirically verifiable physiological or acoustic correlate of either concept, fortis or lenis.

Nonetheless, given the contradictory behaviour that is sometimes observed in speech concerning so-called voiceless and voiced sounds, fortis and lenis are convenient (and widely used) terms. In many languages, in certain phonetic environments, sounds that we usually call voiced can in fact be produced *without* vocal fold vibration. Likewise, sounds that we call voiceless can be produced *with* vocal fold vibration. Labels that avoid mentioning voice overtly are therefore useful – fortis and lenis are two such terms.

In Chapter 7, we learned that the 'voiced' /d/ at the end of English *ode*, is actually devoiced but we still consider it /d/ because of the length of the vowel. In fact, such obstruent sounds in English are only ever fully voiced in a fully voiced environment, in utterances such as [maɪ 'dædi] *my daddy*, for example, where the vocal folds vibrate throughout, as in line 2 of Figure 8.1. If we just say [d̥æd̥] *dad* or [ɪts d̥æd̥] *it's dad*, this so-called voiced sound, adjacent either to silence or to a voiceless consonant, itself becomes partly or fully devoiced (the extent of the devoicing can vary, see for example, lines 3 and 4 in Figure 8.1). The same behaviour can be observed with voiced fricatives and affricates: /zuːz/ *zoos/zoo's* spoken in isolation would be [z̥uːz̥], but in *the zoo's open*, pronounced [ðə 'zuːz 'əʊpən] both z-sounds retain their full voicing; likewise /dʒʌdʒ/ *judge* in isolation would be [d̥ʒʌd̥ʒ̊] – with at least partial devoicing of the affricates – but in [ə 'dʒʌdʒmənt] *a judgement*, both affricates are fully voiced.

German and Dutch have an even more extreme rule: all obstruents in final position in utterances must always be completely voiceless. Thus, /z/ in Dutch

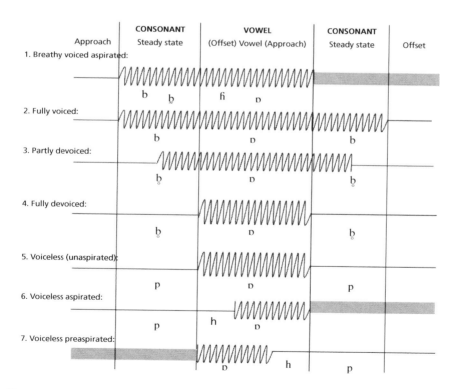

Figure 8.1
Schematic representation of degrees of (de)voicing.

['leːzə] *lezen* 'to read' becomes /s/ in final position [leːs] *lees* 'read' (1st pers. sg.), /b/ in German ['liːbə] *Liebe* 'love' becomes /p/ in final position [liːp] *liep* 'lovely, cute'. This total devoicing is demonstrated schematically at the right-hand side of line 4 in Figure 8.1. In German and Dutch, there is no possibility of contrasting pairs like [p, b] or [s, z] in utterance final position. Phonologists talk about the voicing contrast being **neutralized** here.

This situation differs from the English one. If the voiced phoneme merged with the voiceless one in English, pre-fortis clipping would occur. This does not happen. Looking back at Figure 7.2, even when [d̥] in [əʊᵈd̥] has lost almost all its voicing, it is never confused with final [t] because of the length of the vowel. Retention of full vowel length is clear evidence that /d/ has not literally turned into /t/. Duration of the preceding sonorant is a crucial perceptual cue here for native-speakers of English, distinguishing pairs like *bet/bed, niece/knees*, etc. (This can be called an **enhancing property** attributable to all voiced obstruents in English – a measurable influence they exert over their environment, rather than a primary characteristic carried within the sounds themselves.) No phonetic cuing of this kind occurs in the Dutch or German examples; the final obstruents are true voiceless sounds.

French and Spanish do the opposite, adding voice to sounds which are otherwise voiceless. In each case, this is a form of **assimilation** – the sounds becoming more like some feature in their immediate environment. The French /k/ phoneme, the so-called voiceless velar plosive at the end of the word [ʃak] *chaque* 'each', becomes fully voiced when followed by a voiced consonant such as [ʃak̬ ʒuʁ] *chaque jour* 'each day' (shown here with the 'voiced' diacritic, [̬], beneath the [k] symbol). Similarly, the /s/ phoneme, a voiceless alveolar fricative, heard at the beginning of [sə] *se* 'him-/herself' becomes fully voiced in an utterance such as [ɔ̃ṣvwa] *on se voit* 'one sees' (voicing again triggered by the presence of a following voiced consonant). In fact, the acquisition of voicing by French /k/ and /s/ is so complete, that French phoneticians transcribe them not as 'voiced-k' and 'voiced-s' but as [g] and [z] respectively, acknowledging total equivalence to their voiced counterparts: [ʃag ʒuʁ] and [ɔ̃zvwa]. Any voicing contrast is again neutralized.

Spanish adds voice to its voiceless fricatives /θ/ and /s/. When these occur before a voiced consonant, instead of ['θepa] *cepa* 'hole' and ['kaθa] *caza* 'game', [si] *si* 'yes' and [kasa] *casa* 'house', we find we find [di'eθ̬mo] *diezmo* 'tithe, tenth' and [eṣ'bel̬to] *esbelto* 'tall and slender'.

Dutch also has a voicing assimilation process whereby voiceless obstruents become fully voiced. This is triggered by word-initial /b/ and /d/. For example, when the word /zɑk/ *zak* 'pocket', ending in a so-called voiceless velar plosive, collocates with /'bukjə/ *boekje* 'little book' to give ['z̬ɑgbukjə] *zakboekje* 'notebook' or with /duk/ *doek* 'cloth' to give ['z̬ɑgduk] *zakdoek* 'handkerchief', [k] from the end of *zak* becomes [g], a voiced velar plosive. Likewise, the other voiceless obstruents – alveolar fricative /s/ at the end of /kɑs/ *kas* 'cash, hothouse' becomes voiced when this word collocates with /b/-initial or /d/-initial words as in ['kɑzbuk] *kasboek* 'cashbook', ['kɑzdrœyvə] *kasdruiven* 'hothouse grapes', etc.

Even English has one instance of adding voice to a segment that we typically consider voiceless – this affects /h/, the voiceless glottal fricative. /h/ is unlike other members of the fricative sub-group of English consonants in a number of ways. One of these is that when we pronounce it between vowels, we never completely switch off the vocal fold vibrations required for the vowels themselves. Instead, we switch briefly to breathy voice, producing utterances such as [ə'ɦeḓ] *ahead* rather than [(ðıs) heḓ] *(this) head,* where, initially in the utterance or adjacent to a voiceless consonant, /h/ retains its voicelessness. (This happens to no other voiceless obstruent in English.)

Given such behaviour, the terms voiceless and voiced are not always the most appropriate way to describe these particular sounds. Accordingly, phoneticians often refer to them by the names fortis and lenis instead.

Ex 8.1 **Apply the following rule, supplying the appropriate symbols to complete these transcriptions of Dutch words in the following table.**

Rule: Voiced obstruents become voiceless when they occur in word-final position; intervocalically they remain fully voiced.

	Obstruents	Intervocalic variant	Word final variant
1	Uvular fricatives	['l ɪ __ ə]	[l ɪ __]
2	Alveolar plosives	['b ɛ __ ə]	[b ɛ __]
3	Labiodental fricatives	['d r œy __ ə]	[d r œy __]
4	Bilabial plosives	['h ɛ __ ə]	[h ɛ __]
5	Alveolar fricatives	['r ɛi __ ə]	[r ɛi __]

Variable end-position voicing is summarized in Figure 8.1, at the right-hand side of lines 2 to 4.

8.1.2 Murmured stops

Looking again at Figure 8.1, in line 1 we can see the effect of breathy rather than modal voice in oral stop consonants. This phonation difference is responsible for **voiced aspirates** or **murmured stops**. These are voiced consonants, usually plosives, where the onset of an immediately following vowel sounds like a voiced h-sound, a vowel with breathy voice. The extent of voicing during the hold phase of the stop (labelled 'steady state' here, since the diagram is valid for any kind of obstruent) varies (see Ladefoged and Maddieson (1996: 58–63), for example). Such sounds are widespread in Indo-Aryan and Dravidian languages. Hindi, for example, contrasts unaspirated voiced stops (including one phonetic affricate) with aspirated ones, as in [bal] 'hair' vs [bʰal] 'forehead' and [d͡ʒɐl] 'water' vs [d͡ʒʰɐl] 'glimmer'. Voiced aspirates of this kind are predominantly obstruent consonants but there are records of languages with sonorant consonants which also display this characteristic, including Hindi which contrasts [ɽʰ] with other consonants, as in [bəɽʰa] 'increase' (imp.) vs [bəɽa] 'big' or [bətʃa] 'save', for example (Ohala (1999: 101)).

8.1.3 Voice onset time

The left-hand side of lines 4 to 7 in Figure 8.1 offers a summary of **voice onset time** (VOT) characteristics, showing positive, zero and negative VOTs.

The norm for voiceless obstruents is represented in line 5 which shows **zero VOT**. Here, vocal fold behaviour is indistinguishable from that associated with a fully devoiced lenis obstruent. The vocal folds only start to vibrate simultaneously with the removal of the oral constriction (complete closure for stops, or narrow approximation for fricatives). Sounds displaying this pattern are said to be **unaspirated**. Voiceless unaspirated consonants are typified by French, Russian or Hungarian plosives, for example, and French or English fricatives and affricates. This can be represented by means of a parametric diagram, aligning movement by the active articulator with activity of the vocal folds, as in Figure 8.2.

As the norm for all consonants, absence of aspiration is usually unmarked in phonetic transcription. However, if it is useful or necessary to mark this overtly, the chart of extensions to the International Phonetic Alphabet (ExtIPA Symbols for Disordered Speech, *Handbook of the International Phonetic Association*, p. 193) provides a superscript equals sign placed after the affected symbol: [t=], for example, instead of the implicitly unaspirated plain symbol, [t].

If voicelessness continues into the beginning of the following sonorant, after the removal of the consonantal constriction (as in line 6 of Figure 8.1), there is a **long** or **positive VOT**. We can measure in milliseconds the length of time it takes for voicing to begin. What happens here is that the vocal folds remain fully open, effectively devoicing the onset to any following sonorant. If the sonorant is a vowel, as in English *pie, tea* or *car* we hear what we describe as an h-sound. We call this **aspiration**. Languages vary as to which consonants (if any) they aspirate and they also vary with regard to the length of the VOT. The (length of) aspiration may or may not be contrastive.

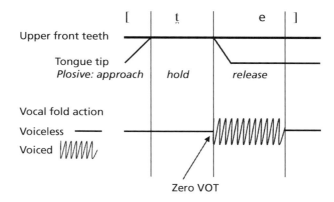

Figure 8.2
Parametric representation of vocal fold action and movement of the tongue tip in the pronunciation of French [t̪e] *thé* 'tea'.

A distinctive characteristic of the MRP accent, always taught to non-native speakers learning the language, is mandatory aspiration of voiceless plosives in syllable initial position. (Aspiration is optional in syllable final position.) Danish, German and Irish also have aspirated voiceless plosives of this kind. This delay in the onset of vocal fold vibration results in a long/positive VOT as shown in Line 6 of Figure 8.1. This is of interest in that it is often only the presence or absence of aspiration that distinguishes initial voiceless plosives from initial so-called voiced ones. If you compare the left-hand side of lines 4 and 5 in Figure 8.1, you will see that without aspiration, there is nothing to distinguish a fully devoiced lenis obstruent from a voiceless fortis one. It is only when we compare these lines with line 6 that we see a difference. Here there is a long VOT, aspiration. So, whereas in final position, English distinguishes fortis and lenis obstruents on the basis of their influence over the length of immediately preceding sonorant segments, in initial position, when dealing with plosives, VOT and its influence over the immediately following sonorant segment is the salient auditory cue. The fact that it comes after the actual plosive, means that this effect is sometimes referred to as ***post*-aspiration**.

Since aspiration is essentially a function of devoicing part of a vowel, we also have two ways to transcribe it – either make the vowel symbol voiceless (so the representation will be different for each different vowel) or use the superscript-h, as provided by the IPA alphabet chart. For the word *tea,* for example, the choice is between [tḭ̊ː] and [tʰḭ̊ː]. The vowel-like nature of [h] can be seen clearly in the spectrograms in Figure 8.3, where the vowel formants are already visible in the intervals of aspiration.

Because it makes for neater narrow transcriptions and because it reflects that the process is the same in each case, this book will use superscript-h. Figure 8.2 representing the pronunciation of French *thé* 'tea' can now be compared with Figure 8.4, representing the pronunciation of English *tea.*

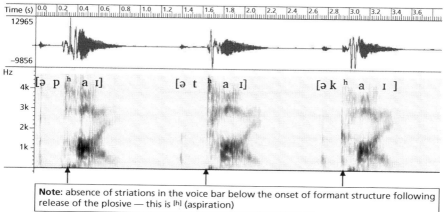

Note: absence of striations in the voice bar below the onset of formant structure following release of the plosive — this is [h] (aspiration)

Figure 8.3
[h]-like nature of aspiration – a voiceless vowel.

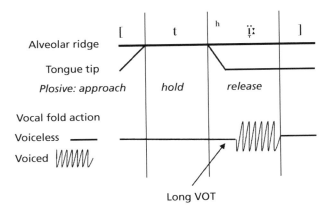

Figure 8.4
Parametric representation of the timing of vocal fold action and movement by the active articulator (the tongue tip) in the pronunciation of English [tʰi̥ː] *tea*.

What you can see here is that although aspiration is a feature of the initial consonant, it is again an enhancing feature. It can't be heard until the active articulator has moved away from the passive one and the plosive is effectively over. For that reason, it is good practice to include its transcription in the vowel column in a parametric diagram, above the voiceless stretch of the vocal fold action line. (Remember that [h] is essentially shorthand for transcribing a voiceless vowel – the vowel segment is therefore the proper place to locate it.)

Although it is most widely a characteristic of plosives, in a small number of languages, aspiration can also be a characteristic of other obstruents. Burmese, for example, aspirates fricatives and affricates. Watkins (2001) lists /s/ vs /sʰ/ in [sa][1] 'writing' and [sʰa] 'to be hungry', and /tʃ/ vs /tʃʰ/ in [tʃa] 'lotus' and [tʃʰa] 'to be inferior'.

Ex 8.2   Draw parametric diagrams to represent vocal fold action suggested in the following short utterances.

(1) [kɛl] *quel* 'what' (French)
(2) [kʰɑːm] *calm*
(3) [p˭eːs] *pace* (English, North Yorkshire)
(4) [ə'tʰæk] *attack*
(5) [puṇto] *punto* 'point' (Spanish)

In English, this long VOT affects immediately following approximants, too. The effect of devoicing an approximant is that we hear the comparable voiceless fricative. Devoiced [l̥] heard in *play* or *clean* in the majority of English accents is phonetically an interval of voiceless alveolar lateral friction (the same as [ɬ]), devoiced [j̥] in *pure*, *tune* or *queue* sounds voiceless palatal friction (the same as [ç]), and so forth.

---

[1]Burmese is a tone language, but for simplicity, the tones are omitted from these transcriptions.

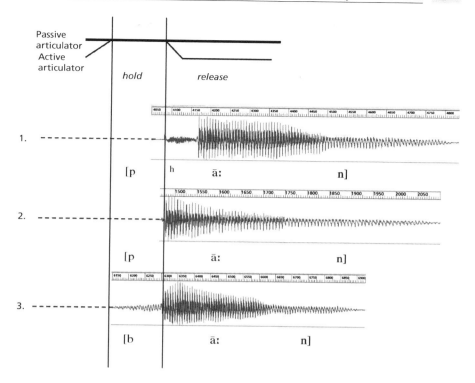

Figure 8.5
VOT in Thai plosives with waveforms integrated into a schematic parametric diagram showing the movements of the articulators in the production of the initial plosives (speaker Kaseam Jongpitakrat).

Length of VOT is also contrastive in a few languages. Thai, Korean and Burmese each operate a three-way VOT contrast in their plosive/affricate subsystem(s). Speech waveform data integrated into the parametric diagram in Figure 8.5 exemplifies these contrasts in Thai by means of bilabial /pʰ/ vs /p/ vs /b/ as in [pʰāːn] 'belligerent', [pāːn] 'birthmark', and [bāːn] 'to bloom' (all spoken with a mid tone, represented here by the macron over the vowel).

Finally, if vocal fold vibration ceases before the obstruent stricture is fully formed, this gives rise to **negative VOT** (as in line 7, Figure 8.1), devoicing the off-set of the previous sonorant. Called *pre*-**aspiration**, this is characteristic of languages such as Irish, Scots Gaelic, Icelandic and Faroese, for example. Here, [h] is heard *before* the consonant stricture is formed.

8.1.4   Glottalization and the glottal stop

8.1.4.1   The glottal stop

We identified the voiceless glottal plosive in Chapter 2, but not much was said about its behaviour in languages. Often referred to as the glottal stop, [ʔ] functions at a phonemic level in many languages, being used to change meaning. Maddieson (1984) lists nearly 150 languages with the glottal stop in their consonant phoneme inventory, including Arabic and Oriental Hebrew. Contrasts include Modern Standard Arabic [saʔala] 'asked' vs [saʕala] 'coughed' and Oriental Hebrew (also contrasting in this example with the voiced pharyngeal fricative) [ʔor] 'light' vs [ʕor] 'skin'.

In more languages again, the glottal stop is a phonetic characteristic and does not change meaning. This is the case in German where its use produces the effect often referred to as **hard attack**. It is used by speakers of German at the beginning of words or morphological stems that would otherwise start with a vowel. Kohler (1999) gives [ʔɛɐ'ʔaɐbaɪtn] *erarbeiten* 'achieve through work' as an example of this characteristic.

The t-glottalling process whereby final /t/ is replaced by [ʔ] in certain regional accents of English was addressed in Chapter 2. This is also found, albeit less extensively, in MRP English, where syllable final, pre-consonantal instances of the /t/ phoneme can be realized as [ʔ], *not quite* becoming ['nɒʔ 'kwaɪt]. The glottal stop is used instead of the first /t/, but cannot replace the final one in this accent.

8.1.4.2   Glottalization

We have already seen the role of the vocal folds as an airstream initiator (Chapter 5), as a place of articulation (Chapter 3), and we have just briefly compared the role of [ʔ] in certain languages. However, **glottalization** – variously termed **glottal reinforcement, pre-glottalization** or **laryngealization** – is different again.

Use of these multiple terms in the literature can be confusing, but arises partly from the lack of uniformity in the phenomenon itself. Some authorities only use glottalization (Roach (1973), for example, prefers this term), some laryngealization (Laver (1994)). Laryngealization is the preferred term, too, in Ladefoged and Maddieson (1996), but they also make reference to 'glottalized' voiceless stops (Ladefoged and Maddieson (1996: 73)) and the so-called 'glottalized' sounds in Hausa (Ladefoged and Maddieson (1996: 86)).

The fact of the matter is that laryngeal coarticulation of this kind is scalar and a single term – a 'one size fits all' approach – may be inappropriate. At one extreme, it involves the formation of a complete glottal closure which is sustained for a measurable period of time (almost certainly the origin of the use of the terms glottalized and glottal reinforcement) while at the other, it is a sustained interval of creaky voice (the origin of the use of the term laryngealization). Between these extremes there is considerable variation and both terms are useful. My preference is to use glottalization to refer to phenomena that can be shown to involve the formation of complete glottal closure (brief or sustained) and laryngealization for those that don't or do so rarely (such as the phonation differences discussed in the following section).

One characteristic of English speech involves the formation of glottal closure just before the formation of the oral closure for certain syllable-/word-final voiceless plosives. This is known as glottalization or glottal reinforcement. Earlier in this chapter, we identified MRP English /p t k/ as being aspirated in syllable initial position – each has an aspirated allophone. Each also has a glottalized allophone which can be used after sonorants either before a pause or before the end of speech (e.g. *Stop!* [stɒˀp], *Wait!* [weɪˀt]), or at the end of a syllable, given an appropriate phonetic environment (word-finally if the next word starts with a consonant, *look round* [lʊˀk ɹaʊnd], word-internally if the next syllable begins with an obstruent, e.g. *dictate* [dɪˀk'teɪt] or a nasal, *topmost* ['tɒˀpməʊst]). Effectively, the voicelessness of /p t k/ is being assisted or **reinforced** by the formation of this precursive glottal closure. Typically, once the oral closure is in place, the glottal closure is released and compression takes place in the normal way. The glottal stop does not replace the [p t k] sounds, it merely supports/reinforces them.

The parametric diagram in Figure 8.6 shows the timing of the articulatory gestures:

1. During the vowel, the oral articulators begin to move towards their hold-phase position, beginning the approach phase.

2. As the approach phase continues, the vocal folds form complete glottal closure, terminating voicing (and in consequence, ending the vowel).

3. Shortly after the formation of glottal closure, the oral articulators also form complete closure.

4. The oral closure established, the glottis re-opens and egressive pulmonic airflow continues…

5. …the air being compressed behind the complete oral closure in the normal way.

6. After a silent interval of compression (this only affects voiceless plosives and so there is nothing to hear during the hold-phase), the oral articulators separate and audible plosion is heard.

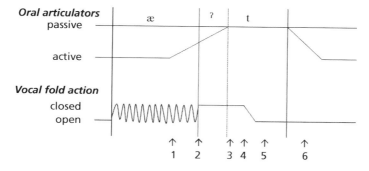

Figure 8.6

Parametric diagram showing glottal reinforcement of the /t/ in *at*, pronounced [æˀt].

Ex 8.3   Try to identify plosives in the following sentences which could be produced with glottal reinforcement by a speaker of MRP English. Each sentence is broken down into intonational phrases (marked by | and ||). Treat each phrase as a separate utterance with a pause at the end.

1. Jack rang the bell [a]| but when nobody answered [b]| he went round to the back door [c]||
2. Becky was upstairs [a]| making the beds [b]| and putting away washing [c]||
3. 'I didn't hear you knock,' she said ||
4. Jack replied, 'I didn't knock [a]| I rang the bell [b]| at least three times.' [c]||
5. 'The bell's broken', said Becky [a]| 'I keep meaning to pin a notice on the door [b]| Knock loudly [c]| Bell out of action.'[d]|

Glottalization in English also affects the voiceless palatoalveolar affricate/tʃ/. /tʃ/ can be glottalized in all the same environments as the voiceless plosives, but, unlike the plosives, it can also be glottalized between vowels. This is interesting because it immediately raises questions about whether affricates are single consonants or whether they are really a sequence of two consonants. Given that we can glottalize /tʃ/ in words like *butcher* ['bʊʔtʃə] (but not /t/ in words like *butter*), is it really the case that in *butcher* we are actually glotallizing /t/ followed by another obstruent (that is, /t/ in word-internal, pre-obstruent position, equivalent to /t/ in *hatpin* ['hæʔtpɪn], or /k/ in *dictate* [dɪʔk'teɪt], above)? This is something to think about.

In its most extreme form, Danish stød can also be described as glottalization or glottal reinforcement, although there is considerable variability in this. Stød results in minimal pairs such as [hun] *hun* 'she' vs [hunʔ] *hund* 'dog'. However, this is an example of what Fischer-Jørgensen (1987: 181) calls *exaggerated stød*. No complete glottal closure is visible in the waveform in Figure 8.7. But even in this less exaggerated form, (stød manifests through a transient creak, to creaky voice

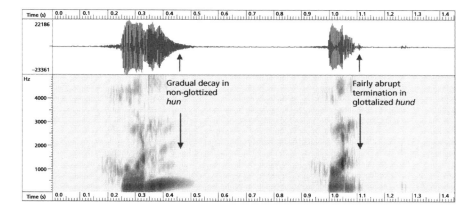

Figure 8.7
Speech waveforms comparing Danish *hun* [hun] and *hund* [hun̩] (speaker Inger Mees).

which affects not just the termination of one vowel or one consonant but what Fischer-Jørgensen calls a *certain stretch of voicing* (ibid, p. 58)) the absence of the more gradual decay visible in the non-glottalized *hun* 'she' is clearly visible. This would more appropriately be represented by the use of the creaky voice diacritic below the affected segment ([huṇ], for example), and would warrant description as laryngealized rather than glottalized (as suggested above).

8.1.5   Phonation contrasts

Creaky voice (also termed laryngealization) and breathy voice (both outlined above in Chapter 2) are just two phonation types that languages sometimes select alongside modal voice to extend their range of consonantal contrasts. Creaky voice persisting throughout the duration of a consonantal articulation is illustrated by Ladefoged and Maddieson (1996: 54) in the Niger-Congo Fula language contrasting [d] vs [ḍ] in the phrases [o dari] 'he stood' vs [o ḍaːnike] 'he slept'.

8.2   FURTHER VARIATIONS BASED ON PLACE OF ARTICULATION

8.2.1   More secondary articulations

Chapter 4 introduced and explored labialization, a secondary articulation defined as a vowel-like gesture (an articulatory gesture with wide approximation) that co-occurs with another articulation which has a less wide degree of stricture. The relatively open lip-rounding, called labialization, that co-occurs with the [s] of *saw* in English was seen to be one such secondary gesture.

In English, labialization of this kind is phonetic, the product of assimilation – [s] accommodates to the lip-position required for the following vowel. In many languages, however, it is added deliberately to bring about contrast. One such language is Tera, a Chadic language spoken in Nigeria, which contrasts plain /g/ in [gàːri] *gaari* 'bush' with labialized/gʷ/ in [gʷàri] *gwari* 'prosper' (Tench (2007:228-9)).

8.2.2   Palatalization and velarization

Palatalization and velarization involve, respectively, front and back close vowel resonances being added to consonants.

The pronunciation given to the voiced alveolar lateral in both Scottish English and General American English is a good example of velarization. The same pronunciation is also used in MRP, but only when the lateral occurs after a vowel, either at the end of an utterance or immediately before another consonant (in utterances like *all, felt* or *welcome*, for example); elsewhere, the MRP lateral has no velarization.

To understand this, we first need to remind ourselves that a back close vowel involves the back of the tongue rising as near to the soft palate as possible, without producing audible friction. In the case of the English lateral, this means that at the same time as the tongue tip rises to contact the alveolar ridge (the side rims remaining low, leaving a space of wide approximation below the upper molars), the back of the tongue assumes a raised, [ɯ]-like position below the soft-palate. In between these two articulatory points, the front and centre of the tongue remain as low as possible – they are not actively involved in this articulation at all. The egressive pulmonic airstream first passes over the raised back of the tongue, creating the back close vowel resonance, and then exits the vocal tract over the lowered side rims of the tongue, going around the central obstruction at the alveolar ridge and acquiring lateral resonance as it does so. Thus we have a voiced velarized alveolar lateral approximant as shown in Figure 8.8. (This diagram is supported by an additional vowel diagram, illustrating the precise vocalic resonance that has been added.)

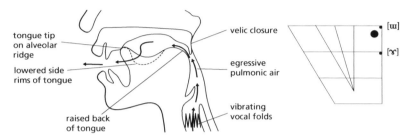

Figure 8.8
Vocal tract diagram showing the position of the articulators during the production of a voiced velarized alveolar lateral approximant with accompanying vowel diagram showing the [ɯ]-like resonance of [ɫ].

The IPA offers two ways of transcribing this. The preferred transcription for many people is the alveolar lateral symbol with a tilde horizontally through the middle, [ɫ]. Unicode fonts supply quite a few velarized values, including [ƀɖ f ɱ ᵾpɼ ɼ s ɫ z]. Partly in response to the typographic difficulties that used to be posed by such symbols, at the last major review of the IPA alphabet chart in Kiel in 1989, phoneticians agreed by a majority vote to an alternative representation of velarization using a superscript gamma, e.g. [lˠ]. This was not entirely non-contentious. The gamma symbol shape, [ɣ], is associated with the presence of voicing, but a velarized *voiceless* alveolar plosive [ɫ], for example, has none. The symbol shape is also associated with friction, but a sound such as a velarized voiced alveolar nasal, [ᵾ], has no audible friction. Nonetheless, criticisms aside, this is a convenient diacritic and it is extremely easy to transcribe: [tˠ], [nˠ], etc.

Ex 8.4   Go carefully through the following text and find all the laterals that would be velarized in an MRP accent.

London's a lovely place for a holiday. Lots of shops and leisure outlets as well as all the museums and galleries. I generally loathe cities but living all the year now in Cornwall, I really miss the hustle and bustle and I look forward to the occasional long weekend in the capital.

Ex 8.5   Draw vocal tract diagrams for (a) a voiced velarized bilabial plosive and (b) a voiceless velarized alveolar fricative.

Although this is not widely acknowledged and is not considered to give rise to major allophonic variants, all English consonants typically undergo a small amount of velarization at the end of a word. The sounds in this exercise might therefore be found in words like *rob* or *loose*.

Palatalization involves the addition of front close vowel resonance. Instead of the back of the tongue being active, the front of the tongue articulates simultaneously with some other, closer, pre-palatal gesture. Palatalized sounds are transcribed by adding a superscript [ʲ] after the primary symbol. The lateral in English *leaf* might well be palatalized as the front of the tongue prepares for the front close vowel during the articulation of the apico-alveolar lateral, [lʲ].

The deliberate use of these secondary articulations to bring about a change of meaning by languages is not unusual. Like English, in some languages secondary articulations are purely allophonic (they don't change the meaning of a word), but some languages exploit this in order to make phonemic contrasts. Such a language is Russian, where palatalized (so-called *soft*) variants of most of the consonants contrast with plain or *hard* ones, such as [sʲok] 'he lashed' *vs* [sok] 'juice'. (Note that though Russian has traditionally been described as having all consonants either palatalized or velarized, recent data suggests that the velarized gesture is only used with laterals giving a phonemic contrast between /lʲ/ and /ɫ/ as in 'coal' pronounced ['ʊɡəlʲ] and 'corner/angle' (n.) pronounced ['ʊɡəɫ].)

A language which contrasts the two types extensively is Irish. Here, the velarized vs palatalized contrast operates across five different manners and four or five different places of articulation, including [bʲi] *bí* 'imp' but [bˠi] *buí* 'yellow', [mʲi] *mí* 'month' but [mˠi] *maoigh* 'boast' (imp), and [fʲi] *fí* 'weaving' but [fˠi] *faoi* 'under'.

In MRP English, the two types are in **complementary distribution**. Each has its own unique environment, palatalized before close front vowels or /j/ and velarized in final or pre-consonantal post-vocalic positions. They never change meaning.

8.2.3   Pharyngealization

The fourth and final secondary articulation is pharyngealization. Simultaneously with a more forward and narrower constriction, the tongue root retracts, narrowing the pharynx and producing a vocalic resonance akin to pCV5, [ɑ].

This is again represented by the addition of a diacritic to the primary symbol and the IPA chart provides a superscript voiced pharyngeal fricative for this purpose, [ˤ]. The same arguments regarding lack of transparency and possible confusion apply to this diacritic as applied to the use of [ˠ] to represent velarization. In the past, application of the tilde through the middle of the symbol (see above) was routinely extended to pharyngealization as well. This option is still given in the diacritics table of the IPA chart.

Arabic is the language most widely cited as contrasting plain consonants with a small set of four pharyngealized consonants (known impressionistically as *emphatics*). The subsystem as a whole includes [tˤ], [dˤ], [ðˤ][2] and [sˤ]. A fifth emphatic, the pharyngealized alveolar lateral approximant, is used only in its long form in [alˤlˤɑɑ] *Allah* 'God'. (For more on duration in consonants, see Section 8.4.)

---

[2]Contemporary sources are agreed with regard to the pharyngealized voiced dental fricative here, but see Mitchell (1962) where this is recorded as a pharyngealized voiced alveolar fricative, as in ['zaːjir] 'visitor' vs ['zˤaːhir] 'clear'.

Contrasts include [ṭiːn] 'figs' but [tˤiːn] 'mud', and [saḍ] 'to prevail' but [sˤaḍ] (the name of the letter that sounds [sˤ]).

Depending on the variety of Arabic, the actual degree of pharygealization in the production of these consonants varies as does the precise position in the pharynx at which the articulatory gesture occurs (which can be near the top, in the middle or even towards the bottom). Some varieties use velarized rather than pharyngealized *emphatics*.

8.3　FURTHER VARIATIONS AFFECTING MANNER OF ARTICULATION

8.3.1　Weakening of strictures

Reference to the scale of strictures set up in Chapter 4 becomes relevant again when explaining alternations observed (especially in running speech) between plosive and fricative gestures, and between fricative and approximant gestures, and even plosive and approximant gestures.

Lenition or weakening, a widening of stricture, is often a function of what is called articulatory undershoot. Such processes form a bridge between segmental phonetics and the phonetics of connected speech. Often such weakening affects non-sibilant fricatives. In English, for example, when the /ð/ phoneme is used in unstressed environments such as *the* and *other* in [ði ʌðə 'deɪ] (*the other day*), the proximity of the articulators and the relative strength of the airflow can fail to achieve audible friction and the pronunciation is that of a voiced dental approximant – one step lower down the rank scale of strictures than the phonemic identification would have us expect. The same happens to Greek /ɣ/ which often lenites to [ɰ], as in [aɰape] 'agape/love, love feast'. In Spanish, the weakening can be even more extreme. Voiced plosives which are fully articulated in initial position in the word and following nasals or laterals, weaken to fricatives or even approximants elsewhere (see Table 8.1). The strong and lenited allophones are in complementary distribution in Spanish.

8.3.2　Approach and release of plosives

The three stages of plosive articulation (approach, hold and release) are each subject to variation, either as a consequence of the immediate phonetic environment or for

Table 8.1
Lenition of plosives in Spanish

	Plosive	Fricative or approximant
Voiced bilabial plosive	['basaɾ] *basar* 'to base'	['kaβal, 'kaβal] *cabal* 'just, exact'
	[um bial] *un bial* 'a tree-lined street'	['aβɾil, 'aβɾil] *abril*, 'April'
Voiced dental plosive	['donde] *donde* 'where'	['naða, 'naða] *nada* 'nothing'
	['kaldo] *caldo* 'broth, sauce'	[ma'ðɾið, ma'ðɾið] *Madrid*
Voiced velar plosive	['gata] *gata* 'she-cat'	['ʎeɣaɾ, 'ʎeɰaɾ] *llegar* 'to arrive, reach'
	[uŋ 'gato] *un gato* 'a cat'	[a'ɣɾio, a'ɰɾio] *agrio* 'sour, acid'

contrastive purposes. Approaches and releases can be wide or narrow, for example, in terms of the distance travelled by the active articulator. The norm realization assumes the plosive to be intervocalic as in *upper, letter, figure,* etc. In such cases, plosives are described as having **wide median approach** and **wide median release**. These gestures are represented in the parametric diagram in Figure 8.4.

Sometimes, however, the plosive might be adjacent to a homorganic fricative, as in English [st] *step* or *last,* [zd] *raised,* Dutch [xk] *ga toch kijken* 'do look', etc. Here, the active articulator starts from a position much nearer to the position required to form closure and the approach is described as a straightforward **narrow median approach** (which we could also term **fricative approach**). All the active articulator needs to do is seal the narrow central gap, thereby terminating the production of friction. In many cases, this will involve little more than an increase in muscular tension. The corresponding release gesture (found in English [ts] *cats,* [dz] *red zone,* or Dutch [kx] *ik kook graag* 'I like cooking', for example) is **narrow median** or **fricative release**.

In heterorganic sequences, however, the active articulator differs from one segment to the next as the place of articulation changes (lower lip for [f], but tongue tip for [t] in English *laughed* or back of the tongue for [x] but tongue tip for [t] in Dutch *acht* 'eight', for example). This time, it is no longer a question of only needing to close a gap. So, while the airflow is turbulent during the approach or release phase, this is only one of several differences and such sequences typify **fricativized (median) approach/release**.

Occasionally, plosives are produced with homorganic fricative release regardless of the phonetic environment. Such examples are called **affricated** plosives. In English, affricated plosives are characteristic of regional pronunciation, especially the Liverpool (or **Scouse**) accent. Here, alveolar and velar plosives regularly undergo quite strong affrication, as in *a black tea pot* pronounced [ə 'blækˣ 'tˢiː pʰɒtˢ]. Indeed, there is sometimes complete lenition such that the plosive at the end of *black* would become the voiceless velar fricative [x], [blæx]. /t/-lenition can be even more extreme, being pronounced [h] (instead of the expected [tˢ] or [s]), giving *that pot* [ðæh 'pʰɒh].

Two other common transitions involve contiguous plosives and sonorant consonants (nasal or lateral). Again, the precise nature of the transitions will depend on whether the sounds are homorganic or heterorganic. In homorganic sequences of nasals and plosives ([mp]/[pm], [n̩d]/[dn̩], etc.), a comparison of how the members of each pair are articulated shows just one significant difference. Figure 4.1 confirms that the only difference in the shape of the vocal tract is the position of the velum. Transition between nasal segments and homorganic plosives is effected simply by the opening or closing of the velum. This will be true for every homorganic nasal and plosive sequence, from bilabial right through sequences of palatal [ɲ] preceded or followed by [c] or [ɟ], to uvular [ɴ] with [q] or [ɢ]. Such transitions are called simply **nasal approach** and **nasal release** and the articulatory gesture can be represented in a parametric diagram (see Figure 8.9). Table 8.2 illustrates a selection of plosives with nasal approach.

Heterorganic sequences are also possible. In this case, the oral articulators will change position at the same time as the velum rises or lowers. In such sequences we have what can best be described as **nasalized approach** and **nasalized release**.

In English, this describes the plosive approach phase in sequences such as [-ŋp-] in *ping-pong* or [-md-] in *climbdown*, etc.

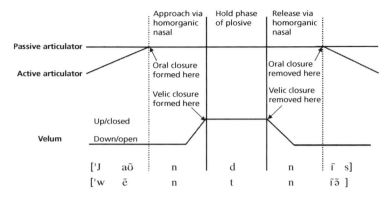

Figure 8.9
Parametric diagram showing the movements of the articulators during the production of a plosive with nasal approach and release, as in *went near* or *roundness*.

Table 8.2
Selected plosives with nasal approach

Language	Examples
English	bilabial *limp, limbo*
	alveolar *lent, lend*
	velar *link, linger*
Dutch	bilabial *ompraten* 'talk round', *omber* 'amber'
	alveolar [-nt] *hond* 'dog', [-nd-] *onder* 'under'
	velar [-ŋk-] *onknap* 'rather pretty'
Italian	bilabial *completo* 'complete', [-mb-] *un ballo* 'a ball''
	dental [-n̪t̪-] *accanto* 'nearby', [-n̪d̪-] *quando* 'when'
	velar [-ŋk] *ancora* 'again', [-ŋg-] *con grazie* 'with thanks'
Spanish	bilabial *campo* 'countryside', *cambio* 'exchange'
	dental *andante* 'walking',
	velar [-ŋk-] *áncora* 'anchor', [-ŋ g-] *un gato* 'a tomcat'

A similar situation pertains when the plosive is preceded or followed by a lateral. As with nasals, these can be homorganic or heterorganic sequences and are known respectively as **lateral approach/release** and **lateralized approach/release**. In English, pure lateral approach/release can only happen in alveolar sequences, in words such as *felt* or *little* ['lɪtl̩], and *old* or *muddle* ['mʌdl̩] because English does not have laterals at any other place of articulation. To understand how lateral approach or release occurs, you need to think about the significant articulatory difference between the articulation of [l] – actually [ɫ] in these examples because it is post-vocalic and pre-consonantal – and that of

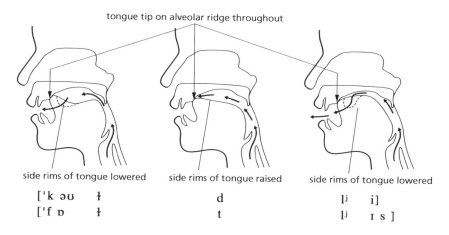

tongue tip on alveolar ridge throughout

side rims of tongue lowered   side rims of tongue raised   side rims of tongue lowered

['k əʊ   ɫ   d   lʲ   i]
['f ɒ   ɫ   t   lʲ   ɪ s]

Figure 8.10

Comparison of the articulatory positions of a homorganic lateral and plosive – alveolar [l] and [t] or [d] – in *coldly*, *fau̱ltless*.

[t] and [d]. The vocal tract drawings in Figure 8.10 show exactly what moves. As with the nasal + plosive sequence, the tongue tip remains firmly on the alveolar ridge throughout this sequence, but this time, the velum remains closed while the side rims of the tongue, which are held low for the lateral at the end of (*col-*), first rise and form a lateral closure to complete the plosive gesture (giving *cold-*) and then lower to switch back to [l] again (completing *coldly*).

All other combinations ([lp] in *gulp*, [gl] in *glow, wriggle* ['ɹɪgl̩], etc.) are **lateralized** sequences.

8.3.3 Hold phase variation

There is less variation possible during the hold phase of a plosive. The only differences likely to occur here happen when the plosives are adjacent to one another. Languages vary as to how they deal with such sequences, but in English, homorganic plosive sequences result in what is called a **long hold phase**, while in heterorganic sequences we may have **overlapping hold phases**.

The simplest example is the long hold phase. In English, this happens in homorganic plosive sequences such as *hop poles, Hard Times* or *back garden*. As in the approach and release variants discussed above, changes in voicing do not affect the basic articulation. In articulatory terms, the active articulator approaches the passive one and then remains in place for approximately twice as long as it would if there was only one plosive. The first plosive in the sequence effectively lacks a release phase and the second lacks an approach phase. This is demonstrated in the parametric diagram in Figure 8.11. The first in each sequence would be said to be **unreleased** or to have **incomplete plosion**. There is no agreed IPA diacritic to represent this absence of a release phase, but one transcription that is sometimes used by phoneticians for this purpose (and widely recognized) is a raised superscript zero, for example ['hɒpᵒ 'pʰəʊlz].

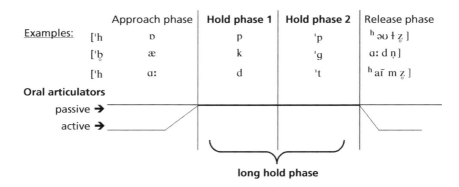

Figure 8.11
Long hold phase typical of medial homorganic plosive sequences in *hop poles*, *back garden* and *hard times*.

With overlapping hold phases, such as happens in heterorganic plosive sequences in English, the situation is a little different. Both plosives have all three articulatory phases, but the second plosive stops us from hearing the release of the first. This phenomenon is called **release masking**. In English, this will be found in heterorganic sequences such as [-pt] at the end of *tapped*, [-kt-] in the middle of *oak tree*, [-gd-] in the middle of *dig deeply*, etc. Although not all languages do this (some release the first stop before forming the second), it is a characteristic of English pronunciation that the first one is maintained until after the second one is established.

Again, this can be demonstrated using a parametric diagram. The diagram in Figure 8.12 shows that by the time the articulators separate for the first plosive (in this utterance, [k], which is velar) there is already another complete obstruction to the airstream in place, in front of the [k]-closure, at the alveolar ridge. Even though the compressed air that built up during the hold phase of [k] is released, we cannot hear this happen, because there is nowhere for the air to go – the flow is obstructed again by [d] at the alveolar ridge. Thus, release of the [k]-sound is said to be **masked** and this is what is meant by the term release masking – articulatory release does take place, but we cannot hear it.

Aspirated and unaspirated release of plosives have already been discussed in an earlier section and so all that remains here is to mention what is called **inaudible release**. Because there is no visible sign of the active articulator moving away from the passive articulator for this kind of release, people often describe such plosives as unreleased. This is wrong. If the plosives were unreleased, that would be the end of the speaker – the plosive must have been released in some way in order for the speaker to continue breathing. So, although we do not hear anything and we do not really see very much either, something definitely occurs. The plosives are formed in the usual way and compression of egressive pulmonic air takes place during a routine hold phase, then, at the point where the active articulator would normally separate from the passive one, causing audible plosion, the speaker instead closes his/her mouth and relaxes all the articulators which return to the rest position, including opening the velum. This way, the compressed air is diffused or dissipated

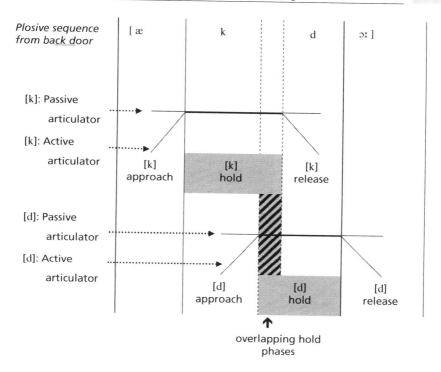

Figure 8.12
Overlapping hold phases in the phrase *back door*.

through the system, and the air pressure in the oral cavity drops as normal breathing resumes. This release is one of three typically used by speakers of English in utterance final position where it is in **free variation** (meaning any one can occur, at random) with aspirated and unaspirated release of voiceless plosives and with unaspirated released of voiced (devoiced lenis) ones. There is a special diacritic to signal inaudible release in the transcription, a superscript right-angle, giving [hɒpˈ] *hop*/[hɒbˈ] *hob*, [hɒtˈ] *hot*/[hɒdˈ] *hod*, etc.

Inaudible release is a routine feature of final plosives in some languages (Korean, Thai and Hakka Chinese, for example).

Ex 8.6 **Look at the phonetic environment of each plosive in the following narrow transcription of the British English version of the beginning of the *North Wind and the Sun* (the test passage used by the International Phonetic Association for language-specific illustrations of the alphabet).**

Give the full phonetic label for each plosive and describe the type of approach and release.
[ðə ˈnɔːθ wɪnd ən ðə ˈsʌn | wə dɪsˈpjuːtɪŋ ˈwɪtʃ wəz ðə ˈstɹɒŋɡə | wen ə ˈtɹævlə ˈkeɪm əˈlɒŋ | ˈɹæpt ɪn ə ˈwɔːm ˈkləʊk ‖]

8.3.4   Grooved fricatives

One further gesture, first mentioned in Chapter 3, and used by many languages, affects fricatives. During the articulation of lingual sounds, the upper surface of the tongue may be smooth, technically termed **slit**, or may have a median depression, termed **grooved**, forming a channel along which the egressive air flows. In the case of languages such as English, German, French, etc., this creates two sub-groups of fricatives which are often referred to a **sibilant** and **non-sibilant**. The sibilant group are all produced with a grooved tongue surface and include alveolar [s z] and palatoalveolar [ʃ ʒ]. The slit and grooved contours are demonstrated in Figure 8.13. The effect on the airflow can be seen by the distribution of arrows in the **palatograms** reproduced in Figure 8.14. In these images, the speaker wears an acrylic palate (like a dental prosthesis for straightening teeth) in which contact electrodes are embedded. The black dots represent the contact of the tongue against the roof of the mouth while speaking. You can see clearly that for dentals [θ ð], there is fairly diffuse airflow across the whole surface of the tongue (no electrodes are black, so there is no surface contact between the tongue and roof of the mouth). For both [s z] and [ʃ ʒ], however, the stream of air is channelled along a central groove, quite narrow for the alveolars, but a little broader for the palatoalveolars. This constricted airstream is deflected down from the alveolar ridge to hit the back of the lower front teeth before exiting the oral cavity. The double strike adds additional noise, and such sounds have much noisier, stronger friction than the slit, dental fricatives. They are known collectively as sibilants.

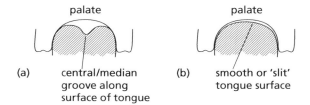

Figure 8.13
(a) Grooved and (b) slit tongue surfaces.

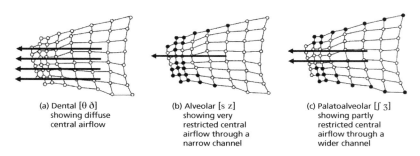

Figure 8.14
(a) – (c) Palatograms showing the passage of air for [θ ð], [s z] and [ʃ ʒ]. Adapted from Cruttenden (2008).

8.4   DURATION IN CONSONANTS

8.4.1   Terminology

The terms **duration** and **length** both refer to how long a particular vowel-sound or a consonant-sound lasts. Duration, however, is a physical, measurable and therefore phonetic concept, while length is a perceptual or impressionistic term (also used by phonologists to refer to the relationship between sounds – in English /iː/ is typically longer than /ɪ/, for example).

The length, or measurable duration, of a given sound is something over and above its basic quality in terms of VPM or BOR. This explains why the length diacritics are located under the Suprasegmental symbols on the IPA chart – length is over and above ('supra') the basic sound type or segment ('segmental'). Such concepts (stress and tone are also in this suprasegmental grouping) are often referred to collectively as **prosodic features**.

8.4.2   Contrastive use of length in consonants

Just as with vowels, languages may choose to contrast the length of consonants and such contrasts are normally two-way, between short and long. Again, however, Estonian is an exception and Jones (1944) provides [lina] *lina* 'flax, sheet' vs [linˑa] *linna* 'of the town' vs [linːa] *linna* 'to the town' as an example of Estonian's three-way length contrast.

Two-way length contrasts (long vs short) are not uncommon, occurring intervocalically, for example, in Finnish. Table 8.3 shows length contrasts involving the 13 native Finnish consonant phonemes.

Table 8.3
Length contrasts in native Finnish consonants

Sound	Short	Long
Voiceless bilabial plosive	[napa] *napa* 'navel'	[napːa] *nappa* (type of leather)
Voiceless dental plosive	[sei̯t̪i] *seiti* 'pollock'	[sei̯t̪ːi] *seitti* 'spider's web'
Voiced dental plosive	[si̪de] *side* 'bandage'	
Voiceless velar plosive	[haku] *haku* 'search' (n)	[hakːu] *hakku* 'pickaxe'
Voiced labiodental fricative	[kuva] *kuva* 'image'	
Voiceless alveolar fricative	[kasa] *kasa* 'pile'	[kasːa] *kassa* 'cashier'
Voiceless glottal fricative	[piha] *piha* 'yard'	
Voiced bilabial nasal	[t̪uma] *tuma* 'nucleus'	[t̪umːa] *tumma* 'dark'
Voiced alveolar nasal	[sana] *sana* 'word'	[sanːa] *Sanna* (girl's name)
Voiced velar nasal		[keŋːæt̪] *kengät* 'shoes'
Voiced alveolar lateral	[ala] *ala* 'area/field'	[alːa] *alla* 'under'
Voiced alveolar trill	[hera] *hera* 'whey'	[herːa] *herra* 'sir/mister'

Source: Data supplied by Minna Salonen, private communication.

Long and short consonants are also found intervocalically in Italian, e.g. ['ɛko][3] *eco* 'echo' but ['ɛkko] *ecco* 'this/that is'), and Arabic (e.g. [kasar] 'he broke' but [kasːar] 'he smashed'). During the discussion of pharyngealization above, it was noted that the pharyngealized lateral in Arabic was only used as a long consonant, transcribed [lˤlˤ]. Arabic otherwise operates length contrasts in medial and final positions as well.

8.4.3   Intrinsic duration of consonants

Just as we saw different vowel types displayed differences of intrinsic duration in Chapter 7, so there are certain generalizations to make about consonant length, too. All three parameters (voice, place and manner) contribute to this. However, it is difficult, if not impossible, to separate universal or general characteristics from language-specific characteristics and probably the least contentious observation that can be made here is that very often, studies suggest that voiced bilabial stops have a rather longer duration than voiced stops at other places of articulation. Laver (1994) attempts to tease out intrinsic durational characteristics, concluding for example that in an affricate, the duration of the fricative release must be shorter than the length that would be perceived as a separate fricative segment. He also points out that the fleeting nature of a tap is such that although it must have a certain minimum duration within which the gesture can be completed, there must also be an upper limit if the tap is not to be perceived by the listener as a plosive (see Laver (1994: 432-6)).

Ex 8.7   Field Notebook: Phonetics in One Word

Entry 8 Use the theory you have just learned in order to continue writing your Field Notebook, applying your knowledge to the detailed phonetic description of the word *completes*.

Go to www.routledge.com/cw/ashby for instructions and feedback.

8.5   SUMMARY

- Chapter 8 described some more detailed variables of consonant production, beyond the basic VPM characteristics identified in earlier chapters.

- Additional contributions made by vocal fold action were outlined, including voicing behaviour within segments (voicing and devoicing) leading to the introduction of the fortis/lenis dichotomy, VOT and aspiration, and glottalization.

- Secondary articulations were explored in greater depth (palatalization, velarization and pharyngealization).

- Manner variables were expanded, including a range of variation found in the approach, hold and release phases of plosives.

---

[3]Preceding short or single consonants, lengthening of the vowel is customary and some authorities mark this explicitly: ['ɛːko]. See, for example, Chapallaz (1979).

Ear-training

Once you have studied this chapter carefully, continue the development of your practical skills by attempting the ear-training exercises for this chapter, available as recordings at www.routledge.com/cw/ashby.

FURTHER READING

Building on the additional reading and study undertaken for consonants so far (see earlier suggestions, especially at the end of Chapters 3, 4 and 5), you can take your studies even further with Chapters 9 and 10 in Ashby (2005), Chapters 6 and 8 in Ashby & Maidment (2005), Chapters 11 and 14 of Ladefoged (2005), and Chapter 10 of Ladefoged & Maddieson (1996). At the more advanced level, Chapters 11 to 14 in Laver (1996) offer a wealth of further information.

9

Connected speech – segment dynamics

Chapter 9 draws together the threads on various topics relating to connected speech, looking in more depth at acoustic cues in relation to voice, place (where it explores formant transitions and locus theory) and manner of articulation. It looks at the relation of acoustic cues to narrow transcription and the concept of juncture, and introduces coarticulation, comparing this with assimilation.

9.1 PHONETIC TRANSCRIPTION AND ACOUSTIC CUES

9.1.1 What are acoustic cues?

Acoustic cues are the means by which we recognize sounds, distinguishing vowels from consonants, sonorants from obstruents, fricatives from plosives, voiced sounds from voiceless ones, etc. They help us to identify the meaning of potentially ambiguous utterances – *peace talks*, for example, rather than *pea stalks*, *cart* rather than *card* – motivating our choice of symbols when we write utterances down in transcription. In other words, acoustic cues are the myriad phonetic details that we have encountered in this book so far, and many more besides.

For example, we discovered how in English, fortis and lenis consonants affect the duration of a preceding vowel (of any preceding resonant, in fact – vowels and sonorant consonants) in the **nucleus** or **coda**[1] of the same syllable. Fortis consonants clip these, shortening their duration when compared with a norm allophone. As we saw, the duration of the vowel is how we tell *cart* and *card* apart, if they are spoken in isolation. Similarly, [ɪ] and [n] in *wince* [wɪns] are both shorter in duration than the same sequence in *wins* [wɪnz]. Sonorant duration thus constitutes an acoustic cue in these contexts. The cue is detected by the listener as a product of connected speech.

When plosive segments like /t/ and /d/ occur at the beginning of the syllable in English, what we rely on to distinguish them is VOT. A devoiced [d̥] is told apart from the voiceless [tʰ] by how long the speaker takes to establish vocal fold vibration in the following sound, rather than by any intrinsic differences in the silent hold-phases of the two sounds themselves. So, acoustic cues are essentially phonetic features. They are embodied in our phonetic transcription of what we have heard.

---

[1]The coda is the part of the syllable following the nucleus (the vowel, or maybe a syllabic consonant). So, in *lengths*, the coda (which can be pronounced in different ways) could include the four consonants [-ŋkθs], giving [leŋkθs]. These consonants together form a four-consonant cluster in the coda of this syllable.

What is effectively happening is that our hearing mechanism is acting as a form of frequency analyser, identifying auditorily details and patterns that we can see in representations like spectrograms and speech waveforms. The selected information is fed to our brain. The brain processes the signal, eventually decoding the meaning in the message. What we attend to is not absolute values and every detail, but patterns and relationships between components of the signal. As well as no two utterances ever being identical, when we listen, we also compensate for differences between men and women, adults and children, accents, ambient noise conditions, etc. Many of these differences that we as human listeners take in our stride pose immense problems for speech recognition technology. A computer is programmed to respond to a particular range of variants, so as soon as a speaker comes along with a different set of variants, the machine can no longer recognize what is being said. A machine can even be confused by a known speaker if he or she turns up with acute laryngitis or a common cold – conditions which change the articulators also change acoustic features in the speech output and if these are features the machine has 'learnt' to look for, communication will break down. There is a massive research literature in this field and the field goes well beyond the scope of this present volume, but you already know enough to be able to follow basic introductions like the comprehensive chapter on speech perception offered in Raphael *et al.* (2006), for example.

For our present purposes, research shows that many of the salient perceptual cues correspond to elements of the narrowly transcribed representations that we make of speech (aspiration, vowel length, devoicing, etc.). Other cues include the intensity and frequency of friction which are used by listeners to assist in determining voiceless from voiced fricative sounds and their various places of articulation, as in Figure 9.1. Here, you can see two factors at work. First, [s z ʃ ʒ] all have darker images than

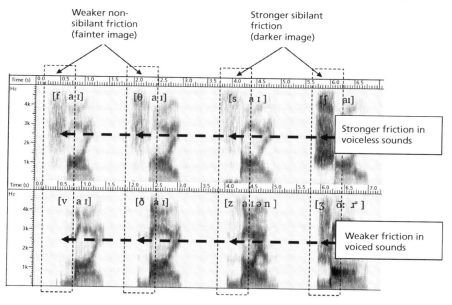

Figure 9.1 Spectrograms of English fricative pairs – voiceless above and voiced below (Speaker PA).

[f v θ ð], indicative of their being louder, altogether noisier sounds. The first four are sibilants (see Chapter 8), produced with a groove along the median line of the active articulator. Second, you will see that the voiced member of each pair (the bottom row) is fainter than the voiceless member (the top row). This tells us something about the airflow again: airflow in voiced (lenis) sounds is reduced in comparison with airflow in voiceless (fortis) sounds. As we saw in Chapter 8, in voiced sounds, the vibration of the vocal folds modifies the airflow into a series of little puffs, the flow stops momentarily each time the folds close. In voiceless sounds, the full stream of air escapes the whole time. The more reduced or weaker the airflow, the less intense (loud) the sound seems to the listener and this is visible in the paler, weaker image in the spectrogram.

One other acoustic characteristic visible in these images is the frequency level and spread of the friction. This relates to the place of articulation of the sound. The palatoalveolars have friction across a wide spectrum, from the very top of the visible frequency scale (around 4kHz) right down to around the 1kHz level. By comparison, the alveolars have much higher frequency of friction, at its most intense in the 4kHz region.

All of these gross distinctions are reflected in our choice of base symbol, demonstrating recognition of the basic sound type – high frequency friction of [s], for example, as opposed to lower frequency friction of [ʃ], or greater intensity [s] as opposed to weaker intensity [z] or [z̥].

A further range of acoustic cues helps us to distinguish between different sonorant sounds. The first of these is intensity again, energy. Spectrograms do not provide absolute measurements of intensity – instead, we make relative judgements based on the darkness of the image. The most intense signals associate with vowel sounds. As we saw in Figure 6.9, the formant structure which characterizes these voiced sonorants is usually visible throughout because there is sufficient energy, giving such sounds sufficient amplitude. The main reason for this is that all the air is travelling in a single, unimpeded stream through the vocal tract – all the energy is being concentrated into one action.

By comparison, approximants tend to have a much weaker spectrographic image. The energy in the airstream is weakened by the consonantal gestures resulting in much fainter formants as in Figure 9.2. You can see the strong [ɑ] vowel formants

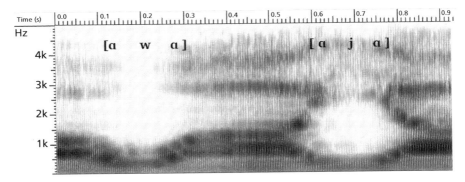

Figure 9.2
Spectrograms of [w] and [j] (Speaker PA).

here with the fainter approximant consonants – the semi-vowels [w] and [j] – in between. The weakest, faintest image of all (see Figure 9.3) is that produced by nasal consonants, where some of the air is flowing into the oral cavity while the rest flows through the nasal cavity – the air is effectively doing two jobs at the same time, exciting two quite separate cavities instead of just one.

(Interestingly, too, in the spectrograms in Figure 9.3, you can see the [æ]-like quality of [h], the formant structure in the voiceless friction matching that of the vowel.)

One further point regarding approximants is the distinction between [ɹ] and [l]. As we know, many languages fail to distinguish these two sounds and speakers may even confuse them when confronted with a language that treats them as separate phonemes. As with all sonorant consonants, the image is faint, but in Figure 9.4, the subtle acoustic difference between the two sounds is clearly visible. It is the frequency dip in the third formant of [ɹ] (indicated) that distinguishes it from [l], in which F3 remains at a steady frequency. It is this dip that makes us hear *write* or *right* rather than *light* in English, for example. Speakers of languages that do

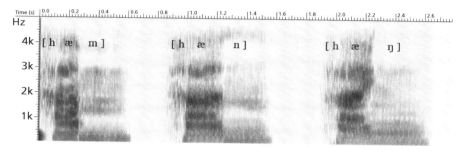

Figure 9.3
Spectrograms of English nasals [m], [n] and [ŋ] in *ham, Han, hang* (Speaker PA).

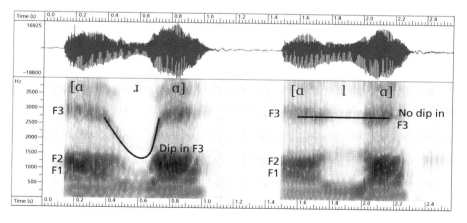

Figure 9.4
English [ɹ] and [l] (speaker PA).

not use such a contrast – speakers of Japanese, for example, Thai, Chinese, Lao – therefore tend to be insensitive to this very small acoustic difference that holds such significance for English ears.

9.1.2   Locus theory

A rather different cue that we have not yet considered at all is used to determine place of articulation differences. This relates to our decoding of transitions in the second formant of an adjacent vowel. In Figure 9.5, spectrograms of [bɛ], [dɛ] and [gɛ], you can see that as the vowel begins after release of the initial plosive, there are transitions (bends) visible at the beginning of the formants. For each sequence, because the consonants are voiced sounds, the beginning of F1 has a curve rising from a lower value to its steady state value (called a **negative transition**), but F2 bends in different directions.

In the [bɛ] sequence, F2 also has a negative transition (it rises up from a lower frequency to a higher one). If we projected the line traced by this curve back through the hold-phase of the plosive, measuring the point at which it reaches the frequency scale, it would hit the scale at somewhere around 700 Hz. This is true for the F2 of all bilabials, [b], [p] and [m], and this value is the **locus frequency** (literally the 'place frequency', locus being the Latin word for place, location) for the bilabial place of articulation.

Alveolars have a much higher locus, around 1.8kHz. This is reflected in Figure 9.5 by the fairly flat profile of F2 in the [dɛ] sequences, which being around 1.8kHz itself does not need to move. For velars, however, the locus varies depending on the vowel. This is partly a function of the fact that the point of closure differs depending on the context. Velar articulations front to a more palatal position before (close) front vowels (as in *key,* for example) and may even retract slightly before open back vowels (as in *car* or *cod*), so velars do not associate with a single point of closure in quite the same way as bilabials and alveolars do. The **positive transition** here (F2 curves down from a higher value to reach the steady state value for [gɛ]) points towards a high locus,

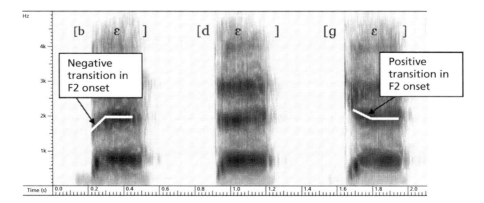

Figure 9.5
Spectrograms of [bɛ], [dɛ] and [gɛ] showing F2 transitions indicating place of articulation (Speaker PA).

around 3kHz, which is typical of velars adjacent to front vowels. (For back vowels, this drops to around 1kHz.)

These transitions visible in Figure 9.5 are transitions which occur as the articulators move away from the constriction in CV sequences. If the sound sequence was reversed, VC, we would see a mirror image of the formant movement. What listeners are picking up here is not the absolute values characteristic of particular places of articulation, but the general shape or direction of formant movement. The shape of transitions is a function of not only the place of articulation of the consonant but also its manner and the F2 of the immediately adjacent vowel. It is this constellation of facts that tells the listener 'alveolar', 'palatal', etc.

9.1.3 Rate of formant transition

The rate (speed) of the transition adds manner information. A very swift transition of the sort that was visible in Figure 9.1 is typical of true consonants, in this case, plosives. A more gradual transition is perceived as an approximant and the slowest of all as a vowel sequence, a diphthong. These differences are demonstrated in Figure 9.6.

Again, these are all acoustic cues that affect our selection of the base symbol, informing our choice of manner of articulation. With a locus of around 700Hz, the speed of the movement to the F2 of the following vowel will determine whether I hear [b] or [w] in a CV sequence, or whether I hear VV, [u] + vowel.

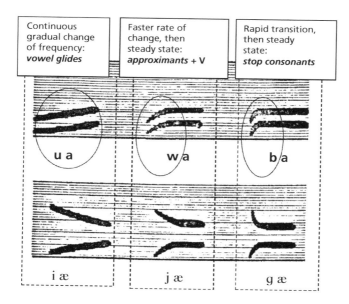

Figure 9.6

Schematic spectrograms[2] showing manner of articulation as a function of formant transition rate
Source: Haskins Laboratories, New York.

[2]These schematic spectrograms were originally hand-painted images used to synthesize speech on a Pattern Playback machine in the Haskins Labs, New York.

Ex 9.1   What features can you detect in the two spectrograms below? Find:

(a) formants (energy bands) that suggest a vowel sound is present;

(b) formants that look as if the sound quality is changing dramatically (as in a diphthong)

(c) formants that stay parallel (as in a simple vowel);

(d) random patterns that might indicate friction – can you say whether the friction is voiced or voiceless?

(e) blank spaces that could be plosive or affricate hold phases.

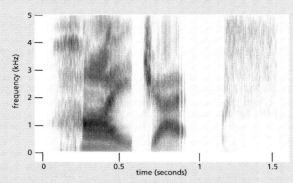

Spectrogram 1

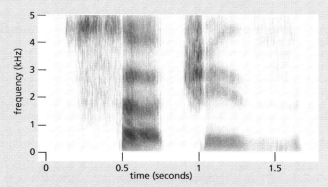

Spectrogram 2

If you were told that one of the spectrograms represents the utterance *searches* and the other represents the utterance *hijacks*, can you begin to figure out which one might be which? (Tip: make a predictive transcription of each utterance first, so that you can decide what features to look for and which order they might occur in – presence or absence of voice, friction, etc.)

9.2 COARTICULATION

9.2.1 The function of coarticulation

Coarticulation, as we have seen, is the name given to the ways in which sequences of discrete 'target' segments are fused together into continuous speech. The term refers to the overlapping of articulatory gestures in time, the spreading of features from one segment to its neighbours. Such changes are largely low-level, phonetic changes. This contrasts with what we usually mean when we use the related term, assimilation, where the changes tend to be higher level, phonemic changes and often involve a complete change of target. The function of the spreading or weaving of phonetic features is to create a continuum – a stream of speech without gaps.

9.2.2 Major allophones and the nature of coarticulation

Not everything we do when we speak is under our conscious control (nasalization of vowels adjacent to nasal consonants is involuntary, for example, likewise the labialization of consonants before rounded vowels). Moreover, not everything that happens is necessarily discernible, especially not to the unaided human ear. When we make phonetic transcriptions we are relying exclusively on our ears. We make auditory judgements of what we hear. We can later check this by looking at waveforms or spectrograms to find evidence to support what we have heard, but we cannot spot something in a spectrogram that we have not heard or cannot hear and then add this to our transcription – if you cannot hear it and judge it, it is outside of anything relevant for speech purposes and so it doesn't matter whether or not the machine has picked it up. So, for example, we can all hear aspiration of voiceless plosives at the beginning of a stressed syllable in English, [pʰɔː], [tʰɔː], [kʰɔː] *pore, tore, core*, and we are equally certain that aspiration is not present in [spɔː], [stɔː], [skɔː] *spore, store, score*. But the weaker aspiration of such sounds in unstressed positions is something we often tend not to notice at all. This may well be because the length of the VOT is just too short for us to pick it up, rather than any lack of concentration on our part, but the tiny h-like interval may still be visible in an acoustic analysis of the signal. However, unless we can genuinely hear it, we cannot transcribe it – transcriptions tell the reader what *we* can *hear*, not what a machine can analyse.

The same is true for any kind of coarticulatory activity. Coarticulation happens all the time – coarticulation holds the speech continuum together – but that doesn't mean to say we are consciously aware of it all. There is a danger in making narrow transcriptions which include everything you imagine should happen – that is fine as a demonstration of understanding of theory, but it is not necessarily a true reflection of real speech, and on any given occasion it may not even be true at all. All possible variants are not necessarily equal. They do not all constitute what we might want to call a major allophone of a given phoneme or sound type.

For example, when allophonic velarization of the MRP lateral was described in the previous chapter (a variant often called *dark-l*), I mentioned that all English consonants tend to be velarized in final, post-vocalic position. However, we tend not to consider this velarized variant as a major allophone for any consonant other than /l/. Look at accounts of each sound in Cruttenden (2008), for example. But this is not the same as saying they don't exist or that they would never occur. They do undoubtedly exist and they may frequently occur, but we are not sensitive to them. I am confident, for example, that when I say *sweet* the initial s-sound is different from the one I use at the beginning of *seem* or *suit* (/sjuːt/) – in *sweet* I have what I might want to call a 'dark-s', a velarized allophone, the body of the tongue preparing for [w] creating an apico-alveolar narrowing with simultaneous back tongue coarticulation of an [u]-type gesture, [s]. In /sjuːt/, by comparison, it is the front of the tongue that coarticulates, preparing [j] during the steady state of [s] and adding a palatal resonance, [sʲ]. However, I cannot say that these are always the case, nor that they are always sufficiently marked for even the trained ear to pick it up. Indeed, there may be occasions when there is no coarticulation of this kind at all. These variants, therefore, although phonetically interesting, are not major allophones in the same way as aspirated allophones of /p t k/ or devoiced allophones of /b d g/, /v ð z ʒ/, or /dʒ/.

9.2.3   Coarticulation and assimilation

In very many cases, coarticulatory gestures are attempts at streamlining articulatory movement and avoiding hiatus. The effect of this is often to make one sound more like another (facilitating economy of articulatory activity and increase of speed). This is also, literally, a definition of assimilation, and yet we do not treat these terms as synonyms. The general convention in phonetics is to term coarticulation anything that will only show up in narrow phonetic transcription, reserving the term assimilation for changes involving a complete change of target. Often, assimilations are so extreme that they can be recorded in a much broader transcription, a phonemic transcription. Nonetheless, the terms are not used altogether discretely in the wider literature. You will need to be sensitive to this overlap in order to understand that coarticulatory gestures mean that one sound can be said to have become more like – assimilated to – another, even if this does not result in a complete phonemic overlap of the kind that is reflected by the final /n/ of *one* being realized by a velar gesture, [ŋ], in *one girl* /'wʌŋ 'gɜːl/.

> Ex 9.2   Try saying the words *car, cur, key* silently to yourself and then try to describe
> what you can feel for the k-sound at the beginning of each word. How does this
> compare with what you can feel for the g-sound at the beginning of *guard, girl,*
> *ghee* (/giː/ – a form of clarified butter used in Indian cookery).

Coarticulation can operate in either direction. That is to say, a speaker may be anticipating a sound that is yet to come, or a feature from an earlier sound may be retained, resulting respectively in **anticipatory** and **perseverative** coarticulation.

In the case of anticipatory coarticulation, the direction of influence is right-to-left (L ← R). The first segment in a string is influenced by a characteristic of the second segment which is later in the string. This compares at the phonemic level with **regressive assimilation**. (Anticipatory coarticulation, where a sound 'anticipates' or 'prepares for' something coming up in the near future is also called 'forward coarticulation' in many American texts.)

In perseverative coarticulation, the direction of influence is left-to-right (L → R). In this instance, a characteristic of the first segment in a string stays on and affects the second segment which is later in the string. A comparison can be made this time with **progressive assimilation**. (Perseverative coarticulation, where some phonetic characteristic stays present or perseveres/continues is given the name 'backward coarticulation' in many American texts.)

Examples of perseverative and anticipatory coarticulation are summarized in Table 9.1.

Table 9.1
Coarticulation: direction of influence with selected examples from English

Direction: Gesture, e.g:	L ← R anticipatory	L → R perseverative
Nasality	Vowels and approximants undergo nasalization when before a nasal, e.g: *sang, helmet, kiln*, etc.	Vowels and approximants undergo nasalization when after a nasal, e.g: *mile, runway, can you*, etc.
Lip rounding	Consonants undergo varying degrees of labialization when before a rounded vowel or approximant, e.g: *torn, saw, queen, cream*, etc.	(Lip rounding affects consonants that occur after a rounded vowel or approximant to a much lesser extent in English.)

Ex 9.3 **The following MRP English utterances contain assimilations. Identify what has changed (you will need to compare the isolated, citation forms of each word with the contextualized versions in these phrases) and say whether the direction of influence is anticipatory or perseverative.**

(1) Fried banana pronounced ['fɹaɪb bə'nɑːnə]
(2) Town crier pronounced ['tʰaʊŋ 'kɟaɪə]
(3) Hit them pronounced ['hɪt̪ ðəm]
(4) Court martial pronounced ['kʰɔːp 'mɑːʃəɫ]
(5) Cornflakes pronounced ['kʰɔːm̩ fleɪks]
(6) Red rose pronounced ['ɹed 'ɹəʊz̥]
(7) Front gate pronounced ['fɹʌŋk 'ɡeɪt]
(8) This shop pronounced ['ðɪʃ 'ʃɒp]
(9) Well thought of pronounced ['weɫ 'θɔːt ɒv̥]
(10) Tent pole pronounced ['tʰemp 'pʰəʊɫ]

This data is representative of a general process of assimilation in English. Can you say what this is?

Ex 9.4 **Identify instances of coarticulation in each of the following utterances. Are these perseverative or anticipatory?**

(1) May leave pronounced [ˈmẽ̞ɪ ˈl̪iːv̥]
(2) Door-knob pronounced [ˈd̪ʷɔ̃ nᵑɒb̥]
(3) Phone call pronounced [ˈfə̃ʊ̃ŋ kʰʷɔːɫ]
(4) Foolproof pronounced [ˈfˣuːɫ ˈpˣɹ̥ˣuːf]
(5) Steam room pronounced [ˈsʲtʲĩ̃m ɹˣõm]

9.2.4 Parametric diagrams

This temporal co-ordination of articulatory movements is brought out in the traditional type of **articulatory description** and illustrated in **parametric diagrams**. The ones we have used in this book are very simple, plotting just the movements of the vocal folds and the velum and the occasional active articulator. But diagrams can have any number of 'channels' – a line for the lips, for the tongue tip, the side rims of the tongue, the back, the front, a line for the lower jaw, and even lines reflecting airflow (nasal or oral), and so forth. Such diagrams like the one in Figure 9.7 are schematic representations of machine outputs of the kind you would achieve in a speech production laboratory with subjects wired up, using electrodes, airflow masks, etc., to record the movements of selected articulators. Each separate record has its own trace. Some of the most elaborate are the product of a technique known as cinefluorography[3] producing

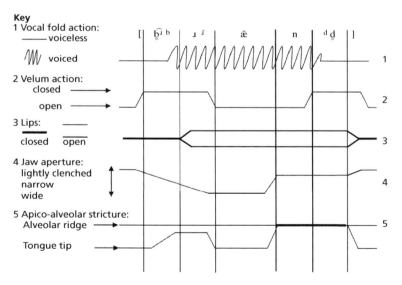

Figure 9.7
Parametric diagram of vocal fold, velum, lip, jaw and tongue tip movements during the articulation of 'brand'.

[3]Also called cineradiography and used in medical diagnostics, this involves use of a movie camera to film movements of organs which have been injected with a non-toxic radiopaque substance. Their image is then visible on a fluorescent screen as they move.

elaborate webs of trace lines as in the image in Figure 9.8. This image tells it like it is, including surprising features such as a nasal segment corresponding with the presence of near closure of the velum (see the [m] in the [mp] sequence of *camping*). Many, however, are schematic, like the ones used in this book (see Pike (1947), Brosnahan and Malberg (1970), O'Connor (1973), Tench (1978), for example) and represent what we believe should happen when theory is put into practice. Comparison with the real thing, though, shows us that we may well be mistaken. Nonetheless, without an understanding of the theory, it would be impossible to read and evaluate the tracings in Figure 9.7 at all, and so as a learning aid, schematic parametric diagrams still have a value (and, of course, much of the time, reality and theory coincide). The technique of parametric representation is outlined and appraised in Laver (1994).

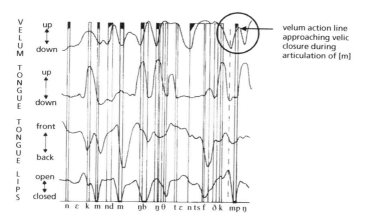

Figure 9.8 Movements of the velum, tongue, and lips recorded by lateral cinefluorography during the sentence "Next Monday morning bring three tents for the camping trip". *Source*: Kent (1983).

Ex 9.5 Look at the following parametric representation of the utterance *brand* /brænd/, pronounced [b̥ɹ̊ʲænᵈd̥]. Explain the coarticulatory activity that is happening at points 1, 2 and 3.

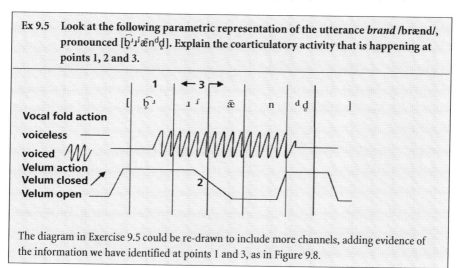

The diagram in Exercise 9.5 could be re-drawn to include more channels, adding evidence of the information we have identified at points 1 and 3, as in Figure 9.8.

Ex 9.6

---

(1) Make a narrow phonetic transcription of the utterance *in luck* and draw a parametric diagram showing velum action. Remember that you will now need to include all the different details discussed so far.

(2) Make a narrow phonetic transcription of the utterance *clever* and draw a parametric diagram showing vocal fold action.

(3) Make a narrow phonetic transcription of the utterance *plans* and draw a parametric diagram showing the actions of the velum and the vocal folds.

9.2.5   Juncture and narrow transcription

Not only do we perceive all these details when we listen to speech but, as I have said, we are also capable of extracting the meaning, including meaning dependent on very small phonetic differences between utterances which, at the segmental or phonemic level, might appear identical. Returning to the pair of utterances *peace talks* and *pea stalks* for a moment, if we made a broad phonetic transcription of these, the segments would be identical: /p iː s t ɔː k s/. Different positions of the word boundary, however, trigger the use of different allophones, and the listener can distinguish /piːs + tɔːks/ from /piː + stɔːks/. **Juncture** is the name given to these relationships.

For example in /piːstɔːks/, depending on the junctural relationship between the /s/ and /t/ segments here, we will understand either *peace talks* or *pea stalks*. We can begin to see why by making narrow phonetic transcriptions of the two different utterances:

1. *peace talks* [ˈpʰi̠ˑs + tʰɔˑks]

2. *pea stalks* [ˈpʰi̠ː + stɔˑks]

Of course, the two utterances have a certain amount in common. If we compare the two transcriptions we can see that they share the initial [pʰ] and the final [ɔˑks], so the beginning and end parts are indistinguishable and will not play a part in helping us to determine the meaning. In the middle, however, the location of the syllable/word boundary (marked here by +) triggers different allophones of the boundary-adjacent phonemes and these, in turn, create a different auditory signal – they sound different to the listener.

In (1), we have what is called **open juncture** between /s/ and /t/ – that is, they are on opposite sides of the syllable boundary. This has two consequences:

- /s/ is the final segment in the first syllable and because it is a fortis consonant, it clips or shortens the preceding vowel. Long /iː/ is realized here as [i̠ˑ]. There is *pre-fortis clipping* (vowel length reduction caused by the syllable-final /s/).

- /t/ is syllable initial (at the beginning of the second syllable) and so it is followed by a long VOT – the aspirated allophone is used, [tʰ]. We hear the voiceless, [h]-like friction that we call *aspiration*.

We would describe the relationship between /iː/ and /s/ and that between /t/ and /ɔː/ as being instances of **close juncture** – sounds adjacent, within the same syllable.

In (2), we have open juncture between /iː/ and /s/ and close juncture between /s/ and /t/. This causes different allophones to be selected and brings about a change in the pronunciation, giving different auditory cues to the listener:

- /iː/ is now the final segment in the first syllable and it is therefore fully long, realized this time as [i̥ː].
- /s/, however, is now syllable initial at the beginning of the second syllable and is in a consonant cluster with /t/. As we have seen, when voiceless plosives are preceded by /s/ in the same syllable in English, the aspiration is absent, so now we have a situation where there is no delay in the onset of voicing following the release of /t/. The allophone of /t/ used here is unaspirated.

These so-called junctural cues are the auditory differences that enable listeners to distinguish the two different noun phrases (*peace talks* and *pea stalks*) when they are spoken aloud.

Ex 9.7	**Decide how many different interpretations each of the following might have and make narrow transcriptions to demonstrate the different junctural cues:**
1 /aɪskriːm/ 2 /ɡreɪteɪp/ 3 /brɑːstræps/ 4 /waɪtʃuːz/	

Languages have different junctural characteristics and processes. In Italian, for example, particularly in central and southern Italy, a process known as **raddoppiamento sintattico** is triggered by specific junctural sequences. Subject to certain constraints, when a short stressed vowel at the end of one word precedes certain word initial consonants at the beginning of the next, the initial consonant is doubled, becoming a long consonant. This is found, for example, in the pronunciation of the name of the coffee retailer, *Caffè Nero* [kafˈfɛ nˈneːro].

Ex 9.8	**Field Notebook: Phonetics in One Word**
Entry 9 Use the theory you have just learned in order to continue writing your Field Notebook, applying your knowledge to the detailed phonetic description of the word completes.	
Go to www.routledge.com/cw/ashby for instructions and feedback.	

9.3 SUMMARY

- This chapter has moved away from the detailed description of individual speech sounds to look more widely at how sounds behave and change in connected speech.

- Using English illustrations, the chapter considered the nature of acoustic cues that allow us to recognize different speech sounds.

- The coarticulatory nature of connected speech was investigated, introducing parametric diagrams.

- The chapter also began to develop your narrow phonetic transcription skills, showing how narrow transcription captures the auditory and articulatory characteristics of the speech continuum.

⑨ Ear-training

Once you have studied this chapter carefully, continue the development of your practical skills by attempting the ear-training exercises for this chapter, available as recordings at www.routledge.com/cw/ashby.

FURTHER READING

To learn more about connected speech, additional basic reading can be found in Chapters 10 and 12 of Cruttenden (2008) — these look particularly at connected speech in English — Chapter 7 of Lodge (2009), and Chapter 16 of Ladefoged (2005).

Wider reading on aspects of representation, transcription and segmentation can be found in Chapters 4 and 5 of Lodge (2009) and Chapter 3 of Ogden (2009). A more advanced acoustic account of consonants is provided by Chapter 7 in Hayward (2000).

Beyond the segment

Over and above the speech sounds themselves, the speech signal includes information transmitted in the form of loudness, timing, pitch changes, etc. Chapter 10 investigates the realms of these suprasegmentals – features that co-occur with segments but which are separate from them. This chapter will look briefly at stress and rhythm, accent, tone and intonation.[1]

10.1   SUPRASEGMENTALS

Right at the beginning of this book in Chapter 1, we talked about the concept of stress and we looked at the typical rhythm that is set up by stressed beats in poetic forms like the limerick. All through the accompanying ear-training materials, you have been marking the stress in English dictations and you will have been including this in English transcriptions, too, when working from written sources.

Stress, as a glance at the *Suprasegmentals* section of the IPA chart (page xiv) shows, is a suprasegmental, likewise tone and intonation (including tonality), duration of speech sounds, and linking. Crystal (1969) takes this further in his description of **prosodic systems**, adding matters of voice quality, tempo, and continuity (involving the duration, incidence and type of pauses). This is a vast area of study in its own right but it is still part of phonetics and so we will touch on some of these concepts here, in this final chapter.

10.2   STRESS

10.2.1   Physical correlates of stress

We often have some sort of feeling for rhythm, intuitions about what is or isn't a stressed syllable or a rhythmic beat. Curiously, though, there is no single physical correlate for stress. We have examined correlations such as changes in the rate of vocal fold vibration with perceived changes in pitch, formant patterns with vowel qualities, and various other identifiable characteristics correlating with our perception of voice,

---

[1] The subject matter of this chapter is such that you will be able to undertake less by way of directly related practical work. The smaller number of exercises make this an ideal opportunity for reviewing and consolidating all the basic English transcription skills that you have developed so far and you are recommended to re-do earlier exercises that you found particularly difficult or in which you feel you did less well.

place or manner of consonants. But there is no such correlate for stress. Stress is a composite, deriving from measurable intensity (how loud the syllable seems to be, in relation to surrounding syllables), duration (how long the syllable seems to last, in relation to surrounding syllables), and frequency (the impression of pitch conveyed to the listener – the higher, the more prominent, but changing or dynamic pitch is the most noticed of all). These three characteristics can all be seen clearly in Figure 10.1 showing the speech waveform and the Fx line (the pitch track) for the utterances *barber* ['bɑːbə] and *babaar* [bə'bɑː] (a nonsense word, reversing the stress and vowel qualities of *barber*, giving the vowel and stress pattern of *bazaar*).

In the 1950s, Dennis Fry conducted a series of investigations demonstrating that of these three factors, pitch was the most important for the perception of stress, length the second most important contributor, and loudness the least important (see Fry (1958)). The **relative** values of all these things are important, though, because in isolation you would not be able to say whether a syllable was stressed or not. We detect stress by making comparisons.

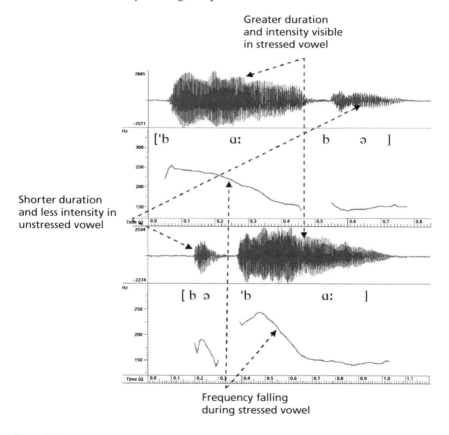

Figure 10.1
Annotated speech waveforms and Fx lines for the utterances *barber* and *babaar* [bə'bɑː] demonstrating relative intensity, duration and frequency in the speech signal (speaker PA).

10.2.2 Word stress

10.2.2.1 *Fixed stress and free stress*

The position of stress in a word can be **fixed** or **free**. A language will have one or the other of these stress types. Fixed stress means that stress almost invariably turns up on exactly the same syllable in every word, regardless of word length – the first, for example, or penultimate, the last, and so forth. In such cases, the position of the stress is predictable. It is quite literally fixed in that position. In the opposite situation, stress is completely unpredictable. Unless we know huge amounts about the etymology and morphology of the language (and even then stress placement may turn out not to be entirely regular), we cannot for the most part predict which syllable will carry the stress because the stress is quite free to occur on any syllable at all.

In fixed stress languages, stress fulfils a demarcative function. If you know, for example, that stress always occurs on the first syllable of words in a language (this is true of Finnish, for example, or Hungarian), every time you hear a stress you know that a new word has begun – with training, you can hear this even if you do not speak the language. Polish and Welsh are two languages that typically have penultimate stress (stress on the last but one syllable of a word), so you would know that there is just one more syllable and then a new word begins. Regardless of word length, and exceptions apart, in such fixed stress languages the position of the stressed syllable can be predicted.

In free stress languages, however, such as English or Russian (or even Spanish and Italian to some extent), you cannot predict the position of the stress. Stress is part of the phonetic make-up of the word and along with the segments (the vowels and consonants) must be learnt as part of the package. Of course there are rules, such as the fact that when an English word has the *–ation* suffix (*civilization, coronation, fixation,* etc.), the main stress falls on the first syllable of the suffix, regardless of the length of the word (*civili'zation, coro'nation, fix'ation*), or that words ending *–ity* have antepenultimate stress (*'equity, com'plexity, regu'larity,* etc.). But these rules are extensive and complex – not something we consciously memorize and operate. (See Fudge (1984), for example.)

It is worth noting here that in English, as an inherent property of the word, word stress patterns also identify the syllable(s) on which a rhythmic beat can occur when the word is used in connected speech (see Section 1.1.6 on p. 6).

10.2.2.2 *Primary stress and secondary stress*

Especially in longer words, we often have the impression that there is more than one stress. This may indeed be the case. In such instances, we need to distinguish between what are called **double stress** words and words which have a **secondary stress** as well as the identifiable main stress, called the **primary stress**. In words with only one stress, this is the main or primary stress: *re'mark, de'fine, e'stablish.* But in longer words – *unremarkably, indefinable, antidisestablishmentarianism –* there often seems to be more than one prominent syllable. Such words can be shown to have not only a primary word stress, but also one or more secondary word stresses: ‚unre'markably, ‚inde'finable, ‚antidise‚stablishmen'tarianism. The lowered stress mark is a convention typically used to indicate secondary word stress (see IPA chart, page xiv). This gives us effectively three degrees of stress: primary stress, secondary stress and unstressed. For most purposes, that is enough. These stresses fulfil two main roles – they are a defining characteristic of the word itself (word stress) and they also identify the points in the word that can or may carry a rhythmic beat when the word is used in a longer utterance as part of an intonational phrase (sentence stress).

10.2.2.3   Word stress and meaning

Some languages – English and Italian, for example – use word stress to make changes of meaning. This is part of the role of word stress (sometimes called **lexical stress**) in such languages. In English, for example, a word pair like *billow* and *below* are distinguished exclusively by the position of the stressed syllable – initial stress in ['bɪləʊ] (*billow*) and final stress in [bɪ'ləʊ] (*below*). Similarly, *(an) import* pronounced /'ɪmpɔːt/ but *(to) import* /ɪm'pɔːt/. A comparable pair in Italian would be *fini* 'ends' and *finì* '(he) finished', pronounced respectively ['fiːni] and [fi'niː] (vowel length here being affected by stress, but without any change in vowel quality). English, too, has some pairs in which vowel length alternates as a corollary of stress movement, including /'riːmɪt/ *remit* (n) and /ri'mɪt/ *remit* (vb), and *Kermit* (the frog from the *Muppet Show*) ['kɜːmɪt] but *commit* [kə'mɪt].[2] While the many noun vs phrasal verb pairs retain identical segmental sequences regardless of stress position (*a dropout* /'drɒpaʊt/ but *to drop out* /drɒp 'aʊt/, *a runaway*/'rʌnəweɪ/ but *to run away* /rʌn ə'weɪ/, etc.) further comparable pairs in English will be seen usually to incorporate strong/weak vowel alternations, as in *record*, where the noun (with first syllable stress) is /'rekɔːd/, but the verb (with second syllable stress) becomes /ri'kɔːd/, or object which is /'ɒbdʒɪkt/ as a noun, but /əb'dʒekt/ as a verb. The nearest Italian comes to this is the relationship between the mid vowels /ɛ, ɔ/ and /e, o/ – if a stressed syllable with /ɛ/ loses its stress, the vowel changes to the closer /e/ quality (likewise with the pair of back vowels). This behaviour is heard in the pronunciation

---

Ex 10.1   Add suitable sentence stress to the following MRP English utterances. (This exercise also offers practice in reading transcription.)

(1) /hi əbdʒektɪb wen ðə sʌbdʒɪkt wəz reɪzd ‖/
(2) /ju niːd ə rɪtəm pɜːmɪt | ɪn ɔːdə tə ritɜːn ‖/
(3) /ɪts ə drɒpɪn sentə fə drɒpaʊts ‖/
(4) /wi gɒʔ tɪkɪts fə ðə flaɪpɑːst ‖ ən sɔː ðə red ærəʊz flaɪ əʊvə ‖/
(5) /ðeɪ faʊn ðə rʌnəweɪ | haɪdɪŋ nɪə ðə rʌmweɪ ‖ bət i wʊdn̩ seɪ waɪ i wəz rʌnɪŋ əweɪ ‖/

---

[2] I have switched to phonetic transcription for this example because the parallel is less visible in the broader, phonemic form where *Kermit* is /'kɜːmɪt/.

of pairs like *meta* 'goal, aim' pronounced ['mɛta], but *metà* 'half' pronounced [me'ta], or *parlo* 'I speak' ['parlo], but *parlò* 'he spoke' [par'lɔ].

Dutch, German, Greek, Russian and Spanish are further examples of languages that sometimes use stress to change meaning. German does this typically with stress on certain prefixes (for example *'umschreiben* meaning 'to re-write', as opposed to *um'schreiben* 'to paraphrase').

10.2.2.4 Double stress words and stress shift

A sub-group of English words with multiple stresses are known as double stress words. These are words like *afternoon, Chinese, unknown, coronation,* etc. In Wells (2008), these are indicated by a special typographic convention like a left-pointing arrowhead: ˌɑːft ə 'nuːn ◄, ˌtʃaɪ 'niːz ◄, ˌʌn 'nəʊn ◄, etc. In these words, stress is grammatical rather than lexical. It changes word class rather than meaning.

In connected speech, it is normally the case that only one of these two stresses is actually realized. The context (in terms of the syntax) determines which one that is. To understand exactly what is happening here, it will help to be aware of three typically English tendencies found in connected speech. First of all, not every stress that is found in the make-up of individual words gets used in longer utterances. The rhythm of a longer stretch of speech, the intonational phrase, may suppress one or more individual word stresses. The second fact is that in connected speech, English spaces the stresses out, having where possible a small number of unstressed syllables in between each of the stressed ones. And the third point of interest here is that, other things being equal, English places the main stress of a phrase on the final stress position (usually carried in the final lexical item) in an intonational phrase, which can be regarded as the norm, the unmarked position.

So, in the dictionary entries illustrated above, the arrowhead is to remind us that under specific conditions, the primary stress moves back in the word structure and attaches instead to the position originally occupied by secondary stress in the citation form. (The final part of the word loses its stress altogether.) The conditions under which this happens are grammatically constrained and depend on whereabouts in the utterance structure the word occurs. When the item occurs in final position in the utterance (as a grammatical complement, for example), or the end of a particular grammatical phrase within a longer structure (for example, the head of a noun phrase), then the main stress will fall as near to the end of the word in question as possible, assuming the position allocated in the citation form – *the 'soldier was un'known.* However, when the item moves to an earlier position in the phrase structure, taking on the role of an adjective in a noun phrase, for example, the main stress shifts back as well – *the 'unknown 'soldier.* (Retaining the main stress on –*known* would violate the preference for ensuring suitably spaced stresses: *ˣun'known 'soldier.*) This behaviour routinely distinguishes nouns from adjectives in this particular lexical subgroup, as illustrated in Table 10.1, and also ensures that there is a suitable space between stressed syllables.

Table 10.1
Stress shift operating in English double-stress noun/adjective pairs

Examples:	Noun	Adjective
ˌafterˈnoon	ˈlate afterˈnoon	ˈafternoon ˈtea
ˌChiˈnese	ˈMandarin Chiˈnese	a ˈChinese ˈlantern
ˌAnglo-ˈSaxon	ˈearly Anglo-ˈSaxon	the ˈAnglo-Saxon ˈChronicle
ˌcoroˈnation	the ˈQueen's coroˈnation	ˈCoronation ˈChicken

10.2.2.5 Compound nouns in English

Earlier in the chapter, we talked briefly about possible rules for determining stress in English.[3] One further example of a stress rule is that compound nouns in English usually have initial stress, left stress – that is stress on the first item of the compound structure. So, if you put together *water* and *bottle* (both two syllable words with first syllable stress in their citation forms, 'water and 'bottle) the new word, the compound *water-bottle*, is stressed on the first element, 'water-bottle, and the second element loses its stress altogether. This is the general rule for stress in compound words in English (compare also '*frying-pan*, '*windowledge*, '*cornflour*, '*cuttlefish*, '*bluebell*, '*wholemeal*, '*bighead*, etc.).

Ex 10.2   Add suitable sentence stress to the following utterances.

(1) /ði ɑːftənuːn hændəʊvə weŋk kwaɪʔ smuːðli ‖/
(2) • /hi kɑːmp pleɪ | ɪf ɪz nɒʔ mætʃfɪt ‖
        ɒ /hiz əz mætʃfɪʔ naʊ | əz eniwʌn ɪz ‖/
(3) /aɪ ɡɒʔ tɒp kwɒləti kɑːpɪts | ɪn ðə priː siːzn̩ seɪl ‖ aɪ wʊd əʊnli kənsɪdə tɒp kwɒləti ‖/
(4) /təmɒrəʊ ɑːftənuːn | wɪl get ə tʃaɪniːz teɪkəweɪ ‖/
(5) /ɪts kɔːld ði əʊvəsiːz haɪweɪ | bikɒz ɪʔ ɡəʊz əʊvə ðə siː ‖/

Some of these compounds, however, consist of ambiguous strings of segments. Take /b l uː b e l/, for example. Without the stress, we cannot say whether the segments represent the name of a flower, a *bluebell*, or the noun phrase, a bell that is a blue colour, a *blue bell*. In such instances, it is the position of the main stress that distinguishes compound nouns, in this case a '*bluebell*, from noun phrases, in

---

[3]This very complex subject has been widely discussed in the literature for much of the past century. For example, Bloomfield (1933), Chomsky and Halle (1968), Fudge (1984), and Spencer (2003) have all proposed rule-based models to account for these patterns. But no rules cope 100% successfully with the variability found. Most recently, English compound stress became the focus of a large scale investigation (Plag, *et al.* (2007), (2008)) in which probabilistic and analogical models were demonstrated to be more successful than rule-based models in assigning stress correctly (although they did less well than rule-based approaches in the correct assignment of the rarer, 'exceptional', right stresses found in compounds such as *tin hat* or *harvest festival*).

this case (')*blue* '*bell*. Likewise /h əʊ l m iː l/ – is it '*wholemeal (bread)* or (*they ate the*) (')*whole* '*meal?*

English has many sequences of this kind in which the salient cue distinguishing compound nouns from noun phrases is the location of the main stress. A few more examples are illustrated in Table 10.2.

What is happening here begins to reveal the link between word stress and sentence stress. The primary stress in the compound nouns would also be the main stress of the intonational phrase if the item was spoken in isolation. Imagine the following dialogue:

●   Wholemeal or granary?
○   'Wholemeal.

If we compare this with an example using a noun phrase, remembering that English likes to postpone the main stress until as near to the end of the intonational phrase as is possible (or appropriate in the context), we find the focus changing:

●   Will they give us a snack?
○   A whole 'meal ||

The main stress in the intonational phrase coincides in both of these replies with the last or main (primary) word stress. In intonation, this stressed syllable is called the nucleus. (Underlining, also included in Table 10.2, is a common convention used to identify the nuclear syllable.)

Ex 10.3   **Add stress to the following emboldened items in such a way as to disambiguate them in speech in the contexts provided.**

(1) *sit in, sit-in*
    /aɪ wəz 'ɡəʊɪŋ tə **sɪt ɪn** ɒn ðə 'lektʃə ‖ bət ɪʔ wəz 'kænsl̩ b bɪ'kɒz əv ðə **sɪt ɪn** ‖/

(2) *frying steak, frying-steak, braising-steak*
    /hiz 'rɪəli 'ɡʊd əʔ **fraɪɪŋ steɪk** ‖ səʊ aɪ bɔːʔ **fraɪɪŋ steɪk** | 'rɑːðə ðm̩ **breɪzɪŋ steɪk** | fə 'sʌpə ‖/

(3) *cream jug, cream-jug*
    /aɪm 'ɡɪvɪŋ ðəm ə '**kriːm** kʌləd 'dɪʃ | ənd ə 'mætʃɪŋ **kriːm dʒʌɡ** ‖ ðə 'dɪʃ ɪz fə 'ʃʊɡə | bət ðə '**dʒʌɡ** kʊd bi ə 'mɪlk **dʒʌɡ** | ɔːr ə **kriːm dʒʌɡ** ‖/

(4) *light house, light-house*
    /fər ə 'məʊmənt | aɪ 'θɔːt juːb bɔːt ə **laɪt haʊs** ‖ ju miːn ɪts ə 'veri **laɪt haʊs** | wɪð lɒts əv 'wɪndəʊz ‖/

(5) *champagne (n), champagne (adj)*
    /aɪ 'dəʊnʔ nɔːməli 'drɪŋk **ʃæmpeɪn** ‖ bət ə **ʃæmpeɪn** kɒkteɪl əb bi 'naɪs ‖/

10.2.3 Metricality in languages

10.2.3.1 Stress-timing

Some languages – and English is one – use stresses to set up the timing of speech. Such languages are often called stress timed languages. Stress timing is the reason

Table 10.2
Stress distinguishing English compound nouns from noun phrases

Compound noun	Noun phrase
a 'bluebell	a 'blue 'bell
a 'bighead	a 'big 'head
some 'wholemeal	a 'whole 'meal
a 'greenhouse	a 'green 'house
a 'tallboy	a 'tall 'boy
a 'blackbird	a 'black 'bird
some 'highlights	some 'high 'lights

why weak or reduced forms of grammatical items exist (*the* realized as /ðə/ instead of the strong, stressable form /ðiː/, for example, or *a* pronounced /ə/ instead of /eɪ/). We need weak forms because there is only a finite amount of time in any given intonational phrase between one stress and the next and the more syllables you have to pack into that space, the quicker they will have to be said. We saw exactly this principle at work in Chapter 7 when we talked about rhythmic clipping (see Figure 7.3 on p. 106), and at the same time you will have started to become more aware of weak forms in English when carrying out the ear-training exercises in the podcasts. Many other languages, however, do not use weak forms and do not operate processes such as rhythmic clipping. Instead, each syllable is perceived as having equal duration in time. Such languages are usually regarded as **syllable-timed languages**. Examples of syllable-timed languages include Italian and Spanish.

The concertina-like or *accelerando-rallentando* effect of stress-timing – that perception that there is an equal amount of time between stresses – can be seen clearly in a schematic representation like that in Figure 10.2 which compares a 'stress-timed' and a 'syllable-timed' realization of the utterance *I want you to time the stresses in this sentence*. In the stress-timed delivery of the utterance, each stress unit or rhythm unit (often called a rhythmic foot) takes up the same amount of space, xms. Strategies adopted to facilitate this include the routine use of weak forms of grammatical items as well as quite extreme reduction in the third foot of *in this*, eliding the dental fricative completely. However, if I say that xms is the equivalent of three syllables and then produce the sentence again, ensuring that each **syllable** now takes up the same amount of time (notice that there are no weak forms or schwas any more in the second version – each syllable has a strong vowel which, at least notionally, takes up the same amount of time), because the number of syllables between stresses is different, the amount of time between stresses becomes different as well. The second rhythm unit takes less time than the first because it has two syllables only, rather than three. Likewise the third takes longer because it has an additional fourth syllable. Only the second and last match, with two syllables each.

Stress-timing, however, is only a perception. Taking Milton's line[4] *Méadows trím with dáisies píed*, J. D. O'Connor demonstrated that in fact, the actual timespan

[4]From Milton's *L'Allegro*, 'Meadows trim with daisies pied, Shallow brooks, and rivers wide.'

A stress-timed realization

[aɪ	'wɒntʃu tə	'taɪm ðə	'stresɪzɪnɪs	'sentn̩s]
	x *ms*	x *ms*	x *ms*	x *ms*
Foot	1	2	3	4

A syllable-timed realization

*[aɪ	'wɒnt juː tuː	'taɪm ðiː	'stresɪz ɪn ðɪs	'sentens]
	x *ms*	x − y *ms*	x + y *ms*	x − y *ms*
Foot	1	2	3	4

Figure 10.2

Schematic representation of stress-timed and a possible syllable timed delivery of the sentence *I want you to time the stresses in this sentence.*

between one stress and the next was very different, even though we perceive it as being regular and equal (O'Connor (1965)). The same mis-match was demonstrated in the duration of French syllables in *Excusez-moi, mon cher monsieur*. However, using what they termed a 'closed mouth technique', two Russian speech scientists Kozhevnikov and Chistovich (Kozhevnikov and Chistovich (1966)) conducted an experiment which suggested that although we may be programmed to deliver speech in compliance with these stress or syllable timing algorithms, articulation interferes with this. They recorded people saying specific sentences, with their mouths shut, and when they measured the timings of the stress pulses, they found much closer parity of duration between stress intervals in Russian and in English than when the subject spoke normally. This led to the idea that the need to articulate often very complex sequences of sounds interferes with the timing of the delivery – by denying people the possibility of going through the full articulatory motions, they had a signal which accorded more closely with our perceptions. We seem to hear what we believe to be the case, even when this is demonstrably untrue.

Given the discrepancy, it may therefore be preferable to refer not to stress-timed and syllable-timed rhythms or languages, but instead to ones that are **stress-based** and **syllable-based** (Laver (1994)) or at least to stress-based timing and syllable-based timing.

10.2.3.2 Syllable weight

Before leaving this topic, it is also important to mention that there is a further very small group of languages, often overlooked, that rely neither on the timing of stresses nor on the duration of syllables for their metricality, but on relative **syllable weight**.

We have talked only about open and closed syllables so far in this book, but the segment structure of a syllable is also responsible for syllables having different metrical or rhythmic weights, **light** and **heavy**. These are phonological terms, but a light syllable is one that has a short vowel followed by no more than one short consonant. By this definition, English words such as *it, cat, club* or *spring* are light syllables. A heavy syllable, on the other hand, will have either a short vowel followed by two or more consonants (English *its, cats, clubs* or *springs*, also *twelfth, acts, glimpst*, etc.), or a long vowel only (MRP English *Ah!, straw, sky*, etc.), or a short vowel followed by a long consonant (see Finnish examples in Table 8.3 on p. 141).

Syllable weight is intrinsically linked to a further concept, the **mora**. The most well-known moraic language is Japanese where a short vowel is one mora, a long vowel is two moras, the syllable final nasal is a mora, and the first consonant in geminates or consonant sequences is also a mora. In the two-syllable utterance *Nippon* ('Japan'), therefore, there are four moras, *ni-p-po-n*. This takes us back to Chapter 1 in which we discussed syllable perception and explained why a Japanese listener will tell us that *Skegness* has five syllables – it is not syllables that they are actually counting, but the moras by which their own language is organized and by which their perception of speech is governed. Skegness breaks down into *s-ke-g-ne-s* (the final <ss> spelling, of course, is pronounced as a single [s] consonant sound, so one mora). This gives us a third type of metricality, mora-based timing. Other languages with which the concept of the mora is associated are Luganda and Hawaiian.

10.3 ACCENT

10.3.1 Word stress and sentence stress

Sentence stress was mentioned above in connection with primary and secondary stress and also in connection with the stress of English compound nouns and segmentally similar noun phrases. Sentence stress is the name given to the pattern of rhythmic beats contained within an intonational phrase. Sentence stress is what we were focusing on when we added stresses to limericks in Chapter 1. We have also included sentence stress in every piece of transcription (from dictation or from a written stimulus). Basically, in a stress language like English, sentence stress enhances a selection of the word stresses available in a syntactic string to bring about a discernible succession of rhythmic beats in speech.

10.3.2 Stress and accent

It can be intuited from the noun phrase examples in Table 10.2, that in the phrase – just as in an isolated polysyllabic word – not all stresses are equal. In the noun phrase examples in Table 10.2, there were both stressed and unstressed syllables, but of the two stressed syllables, only one received underlining, so only one was identified as the nucleus. This suggests that in sentence stress, as in word stress, three levels of stress could be sufficient: at the highest level of importance is the nucleus, at the lowest the unstressed syllables, and between the two the remaining rhythmic beats. This is true to an extent, but it needs a little refining.

To carry out this refinement, we need to remember the three physical correlates of stress: loudness, length and pitch. Research has shown that the least relevant of these is loudness. English listeners are, however, sensitive to length, and they are particularly sensitive to pitch. There are two kinds of pitch: level or static pitch, and moving, changing or dynamic pitch. In speech, some of the rhythmic beats carry such pitch information – the stressed syllables are either higher or lower in level than the pitch of an immediately preceding syllable, or they actually incorporate a change (or at least the start of a change) in pitch. Stresses with pitch characteristics of this kind are described as having **pitch prominence** (some older texts refer to **pitch obtrusion**) and they constitute an important subgroup of stresses known as **accents**. Of these two kinds of pitch, static and dynamic, English ears respond particularly to the dynamic variety, noting moving or changing pitch, and it is moving pitch that is the type typically associated with the nucleus. What we are responding to when we distinguish hearing _wholemeal_ from _whole meal_ is the moving pitch contour visible in Figure 10.3. This represents a sudden, dynamic departure change.

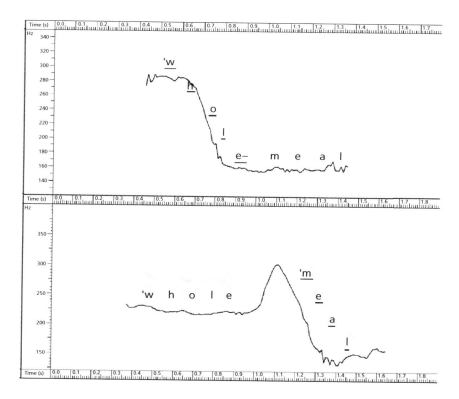

Figure 10.3

Annotated Fx (fundamental frequency) contours showing the position of the nucleus in '_wholemeal_ vs '_whole_ '_meal_ (Speaker PA).

It is exactly the same acoustic cue that is principally responsible for enabling us to distinguish noun verb pairs like *permit* (n)/*permit* (vb), pairs like *billow/below*, and so on.

It is the same pitch prominence that enables us to detect the first stress in each of the noun phrases in Table 10.2. In these examples, the first lexical item is typically said at a noticeably higher level of pitch than that used when articulating the initial determiner. This stress, too, can be classified as an accent, a stress with pitch prominence. You can see these pitch relationships in the intonation contours in Figure 10.3.

As far as English rhythm and intonation are concerned, the division of stressed syllables into routine stresses, on the one hand, and accents, on the other, leaves us with a hierarchy of phonetic syllable types, starting with the vowel type (weak or full) at the lowest level and culminating with accented syllables at the top, those which represent the intonational nucleus and those which, if they occur at all, precede the nucleus in the intonational phrase. This hierarchy can be seen in Figure 10.4.

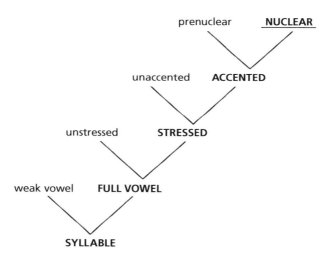

Figure 10.4
Hierarchy of English syllable types.

10.3.3 Pitch accent

Another technical term, sometimes used synonymously with accent as we have just defined it (for example, Laver (1994)), is **pitch accent**. The difference between pitch accent as a technical concept and accent as a stress-type in an intonation language like English remains less than clear, even today. The key distinction would seem to be that in intonation languages like English, pitch and pitch prominences are determined by the intonation (which I am taking to include sentence stress) and the incidence of a (pitch-based) accent on any given word is contextual and not a property of the word itself. Pitch accent languages, however, are closer to true tone languages in that the pitch prominences are an inherent property of the word. That said, the realization of pitch accent in such languages is in no way absolute and, like tones in tone languages, can vary as a function of the context in which a word is used, or as a function of the dialect and regional accent of the speaker (see, for example, Bruce and Thelander (2001)).

There is much debate as to which languages can truly be called accentual languages. Those most usually cited are Norwegian, Swedish, and Japanese. Others include Latvian, Lithuanian, Serbo-Croat,[5] certain Limburgse varieties of Dutch, and Punjabi. More recently, a case has been made for 'Galician Spanish' (a name used to refer to a variety of Spanish spoken by bilingual speakers of Galician and Castillian Spanish, Castro (2003)). While none of these are fully-fledged tone languages in the sense that we will see described below, all use a small number of tones or pitch changes to affect meaning.

The Scandinavian systems are highly constrained, contrasts applying only in words of more than one syllable. In Swedish, Accent 1 (also called **acute** and traditionally marked in Swedish transcription using an acute accent above the stressed vowel: [´][6]) has a single peak in the Fx contour (used, for example, in the word *ánden* 'duck') and Accent 2 (also called **grave** and traditionally transcribed using a grave accent above the stressed vowel: [`]) has a double peak (used, by way of contrast, in the word *ànden* 'the spirit').[7] Accent 2 is always word initial, while Accent 1 is unconstrained and can be placed on any syllable in the word. The Fx associated with citation form realizations of these accents can be seen in Figure 10.5. For English speakers, the presence of the pitch accent gives the impression that the syllable is stressed. What this means in practice is that words falling in the Accent 1 group seem to be stressed and having a fall in pitch on the accented syllable (which can be any syllable in the word), while those in the Accent 2 group are all accent-initial and give the impression

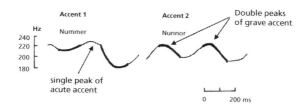

Figure 10.5

Swedish pitch accents (after Bruce 1977) showing citation form pronunciation of the words *nummer* 'number' (with Accent 1) and *nunnor* 'nuns' (with Accent 2).
Source: Bruce (1977).

[5]This name covers Bosnian, Croatian, Montenegrin and Serbian.
[6]These are not a good choice of diacritic in IPA terms, the super-posed acute overlapping one of the IPA possibilities for indicating a high tone, and the super-posed grave overlapping one of the possibilities for indicating low tone. In their application in Swedish, we have to remember that they are used to indicate dynamic pitch, a single fall in the case of the acute accent and a succession of two falls in the case of the grave.
[7]Swedish does not indicate accent in the orthography. The accents are included here simply to demonstrate the type and syllable location.

Table 10.3
Minimal pairs based on pitch accent from Standard Swedish

Accent 1 (acute)		Accent 2 (grave)	
/áksel/	'shoulder'	/àksel/	'axle, axis'
/fá:ret/	'the lane'	/fà:ret/	'gone'
/hé:den/	'the moor'	/hè:den/	'heathen'
/lý:dia/	'Lydia'	/lỳ:dia/	'obedient (pl.)'
/stúken/	'the stucco'	/stùken/	'stung, prodded'
/vré:den/	'the door knobs'	/vrè:den/	'the wrath'

Source: Derived from Elert (1972).

of being stressed and having falling pitch on both the first and second syllables (one syllable corresponding with each of the peaks).

In practice, the use of pitch accent is contrastive in only a small number of words, around 350 minimal pairs in total. Elert (1972) lists about 320 of these pairs, based on pitch accent differences for Standard Swedish. A small number of these are quoted in Table 10.3.

In Japanese, pitch accents map not just onto syllables, but onto moras, meaning that even monosyllabic words can have a pitch accent. In Standard (Tokyo) Japanese, for example, monosyllabic [kā \ɴ] *kan* 'tin or can, sense' is such a word (with \ in the transcription showing the point at which the drop in pitch occurs – in this case on the second mora, the syllable final nasal traditionally represented by upper-case N) with the pitch pattern [˥ ˩]. Moras can be pronounced with either high (H) or low (L) pitch. Effectively, words affected by pitch accent will have a noticeable drop in pitch somewhere in the word (from H on the accented mora itself to L on the following one, then remaining low), for example [ō\ɴ ga ku] 'music' (pitch pattern: [˥ ˩ ˩ ˩]). A word with one unaccented mora before the accented one starts low as in [ha çī] 'bridge' (pitch pattern: [˩ ˥]), but if there are more unaccented moras, the pitch goes to high on the second mora and remains there until the accent occurs, as in [ta ma nē \gi] 'onion' (pitch pattern: [˩ ˥ ˥ ˩]). In unaccented words, the pitch is low on the first mora and high on all successive moras, as in the unaccented [mu zu ka çi i] 'difficult', (pitch pattern: [˩ ˦ ˦ ˦ ˦]). Word final accent can be seen in both [ka kī] 'fence' and [ha çī] 'bridge' in Table 10.4, both with the pitch pattern [˩ ˦] in which no drop is possible because there are no further moras. Unaccented words and words with final pitch accent are therefore ambiguous when spoken in isolation. [ka kī] 'fence' and [ka ki] 'persimmon' both have the pattern L-H. This ambiguity is typically resolved by adding a particle such as the subject marker [ga], [ka kī \ga] and [ka ki ga] for example. This yields phonetically distinct sequences with a pitch drop in the accented word ([˩ ˥ ˩]) and no pitch drop in the unaccented one ([˩ ˦ ˦]).

However, pitch accent in Japanese affects only about 20 per cent of the total vocabulary. The remaining 80 per cent are unaccented words. Within the affected

Table 10.4

Minimal contrasts based on location of pitch accent in Japanese

1st mora accent	2nd mora accent	Unaccented
[hā \çi] 'chopsticks'	[ha çī] 'bridge'	[ha çi] 'edge'
[kā \ki] 'oyster'	[ka kī] 'fence'	[ka ki] 'persimmon'
[sā \ke] 'salmon'		[sa ke] 'sake'

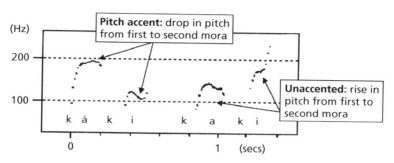

Figure 10.6

Fx lines for [kā \ki] 'oyster' and [ka ki] 'persimmon' (after Abe (1998)).

20 per cent of the vocabulary, minimal pairs and triplets created by accented/ unaccented syllable combinations are not uncommon and selected examples are illustrated in Table 10.4. Akamatsu (1997: 226) points out that those words which have minimal pairs/triplets represent a 'tiny portion of the whole of Japanese vocabulary' but 'receive disproportionately great emphasis by most scholars'. However, although they only represent a tiny portion of the vocabulary, many of the words in common use have such minimal pairs/triplets and so pitch accent plays an important role in lexical access in Japanese (Kayoko Yanagisawa, private communication).

The phonetic reality of Japanese pitch accent can be seen very clearly in the minimal pair illustrated by Fx contours in Figure 10.6.

10.4 TONE

10.4.1 The function and nature of tone

Tone generally refers to the lexical use of pitch to distinguish different meanings. Languages that use tone lexically are called tone languages. The classic example of a tone language is, of course, Chinese. Different varieties of Chinese have different numbers of tones, but without exception, all use tone to differentiate word meaning. Cantonese, for example, can be analysed as having six tones[8] (illustrated

---

[8]Zee (1999) (followed here) describes Cantonese as having six tones only, omitting a seventh, a high-to-mid falling tone, which is included in Man (1985) giving [sî] 'thought', but which has merged for most speakers with high level and is now commonly discounted.

Table 10.5
Cantonese tones

Tone	Description	Interlinear representation	Example*
1	high level		[sí], [si˥] 'silk'
2	mid level		[sī], [si˧] 'to try'
3	low-mid level		[sì], [si˨] 'matter'
4	low-mid to low fall		[sỉ], [si˩] (Zee 1999) or [si̯˨] 'time'
5	low-mid to high rise		[sǐ], [si˩˥] 'history'
6	low-mid to mid rise		[sǐ], [si˨˧] 'city'

Source: Data from Zee (1999).

Note: * Note that the transcriptions using tonal diacritics from the IPA chart are identical with the information conveyed in the stick representations which follow each time. However, in the case of Tone 4, which he described as low and falling, Zee selected ⌄ to transcribe this, and accordingly, I have used the extra low diacritic above the vowel [ˇ].

in Table 10.5), while Modern Standard Chinese (usually called *putonghua* in the PRC, and still sometimes in the West by its old name, Mandarin) has only four (as in Table 10.6). Other (south-east) Asian tone languages include Burmese, Thai and Vietnamese, but many tone languages are also found in Africa (Igbo, Yoruba and Zulu, for example) and in the Americas (languages such as Oneida and Navajo). One part of the world with no reported tone languages at all is Australia.

At the most basic level, tone languages fall into two principal groups, determined by the nature of tone that is used. One group uses level tones produced at different pitches. Such languages are known as **register tone** languages. The other group uses tones with a dynamic or changing pitch profile. These are known as **contour tone** languages. This division is reflected in the IPA chart entry for tone and word accents, where representations are divided into two groups showing two ways of representing level tones on the left and two ways of representing contour tones on the right. However, there are also many languages that use both, as for example, Modern Standard Chinese and Cantonese.

These tables take the opportunity to introduce **interlinear notation**. These diagrams are very simple, schematized representations of pitch movements. The bottom line represents the speaker's lowest pitch and the top line their highest. The dot represents a syllable and any tail represents the direction and approximate extent of any pitch glide produced by the speaker's voice.

Table 10.6
Modern Standard Chinese tones

Tone	Description	Interlinear representation	Example
1	high level		[ʃú], [ʃu˥] 'book'
2	mid to high rise		[ʃʊ̌], [ʃu˧˥] 'ripe'
3	mid to low-mid dip		[ʃʊ̂]*, [ʃu˨˩˦] 'rat'
4	high to low fall		[ʃû] [ʃu˥˩] 'tree'

Source: Data from Lee and Zee (2003), Scurfield (1991).

Note: *There is no officially recommended IPA tone diacritic to represent this movement; since the tone is essentially a fall-rise in nature, I have used a diacritic which reflects the opposite movement from the recommended rise-fall.

As well as distinguishing words, tone can also be used for grammatical purposes, as in Bini (an Edo language spoken in Eastern Nigeria), where tone combinations on the pronoun and verb are used to distinguish tense. Illustrating part of the Bini tense-aspect system, Ladefoged (2001: 236) shows how a low tone pronoun followed by a low tone on the verb produces the timeless form ([ì mà] 'I show') but when followed by a high tone on the verb it becomes the past form ([ì má] 'I showed'); however, if the pronoun is given a high tone and the verb low, the continuous form results ([í mà] 'I am showing').

10.4.2 Register tones

A pure register tone language will usually have no more than four contrastive levels of pitch, and at their simplest, they have just two, usually called high and low. Languages with two register tones are regarded as simple tone languages (Maddieson (2008b). Anything in excess of two levels starts to qualify as complex. There may even be other levels in excess of four perceptible in such a language, but these further levels do not normally result in a change of meaning (Pike 1948: 5-6). Register languages include Bini and Yoruba both with a two-level system. Register languages also occur among the Otomanguean languages spoken in Mexico, including Mixtec with three levels (high, mid and low), and Mazatec with four (high, high-mid, low-mid and low). (These last four were called high, mid, norm and low by Pike (1948: 6).)

In running speech, a characteristic of register tone languages is the perception of contours, gliding tones, which result directly from the juxtaposition of registers, high + low, for example, with the speaker gliding audibly from one level to the next. Such glides would be heard between the mid and low registers in Mixtec [ʒūù] 'stone' or the low to high registers of [nàá] 'mother', sounding a fairly narrow falling tone and a much wider rising tone respectively. The glides, however, have no phonemic significance at all – they are simply the phonetic product of liaison.

10.4.3 Contour tones

Contour tones have already been seen in the earlier Chinese examples where, in both cases, a mix of register and contour tones was found, Cantonese having three registers and three contours, and MSC one register and three contours. Both systems are complex systems.

Pike (1948) made a number of points about the nature of contour tones, one of which was that a contour tone would normally be completed within the syllable, the pitch movement starting on the vowel and completing there or during a following sonorant consonantal segment. He also acknowledged that there may be systems where the tone may stretch across more than one syllable, in the case of a polysyllabic morpheme root, for example. However, the tone:meaning correlation meant that the tone should not cross a morpheme boundary.

A final point of interest that can be made here concerns the actual realizations of contour tones which differ not only in their respective starting points, their targets, the extent of the pitch movement, and whether or not they are terminated by a glottal stop, but also in timing. Such pitch glides may also be produced very quickly or very slowly. Additionally, relative timing of the onset and offset may also differ (a slow start + a rapid conclusion, for example, or the other way round). All of these are open to phonetic investigation and measurement.

10.4.4 Tone sandhi

Tones, just like vowel and consonant segments, are influenced by their environment and just as segments have been seen to assimilate and adapt to adjacent sound qualities, tones do the same. To the outsider, this can often seem bewildering, but to speakers of the language it is no more bewildering than when speakers of English replace /n/ with a bilabial [m] articulation in a phrase such as *one way* /'wʌm 'weɪ/.

For our present purposes, it is enough simply to be aware that this happens and one example will suffice to illustrate this effect. Pike (1948: 85) gave a detailed account of tone sandhi in Fuzhou Chinese, which has nine contrastive tones (four register and five contour). The tones are as follows:

Tone 1 ˧   *High-mid level*

Tone 2 ˧   *Low-mid level*

Tone 3 ˧   *Slow low to low-mid rise*

Tone 4 ˧   *Fast low to mid rise*

Tone 5 ˧   *High to low-mid fall*

Tone 6 ˧   *Low-mid/mid rise-fall*

Tone 7 ˧   *Extra short high-mid level*

Tone 8 ˦   *Mid to high rise*

Tone 9 ˧   *Mid level*

Pike then went on to demonstrate that seven of these nine tones are subject to sandhi:

Tone 1 → Tone 5 / _____ {Tones 2, 3, 4 or 6}[9]

Tone 2 → Tone 8 / _____ {Tones 2, 3, 4 or 6}

Tone 3 → Tone 1 / _____ {Tones 1, 5 or 7}

               Tone 5 / _____ {Tones 2, 3, 4 or 6}

Tone 4 → Tone 1 or Tone 2 / _____ {Tones 1, 5 or 7}

               Tone 5 or Tone 8 / _____ {Tone 2}

               Tone 5 or Tone 7 /_____ {Tones 3, 4 or 6}

Tone 5 → Tone 2 / _____ {Tones 2, 3, 4, 5 or 6}

               Tone 9 / _____ {Tones 1 or 7}

Tone 6 → Tone 1 / _____ {Tones 1, 5 or 7}

               Tone 5 / _____ {Tones 2, 3, 4 or 6}

Tone 7 → Tone 1 / _____ {Tone 1 or 7}

               Tone 2 / _____ {Tones 2, 3, 4, 5 or 6}

The only constants here are Tones 8 and 9 which do not participate in this process at all, and Tones 1 and 2 which remain unchanged before any of Tones 1, 5 or 7. Not all tone sandhi systems are as complex or extensive as this one, but Fuzhou is nonetheless an ideal example of the many kinds of changes that can occur, depending on the phonetic environment. Writers make reference to the **toneme** for the original basic form of the tone (paralleling the use of phoneme for a basic segmental unit), and **allotone** for the variants that occur in different contexts (paralleling the segmental allophone).

10.4.5   Intonation in tone languages

The intonation of tone languages is still an under-researched and thinly documented area compared with other areas of the subject. However, as well as being affected by sandhi, tones are also known to be affected by intonation, which operates over and above the lexical tone system. There is a probably universal tendency to lower pitch

---

[9]Based on transformation rules, each of the following formulae reads 'Tone A becomes Tone B when it is immediately followed by any of Tones C, D, E', etc.

across an utterance. This is called **declination**. However, in tone languages, there is often a more specific characteristic operating that is triggered by the incidence of low tones. This is called **downstepping**.

Downstepping is especially a characteristic of register tone languages in which each successive low tone in an intonational phrase (or a sentence – researchers are not in complete agreement about the extent of the domain involved here) lowers the height of any following high tone, resulting in a gradual declination of the speaker's highest pitch. What is less clear is whether this so-called topline declination is matched by some kind of baseline declination. Yip (2002), quoting from Pulleyblank's (1986) study of Igbo, shows declination of both levels. We can represent this utterance *ó nwè-rè à-kọ́ nà ú-chè* meaning 'she was clever and sensible' in interlinear form to show clearly how such declination works. Having entered the syllables at suitable relative heights in the speaker's pitch range, joining the series of high tone syllables and the series of low tone syllables demonstrates this gradual drifting down of overall pitch within the speaker's actual high to low range:

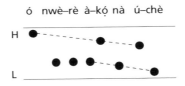

Here, both low and high are different in height at the beginning of the utterance from the height they display at the end. However, a speaker's fully low pitch remains an absolute – there is a pitch below which it is impossible for any given speaker to phonate. (This representation also serves to reinforce the point that our perception of pitch, like our perception of stress, is relative – the impression of height is judged in relation to the height of neighbouring syllables.)

With regard to baseline variation, Cruttenden (1997:121) summarizes the phonetics of the situation, saying that just as there is evidence that the baseline is re-set at the beginning of each new intonational phrase, there is also evidence that unaccented fully low syllables in sentence-final intonational phrases can be shown to be measurably lower than those in non-final intonational phrases.

10.5   INTONATION

10.5.1   The role of intonation

Intonation serves a mainly linguistic or phonological purpose and, as such, is largely beyond the scope of this volume. However, it is the combination of a number of different phonetic features and, as such, it provides a conclusion to our phonetic exploration of suprasegmentals.

Just as the segmental features we have studied have been shown to operate linguistically in languages, so does the combined effect of stress and tone. Before leaving the subject, it is worth seeing just how speakers do this. In the previous section, we looked briefly at some of the phonetic effects of intonation in tone languages, but we did not touch on its purpose. Intonation starts to contribute all sorts of nuances not carried by segments themselves. These include information about focus, grammar, and – most importantly, perhaps – about the speaker's attitude. It is fair to say that in a tone language, intonation will probably do rather less grammatical or semantic work than might be the case in non-tone languages (meaning, and sometimes grammatical information as well, being contributed by the tones themselves), but what is probably universal is the role of intonation in conveying emotional content, attitude. People the world over convey something of what they are feeling through what the layperson often calls their 'tone of voice', through their intonation.

We are all human and it is very difficult to speak in such a way as to convey no inkling of our feelings – happiness or sadness, general well-being or depression, liking or loathing. Social etiquette, of course, often demands that we conceal what we really feel about a person or situation, but I am sure we all know how difficult it is to sound pleased and delighted if that is not what we are feeling at the time. Sometimes, unfortunately, it becomes a question of choice between being untruthful or being ungracious, and when we need to be untruthful, it is often intonation that helps us to tell the lie. So, a common denominator across all languages is that intonation can communicate attitude, feelings.

Variously, it is also used by languages to carry grammatical information (distinguishing statements from questions, for example, or complete from incomplete utterances), and/or to perform a focusing function in terms of drawing attention to the topic (the sort of thing that might be done through use of grammatical particles in a language like Japanese,[10] for example, or varying word order in a language like Italian).

10.5.2   The tools of intonation

We have now met many of the components of intonation, the tools of intonation if you like – stress, accent, pitch levels, pitch movements, the concept of declination, and the **domain of analysis**, the intonational phrase. Mention has also been made of the concept of the nucleus and we've discovered a couple of ways of representing intonation (either transcribing it using the suprasegmental tone and word accent symbols from the IPA chart (sometimes called **phonetic stress marks**), or making it visible by means of interlinear representations – the schematic representations of actual, measurable Fx contours (pitch tracks) we can see using WASP or Praat).

---

[10]For example, in English we would distinguish the 'unmarked/non-emphatic' statement *This is my **book*** from the 'marked/emphatic' one ***This*** *is my book* (meaning this, and not any other...). Japanese does this not by means of intonation, but by choice of particle, selecting the general focus particle *wa* for the unmarked version, *kore wa watashi no hon desu* (literally 'as regards this, it's my book'), but the subject marker particle *ga* for the marked one *kore ga watashi no hon desu* (literally, 'this – and only this – is my book'.)

We've used these tools to make rather general auditorily-based descriptive statements about intonation in impressionistic terms that, in many ways, date back to the nineteenth century and the work of A.M. Bell. We will conclude by considering briefly the domain of intonation description.

10.5.3 Describing intonation

There are many, many names in the literature for the stretch of speech which constitutes the domain of analysis for basic intonation description. My own habit is to use the expression intonational phrase (IP), as in Wells (2006), for example. Cruttenden (1970) talks about **intonation groups,** O'Connor and Arnold (1973) the **word group,** and Halliday (1970) and Kingdon (1958) the **tone group.** Other names include **rhythm group, breath group** and **sense group.** All of these are illuminating when deciding how long a stretch of speech is relevant to the description of intonation tunes and each begins to hint at how intonation bridges from pure phonetics into other areas of linguistic description. IP and tone group are motivated by identifiable recurrent melodic patterns which have nuclear tones at their centre, rhythm group acknowledges that each of these stretches has its own inherent rhythm, breath group tells us that there is a connection with taking breath (an act often performed at a pause between groups), and sense group implies a grammatical and/or semantic integrity.

Chunking, determining and inserting the IP boundaries, is the job of **tonality.** Boundaries, probably universally, seem to co-occur with the end of an identifiable recurrent melodic pattern, almost always at the end of a grammatical unit of some sort, and frequently at a point where it would be possible – although this by no means always happens – to pause for a longer or shorter time. Pauses, when they do happen, may be genuine and silent, but they may also be filled by some kind of hesitation strategy. This last, such as drawing out a sound to an unnatural length *I'll have one more... | biscuit ||* (with an extra long [ɔː]) or *It's an... | iguana ||* (with extra long [n]), may be to allow utterance planning time or it may simply be to ensure you hold your turn and nobody else butts in, but in either case, the pause will be filled and the way this is done can be described in phonetic terms. In spontaneous colloquial speech, boundary evidence is rarely completely clear-cut, but there is usually sufficient phonetic information to enable us to come to a conclusion when engaging in auditory analysis.

In a discourse situation, regardless of the number of speakers, any turn can contain any number of IPs. There is even evidence to suggest that there may be a much larger discourse- or text-based set of rules that make a whole turn, or even a whole dialogue, hang together. A contributing factor is undoubtedly the role of **tonicity,** the technical name for location of the nucleus. For now, however, it is the pure phonetics of the IP that is of concern. IPs in English may be very small – a monosyllabic noun subject, for example *Cats | have whiskers ||* where the subject *cats* has its own IP, or even just an exclamation such as *Ah!* in the old advert *Ah! || Bisto! ||.* Likewise, a phonetic word such as the possessive *Jonathan's* in *Jonathan's | is a blue one ||.* At their shortest, IPs in English can be just one segment: *Mm... ||* or *er... ||.* Alternatively, they can be incredibly long, such as a typical idiomatic introduction to a joke in English: *Haven't you heard the one about the elephant in the telephone box?* || where the whole inversion question – all twelve words – is just one long IP. On average, though, English IPs tend to be about five words in length. Languages will vary, but given that one of the purposes of chunking is to enable the speaker to communicate exactly the message he wants the listener to understand, they are never going to be routinely very long.

Ex 10.4   **Divide the following text into IPs. Try to distinguish between major boundaries – places where you could stop but still make sense, and minor boundaries – where the speaker really needs to continue to complete the message. Add sentence stress. The punctuation has been stripped here to reinforce the idea of the text representing speech. You will need to think about the message you want to put across.**

A	heard any good jokes recently
B	not really no
A	didn't you hear the one about the man who went to the airport
B	no how did it go
A	well the airport didn't go anywhere but the man went by plane
B	oh very funny I suppose you call that some kind of humorous take-off

---

Ex 10.5   **Field Notebook: Phonetics in One Word**

Entry 10 Use the theory you have just learned in order to finish writing your Field Notebook, applying your knowledge to the detailed phonetic description of the word *completes*.

Go to www.routledge.com/cw/ashby for instructions and feedback.

10.6 SUMMARY

- Looking beyond segmental phonetic description, this chapter has discussed the concept of stress, compared word stress with sentence stress, and explored aspects of metricality in languages.

- The relation between stress and accent, and the discussion of tone, together paved the way for an introduction to intonation.

- The chapter concluded this introduction to phonetics by looking briefly at the contribution made by intonation to speech.

 Ear-training

Once you have studied this chapter carefully, continue the development of your practical skills by attempting the ear-training exercises for this chapter, available as recordings at www.routledge.com/cw/ashby.

FURTHER READING

Suprasegmentals are the subject matter of Chapter 10 of Ashby & Maidment (2005), Chapter 6 of Lodge (2009) and (specifically for English) Chapter 11 of Cruttenden (2008).

For information specifically on English, see Chapter 5 of Ladefoged (2001). For information of a more general nature, see Chapter 10 of Ladefoged (2001). Extended and more advanced studies of tone can be found in Yip (2002), on intonation in Cruttenden (1997), and of English intonation in particular see Wells (2006).

Answers to exercises

Chapter 1

Ex 1.2.

The sentence says: 'If I switch at this point to phonetic transcription, you might be surprised to find you can still read a lot of what I write.'

Ex 1.3.

The manufacturers can spell 'fish' as *phish* because elsewhere in English <ph> is used to spell the sound [f] as in *physics, elephant*, etc.

Ex 1.4.

Monophthongs are found in 1, 4, 7, 8, 9.
Diphthongs are found in 2, 3, 5.

The sort of vowel you use in the words 6 *day* and 10 *no* will depend on your accent. Speakers of English from Scotland or from Yorkshire, for example, may pronounce these words with monophthongs while speakers from the south of England or from most parts of America will use a diphthong.

Ex 1.5.

1 CCVC	2 CCVC	3 CVCVCV	4 CCVC	5 CVC
6 VCVC	7 CVCVC	8 CCVCVC	9 VCCCV-CVCC(V)C	10 VCVC(C)C

Ex 1.6.

In the majority of English accents, the words in 1, 3, 4, 7 and 10 will be homophonous while those in 2, 5, 6 and 9 almost certainly will not. The pair in 8 could be either – some speakers pronounce them both with a [k]-sound at the end ([lɒk]) while others make the second one sound more like the Gaelic [lɒx].

Ex 1.7.

Depending upon on your own accent, possible homophones here include:

1 eye: aye, I. 2 tacks: tax. 3 stair: stare. 4 which: witch. 5 taught: tort, torte, taut. 6 site: cite, sight. 7 bail: bale. 8 hi: hie, high. 9 awe: or, ore, oar. 10 Y: why, Wye.

Ex 1.8.

Who from lárynx to líps knew no bóunds.
Her whóle oral cávity
Caused enórmous hilárity;
The cláss laughed so múch they lost póunds.

Ex 1.9.

When dóing transcríption in phónes
I ténd to get lóst on the tónes.
The stréss is quite cléar –
Well, it ís to my éar.
Thank góodness for Dániel Jónes.

Ex 1.10.
Lines 1, 2 and 5 have three evenly spaced stresses, while lines 4 and 5 have two.

Ex 1.11.

1   When I look in the mirror to make the *pa, ba, ma* sequences, I see the two lips closing for the consonant sound and opening again for the vowel; effectively, my mouth is closing (for the consonant) and opening (for the vowel).

2   When I repeat *la* several times I can feel the tip of my tongue touching the roof of my mouth, somewhere just behind my upper front teeth, for each l-sound and moving down away from the roof of my mouth for the vowel. My mouth is open all the time.

3   When I pinch my nostrils, I can no longer make a clear difference between the m-sound and the p- and b-sounds. The m-sound is more like the b-sound.

Ex 1.13.
It quickly becomes clear that you need to be able to interpret the entries when you look things up – you have to learn how to 'read' the LPD and dictionaries like it where typographic conventions are used to compress large amounts of information into small spaces.

1   ə 'nem ə ni tells us there are four syllables, stress on the second and it also tells us (by means of an exclamation mark in a little triangle) that a lot of people mis-pronounce it, switching round the [m] and the second [n]. Finally, it tells us that in the plural, *anemones*, the final <s> is pronounced [z].

2   Apart from telling us how the Poles themselves pronounce this place name, this entry tells us that it is said two ways in British English. Most commonly people say ['vrɒtslɑːv] but you may also hear ['vrɒtslæv]. After this, there is a double bar which is followed by information on American English pronunciation – you can see that there are two possibilities again, but this time it is the stressed vowel that will vary; the last sound in American English is always [f].

3,6 ,biː biː 'siː tells us this utterance has two stresses, but the presence of the little wedge icon after it, ◄, tells us that which one of these is used when we speak is determined by the role the word is playing. As a noun, e.g. *on the B B 'C,* the second stress is preserved; as an ajdective, e.g *on 'B B C '4,* the first stress is preserved. The wedge icon tells us that **stress shift** will occur. (*Unknown* is another word subject to stress shift: the *'unknown 'soldier* but *the great un'known.*)

4,7,9,10 Sometimes, as with the word *inculpatory,* we may not be sure which syllable to stress – LPD tells us that the stress falls on the second syllable. Sometimes, however, we may not even be sure which sounds to use – again, LPD can tell us how to pronounce unfamiliar words such as the name *Legh* or the words *oleic* and *cholla.*

5   LPD tells us that there are two ways to pronounce *exit,* but it also offers us information about our preferences. In the UK we can see our preference is for the variant using [ks] in the middle whereas speakers of American English prefer the variant with [gz].

8   Here, too, the entry includes information about variants (as well as a warning about how ***not*** to pronounce the word in MRP!). This time, the transcription includes a little superscript: wʌn'ˢ. What this tells us is that some speakers say [wʌns] with no t-sound, while others say [wʌnts], inserting [t].

Chapter 2

Ex 2.3.

4   *Think* begins with a voiceless sound and yes, MRP also has the voiced version of this sound which is used at the beginning of words like *the, this, that, those,* in the middle of *other,* etc.

Ex 2.4.

There are lots of sounds to choose from, but typically 'voiced-only' sounds include anything found in the rows labelled *nasal, trill, tap/flap, approximant, lateral approximant.*

For voiceless/voiced pairs, there is an even wider choice, including all the pairs in the rows labelled *plosive, fricative, lateral fricative.* Note that this excludes the singleton [ʔ] in the plosive row.

Ex 2.5.

1   Utterances beginning with a voiceless consonant are 1, 3, 7.
    (Remember that we are thinking exclusively about ***sounds*** here; the spelling is irrelevant.)

2   Utterances with a voiceless consonant between the two vowels are: 4, 5, 7, 8 and 9.

3   Utterances ending in a voiceless consonant are: 2, 6, 8, 9.

Ex 2.6.

1 English *race*

2 English *whirrs*

3 An English "spelling pronunciation" of the German name *Weiss* is what could happen here ([waɪs]), but there is no proper English word.

4 No English word.

5 No English word, although the related noun *breath* ends in a voiceless version of the same sound.

6 English *of*

7 No English word

8 No English word, although some northern accents pronounce this word with a voiced sound at the end anyway; also, the related verb *clothe* has a voiced version of the same sound at the end.

9 English *doze* and *does* (plural of *doe*, a female deer)

10 English *off*

Ex 2.7.

Voiceless	Voiced
p t k	b d g
f θ s ʃ h	v ð z ʒ
tʃ	dʒ
	m n ŋ
	w r l j

Ex 2.8.

1 peg   2 weighed/wade   3 view   4 jump   5 thigh   6 lazy
7 refuse   8 bicker   9 fussy   10 edging   11 fleas   12 card   13 eyes/
i's (plural of 'i')   14 rich   15 hozed (hosed)

Ex 2.9.

The voiceless sounds occur in:

little, cameos, National, Trust, about, its, various, properties, Some,
wonderful, Polesden, Lacey, Quebec, House, Orford, Ness, Canons, Ashby,
House, wish, that, address, delightful, Elizabethan, house.

Ex 2.10.

The symbols for each of the voiceless consonants are:

[p] in properties, Polesden
[t] in little, Trust, about, its, properties, that, delightful
[k] in cameos, Quebec, Canons
[f] in wonderful, delightful, Orford
[θ] in Elizabethan
[s] in Trust, its, various, Some, Lacey, House (x3), Ness
[ʃ] in National, Ashby, wish
[h] in House (x2), house*

Ex 2.11.

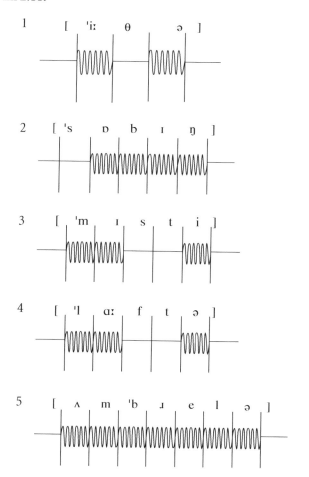

*Note that whether the h-sound is voiceless or voiced will depend in part on how fast you are speaking. The h-sounds in between other voiced sounds in English often acquire voicing as well. (When the h-sound is voiced, the symbol is [ɦ].)

Chapter 3

Ex 3.2.
Labial articulations occur in: <u>b</u>all, gi<u>ve</u>, <u>b</u>ye-<u>b</u>ye, <u>b</u>a<u>b</u>y, <u>M</u>u<u>mm</u>y, u<u>p</u>, <u>p</u>ee<u>p</u>-o, <u>b</u>ikkie (biscuit), <u>m</u>ore, <u>m</u>ilk, stop.
  Just one of these words has a labiodental articulation – the v-sound in give.

Ex 3.4.
The places of articulation that most people will agree on are:

bilabial	voiceless: <u>p</u>lease, <u>p</u>ink; voiced: <u>b</u>rown, <u>m</u>oon
labiodental	voiceless: [f] at the start of <u>ph</u>ysics; voiced: <u>v</u>iew
alveolar	voiceless: <u>s</u>ee, <u>t</u>aste, [t] at the start of <u>Th</u>omas, [s] at the start of <u>c</u>ease; voiced: [n] at the start of <u>mn</u>emonic, <u>d</u>o, <u>z</u>oo, <u>d</u>ate, <u>l</u>ook, <u>n</u>ever, [z] at the start of <u>x</u>ylophone

Depending on your accent, you may disagree about:

postalveolar	<u>r</u>ide - some speakers will use a labiodental [ʋ] here (the celebrity Jonathan Ross has this pronunciation), while others (speakers of Scottish English or South African English, for example), may use an alveolar [r].
dental	not all accents have dental sounds; speakers of a number of urban accents of English will use labiodental [f] in *think* and labiodental [v] or alveolar [d] in *that*; speakers of Irish English may use dental articulations [t̪] and [d̪] respectively, instead of MRP [θ] and [ð].

Ex 3.5.
Alveolar consonants occur as follows:

[t] <u>t</u>old, <u>T</u>ina, da<u>t</u>e, nex<u>t</u>, ou<u>t</u>ing, <u>t</u>o, i<u>t</u>, mee<u>t</u>, pho<u>t</u>os, shoo<u>t</u>, ge<u>t</u>, no<u>t</u>ice, a<u>t</u>.
[d] <u>D</u>avi<u>d</u>, tol<u>d</u>, <u>d</u>ate, Lon<u>d</u>on, He'<u>d</u>, woul<u>d</u>, goo<u>d</u>, boar<u>d</u>.
[l] to<u>l</u>d, <u>L</u>ondon, <u>l</u>ike, ab<u>l</u>e, c<u>l</u>ub.
[s] ne<u>x</u>t [nekst], chan<u>c</u>e, <u>s</u>ome, noti<u>c</u>e.
[z] <u>Z</u>oo, wa<u>s</u>, photo<u>s</u>.
[n] Ti<u>n</u>a, <u>n</u>ext, Lo<u>n</u>do<u>n</u>, cha<u>n</u>ce, <u>n</u>ew, <u>n</u>otice

Ex 3.6.
*Pre-bilabial is physically (and logically) impossible because bilabial itself is the frontmost place of articulation. By the same token, you can not retract a glottal articulation.

Ex 3.7.
Dorsal articulations occur in:

[j] <u>y</u>ou, beautiful ['bjuːtɪfʊl], v<u>i</u>ews, new [njuː].

[k] too<u>k</u>, taxi ['tæksi], Lo<u>ch</u> (you will pronounce this as [k] unless you say [lɒx] with the original Gaelic [x] sound at the end which is also a

dorsal consonant), Mi<u>ch</u>ael, Pentax ['pentæks], thin<u>k</u>, excellent ['eksələnt], excursion [ɪk'skɜːʒn].

[g] <u>g</u>et, <u>g</u>o, photo<u>g</u>raphs.

[ŋ] stayi<u>ng</u>, sighti<u>ng</u>s, doi<u>ng</u>, thi<u>n</u>k.

[w] <u>wh</u>ere (or you may pronounce [ʍ] at the beginning of this word – still a dorsal articulation), <u>w</u>ere, <u>w</u>ith, <u>wh</u>en (or starting [ʍ], see above), <u>w</u>e, <u>w</u>ent.

Chapter 4

Ex 4.1.
Set has a closed velum throughout: [set]

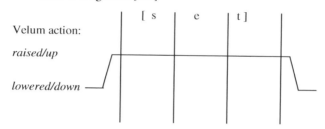

Net begins with an open velum which rises and closes during the vowel, in time for the last sound, [t]: [nẽet]

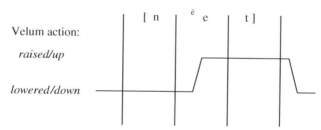

Mend also begins with an open velum which again rises and closes, this time for the last sound, [d] – this time the closure happens on the boundary, and is responsible for the switch from [n] to [d]:

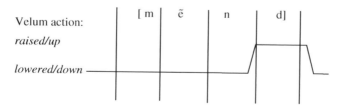

Ex 4.2.

[ŋ] velar; [N] uvular.

The active articulator is the back of the tongue in both cases.

Ex 4.3.

1   Voiced bilabial nasal: Mary, mother's some, small, meter, comb (with silent-b), mirror, empty, make-up, money

2   Voiced alveolar [n]: ninety-nine, hundred, One hundred, No wonder, knees (with silent-k)

3   Voiced velar nasal: hungry, starving, think, something, long

Speakers from London and the south-east of England may find they use an alveolar nasal in the –ing suffix (e.g. *starvin'*, *somethin'*, etc).

Ex 4.4.

	Voice	Place	Manner
[p]	voiceless	bilabial	plosive
[d]	voiced	alveolar	plosive
[c]	voiceless	palatal	plosive
[ɢ]	voiced	uvular	plosive
[t̪]	voiceless	dental	plosive

Ex 4.5.

Plosives occur in: car, atom, queue, Thomas, forgive, bomb, orchid, X-ray, door.

The word *lough* has two ways of being pronounced. One is homophonous with *lock* and contains a plosive; the other is closer to the Irish ([lɒx]) and does not contain a plosive – your answer will depend on your pronunciation.

Ex 4.6.

1 (c) This matches the voiced alveolar plosive indicated in the syllable [de] but with the 'voiced' marker missing.(Compare the characters for [zo] and [so], [ka] and [ga], where consonant voicing is indicated by two small strokes – reminiscent of quotation marks – to the top right of the main shape.)

2 (b) (Compare the syllable [to].)

3 (c) [sake] starts with a voiceless alveolar fricative and only (b) and (c) start with a voiceless segment; additionally, only (c) has the second syllable also beginning with a voiceless segment (and [k] is a voiceless velar plosive.) The answer is therefore (c). (Check out the corresponding syllables [za] and [ga].)

Ex 4.7.

	Voice	**Place**	**Manner**
[ɸ]	voiceless	bilabial	fricative
[z]	voiced	alveolar	fricative
[h]	voiceless	glottal	fricative
[χ]	voiceless	uvular	fricative
[ʒ]	voiced	palatoalveolar*	fricative

*Refer back to Table 3.1 if you are puzzled by this term – you may have written postalveolar, which is OK, but palatoalveolar is better/more precise when dealing with English.

Ex 4.8.

1 [b͡β]   2 [ɢ͡ʁ]   3 [g͡ɣ]   4 [t͡θ]   5 [c͡ç]

Ex 4.9.

Lateral approximants

1 From left to right: voiced alveolar lateral approximant; voiced retroflex lateral approximant; voiced palatal lateral approximant; voiced velar lateral approximant.

2 [l̥].

Central approximants

1 [ʋ]

2 [ɭ]

3 [j]

4 [ɥ]

5 [w] Note that this double articulation is located under 'Other Symbols'

Ex 4.10.

1 [d]   A voiced bilabial plosive is to a voiced bilabial nasal as **a voiced alveolar plosive** is to a voiced alveolar nasal.

2 [d͡ʒ]   A voiceless palatotalveolar affricate is to a voiceless alveolar plosive as a **voiced palatoalveolar affricate** is to a voiced alveolar plosive.

3 [d]   A voiced bilabial nasal is to a voiced alveolar nasal as a voiced bilabial plosive is to a **voiced alveolar plosive**.

4 [w]   A voiced palatal approximant is to a voiced velar approximant as a voiced labialpalatal approximant is to a **voiced labialvelar approximant**.

5   [s]   A voiced alveolar fricative is to a voiced alveolar plosive as a **voiceless alveolar fricative** is to a voiceless alveolar plosive.

Chapter 5

Ex 5.1.

1   voiceless bilabial ejective plosive

2   voiceless alveolar ejective fricative

3   voiceless palatoalveolar (or postalveolar) ejective affricate

4   voiceless alveolar ejective lateral fricative

5   voiceless palatal ejective plosive

Ex 5.2.

1   [t̪']

2   [t͡s']

3   [kʷ']

4   [t͡ɬ']

5   [ṯ']

Ex 5.3.

There is **velic** closure, preventing airflow via the nasal cavities. The lower lip rises and rests lightly against the upper front teeth. Simultaneously, the **vocal folds** close, preventing airflow to and from the **lungs**. The larynx **rises** fractionally, putting momentary pressure on the body of air contained in the speaker's **pharynx** and causing a small rush of air through the oral cavity which exits through the narrow constriction between the lower lip and the **upper front teeth**. There is a narrow jaw aperture throughout. A voiceless, **labiodental**, ejective **fricative** is heard. This sound is represented in transcription by the symbol [f'].

Ex 5.4.

1   voiced dental implosive

2   labialized voiced palatal implosive

3   voiceless bilabial implosive

4   palatalized voiced bilabial implosive

5   voiced retroflex implosive

Ex 5.5.

   1 [ʃ]

   2 [ʞ̊]

   3 [ɗ̥]

   4 [d̪]

   5 [ɗʷ]

Ex 5.6.

The jaw assumes a medium aperture. The **lips** part and assume a rounded position and the velum **rises** and forms **velic** closure. At the same time, the back of the tongue **rises** and forms a firm closure on the **soft** palate. **The vocal folds** are vibrating for normal voice and the larynx **lowers** slightly, momentarily reducing air pressure in the pharynx. Immediately, the back of the tongue moves **down** away from the velum and ambient air may be drawn into the oral cavity to equalise the ambient and intra-oral air pressure. A **labialized, voiced, velar, implosive** is heard. This sound can be represented in transcription by the symbol [ɠʷ].

Ex 5.7.

   1 voiceless bilabial click

   2 labialized nasalized voiced alveolar lateral click

   3 glottalized voiceless palatoalveolar click

   4 voiced postalveolar click

   5 creaky voiced dental click

Ex 5.8.

   1 [k͜ǁ]   2 [g͜ǃʷ]   3 [ŋ̊͜ǃ]   4 [ˀk͜ǁ]   5 [g͜ǂ]

Ex 5.9.

The jaw assumes a narrow aperture. Simultaneously, the back of the tongue **rises** and seals firmly against **velum/soft palate** and the **tip** of the tongue **rises** and seals against the **back** of the upper front **teeth**. This **dental** closure is completed by the side rims rising and sealing against the inside edges of the upper molars. The main body of the tongue then **lowers**, increasing the cavity formed inside the mouth and **lowering/reducing** the air pressure in this enclosed space. At the same time, the velum lowers, assuming an **open** position and the **vocal folds** vibrate for normal voice. A **nasalized voiced dental click** is heard. This sound can be represented in transcription by the symbol [ŋ͜ǀ].

Ex 5.10.

Sound	Pulmonic egressive	Glottalic egressive	Glottalic ingressive	Velaric ingressive
1 [k']		✓		
2 [k͡ǁ]				✓
3 [ɠ]	✓		✓	
4 [t͡θ']		✓		
5 [ɦ]	✓*			
6 [ɡ͡ǃ]	✓			✓
7 [ɗ]			✓	
8 [ŋ͡ʘ]	✓			✓
9 [ʃ']		✓		
10 [ɓ]	✓		✓	

* This symbol represents a voiced glottal fricative – the forward pointing hook on the top of the upright is **not** indicative of an implosive in this instance.

Chapter 6

Ex 6.1.

pCV2 [e]	front half-close spread/unrounded
pCV3 [ɛ]	front half-open spread/unrounded
pCV4 [a]	front open spread/unrounded
pCV5 [ɑ]	back open spread/unrounded
pCV7 [o]	back half-close rounded
pCV8 [u]	back close rounded
sCV1 [y]	front close rounded
sCV2 [ø]	front half-close rounded
sCV3 [œ]	front half-open rounded
sCV4 [ɶ]	front open rounded
sCV5 [ɒ]	back open rounded
sCV6 [ʌ]	back half-open spread/unrounded
sCV7 [ɤ]	back half-close spread/unrounded
sCV8 [ɯ]	back close spread/unrounded

Further comments

- Although the front primary Cardinal Vowel [a] is traditionally described as having spread lips, by the time the jaw is this wide open, the lip position is actually fairly neutral. The same is true for the most open back primary Cardinal Vowel, [ɑ]. I will refer to these values simply as *unrounded*.

- It is equally acceptable to use the terms close-mid and open-mid respectively where these answers use the more traditional half-close and half-open. However, whichever you chose, you should use them consistently – it is not acceptable to speak of close-mid in one label and half-close or half-open in another.

Ex 6.2.

1. (a) a sinewave with a frequency of 200Hz.

   (b) a complex wave with three components: a sinewave with a frequency of 100Hz, a sinewave with a frequency of 150Hz and a sinewave with a frequency of 300Hz. The 100Hz wave had the highest amplitude and the 150Hz wave, the lowest.

   (c) is a complex wave with two components: a sinewave with a frequency of 100Hz and a sinewave with a frequency of 400Hz. The lower frequency wave has the higher amplitude.

2. The complex wave in Figure 6.5 would have the approximately following a/f spectrum:

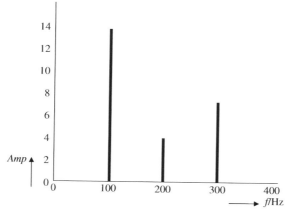

Ex 6.3.

1   MRP [iː] looks as if it must be closest to pCV1 [i]: front close spread

2   MRP [ɔː] looks as if it must be closest to pCV6 [ɔ]: back open-mid (half open) rounded

3   MRP [uː] looks as if it must be closest to pCV 8 [u]: back close rounded

4   MRP [ɑː] looks as if it must be closest to pCV5 [ɑ]: back open unrounded

5   MRP [ɔː] looks as if it must be closest to the central, mid, neutral vowel, schwa, IPA [ə].

Ex 6.4.
All long:

1   Centralized front lowered from fully close unrounded/spread

2   Central mid unrounded neutral

3   Centralized back open unrounded/spread

4   Centralized back lowered from fully close rounded

5   Back mid rounded

Ex 6.5.

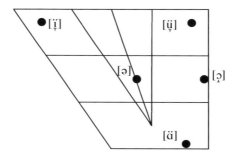

Ex 6.6.

1   Nasalized, central, mid, neutral

2   Back, half-close, unrounded/spread

3   Centralized front, close, rounded

4   Retracted front, half-close, unrounded/spread

5   Voiceless, back, half-open, rounded (Note that the voiceless diacritic can be written above or below the affected symbol.)

Ex 6.7.
All short:

1   Slightly centralized (or ***retracted***) front, lowered from fully open, unrounded (actually, the lips are a little spread for this vowel)

2   Slightly centralized (or ***advanced***) back, lowered from fully open, rounded

3   Strongly centralized (nearer to centre than front), just above half-close/close mid, unrounded (actually, the lips are usually fairly neutral for this vowel)

4 Strongly centralized (nearer to centre than back), just above half-close/close-mid, rounded

5 Front, mid, unrounded (actually, usually fairly neutral lips)

6 Central, mid, unrounded (actually, neutral)

7 Front, mid-way between open and half-open/open-mid, unrounded (actually, neutral)

8 Central, mid-way between open and half-open/open-mid, unrounded (actually neutral)

9 Back, open, rounded

Ex 6.8.

1 [ï] – this is schwi or 'the happy vowel'

2 [ü] – this is schwu or 'weak-u'

3 [ɪ] (You could have used a strongly centralized pCV2 here, [ë], but the IPA chart provides the symbol [ɪ] for values in this sort of area, and selecting that symbol simplifies the transcription.)

4 [ʊ] (As with 3 above, the IPA provides the symbol, [ʊ], which avoids the need to apply diacritics to pCV7, [ö].)

5 [ẹ] (You could also transcribe this as [ɛ̝], but the symbol that most closely reflects the choice of phoneme symbol here is [ẹ].)

6 [ə]

7 [æ] (This is another readymade IPA vowel symbol; using Cardinal Vowels, you could achieve the same value through raising pCV4, [a̝], or lowering pCV3, [ɛ̞].)

8 [ɐ] is the narrow phonetic representation of the norm allophone of the MRP English /ʌ/ phoneme. Although this looks as if it ought to use sCV6 [ʌ], the actual pronunciation of this vowel today is much closer to this very open central vowel value.

9 [ɒ]

Ex 6.9.

(i) front vowels [i y e ø]

(ii) back vowels [ɯ u o ʌ]

(iii) close vowels [i y ɯ u]

(iv) non-close vowels [e ø o ʌ]

(v) rounded vowels [y ø u o]

(vi) unrounded vowels [i e ɯ ʌ]

Chapter 7

Ex 7.1.

In common with many other accents, MRP speakers will make a length distinction (as well as a noticeable difference in vowel quality) in each of the word pairs in this exercise. However, speakers of Standard Scottish English (SSE) tend not to make much of a length distinction between such pairs and there is not always a quality difference either (SSE has no [ʊ] quality of the type in MRP *should*). GAm also tends not to employ a noticeable length difference.

Ex 7.2.

Pre-fortis clipping will occur in 2, 3, 6, 7 and 8.

(If your answers don't agree with this, check out the transcription of the words in LPD – you will see that each ends with a voiceless/fortis consonant.)

Ex 7.3.

Pre-fortis clipping will occur in:

1   Many hands <u>make</u> <u>light</u> <u>work</u>.

2   A bird in the hand is <u>worth</u> two in the <u>bush</u>.

3   A <u>stitch</u> in time saves nine.

4   Many a <u>slip</u> <u>twixt</u> <u>cup</u> and <u>lip</u>.

5   A rolling stone gathers no <u>moss</u>.

Rhythmic clipping may affect the stressed vowels in:

1   *Many* and *hands* which are each followed by an unstressed syllable (underlined here) within the rhythmic foot: 'Many 'hands <u>make</u> 'light 'work ||

2   *bird, hand* and *two* could all be shortened slightly because of the need to include two following unstressed syllables in each rhythmic foot: a 'bird <u>in the</u> 'hand <u>is worth</u> 'two <u>in the</u> 'bush ||

3   *stitch*. Already shortened by pre-fortis clipping, this vowel may also be subject to rhythmic clipping here because of the presence of the following unstressed *in* in the same rhythmic foot: a 'stitch <u>in</u> 'time 'saves 'nine ||

4   *Many, slip* and *cup*. Although not affected by pre-fortis clipping, the stressed vowel in *Many* is followed by two unstressed syllables within the rhythmic foot while the already clipped vowels in *slip* and *cup* are each followed by one: 'Many <u>a</u> 'slip <u>twixt</u> 'cup <u>and</u> 'lip ||

5   *rolling* and *stone* where *roll-* is followed by one unstressed syllable and *stone* by two in the same rhythmic foot: a 'rolling 'stone <u>gathers</u> 'no 'moss ||

Ex 7.4.

MRP typically pronounces 1, 5, 7 and 8 with diphthongs. In spite of their spelling, the rest are monophthongs in this accent. In many other accents, however, including a number of northern accents of English (from what Wells 1982 identifies as the 'middle north' group) and most Scottish English accents, only the vowels in 7 and 8 are diphthongs. Some speakers, however, will also have a diphthong in items

2 and 4 as well (speakers with Australian or broad London (Cockney) accents, for example, or with an accent from parts of the midlands or the north-west of England (such as Birmingham and Liverpool).

Ex 7.5.

   a) All diphthongs in this group glide towards schwi: 1. [e̞ɪ̯], 2. [ä̠ɪ̯], 3. [ɔ̞ɪ̯]

   b) All diphthongs in this group glide towards schwu: 1. [ə̞ʊ̯], 2. [ä̠ʊ̯]
      Note here the different phonetic qualities from which the diphthongs /aɪ/ and /aʊ/ begin. This is only reflected in the narrow phonetic transcription and does not show up in the simplified, phonemic symbols.

Ex 7.6.

Usual answers to this question include the following perceptions:

- With either one or two syllables: 1, 3, 4, 5, 6, 8, 9, 10.

- Within this group, some people will feel that the monomorphemic words have just one syllable, *hire*, for example, or *wire, quire/choir* and *flour* while the bimorphemic *higher, player* and *mower* (high + er, etc.) have two.

- This same argument is sometimes made for the words in *flower growers.* Some people feel strongly that each word has just one syllable or that each word has two while others feel that monomorphemic *flower* has one but bimorphemic *growers* has two.

- *Curious* is even more curious... people will argue for two, three or even four syllables here! People who feel there are four seem to perceive the [ʊə] diphthong as a vowel sequence of [uː]+[ə], making it homophonous with a *queue-er* (someone who queues).

Ex 7.7.

Using slightly less narrow representations of the qualities (some of the detailed diacritics have been omitted where there is no possibility of confusion):

   (1) [aɪə] first becomes [a̠ə] and then [aː]. The smoothing process here eventually results in a new simple vowel.

   (2) [əʊə] immediately becomes [əə] which is another way of writing [əː]. Immediately, therefore, smoothing brings about an overlap with the existing long vowel [əː] (phonemically transcribed /ɜː/).

Chapter 8

Ex 8.1.

  1 ['lɪʁə], [lɪχ] (*to lie, lie (1st pers. sg.)*)

  2 ['bɛdə], [bɛt] (*beds, bed*)

  3 ['drœyvə], [drœyf] (*grapes, grape*)

  4 ['hɛbə], [hɛp] (*to have, have (1st pers. sg.)*)

  5 ['rɛizə], [rɛis] (*to travel, journey*)

Ex 8.2.

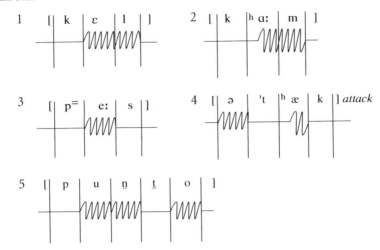

Ex 8.3.

The plosives which could have glottal reinforcement are transcribed.

Ja[ˀk] rang the bell, bu[ˀt] when nobody answered, he wen[ˀt] round to the ba[ˀk] door. Becky was u[ˀp]stairs, making the beds and putting away washing.

"I didn[ˀt] hear you kno[ˀk]", she said.

Ja[ˀk] replied, "I didn[ˀt] knock, I rang the bell – a[ˀt] leas[ˀt] three times."

"The bell's broken," said Becky. "I kee[ˀp] meaning to pin a notice on the door: Kno[ˀk] loudly. Bell out of a[ˀk]tion."

Ex 8.4.

The velarized allophone of the lateral will occur in: well, all, Cornwall, hustle, bustle, occasional, capital.

Ex 8.5.

(a) Voiced velarized bilabial plosive [ɓ] (or [bˠ])

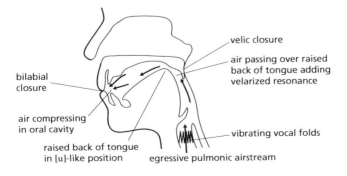

(b) Voiceless velarized alveolar fricative [s] (or [sˠ])

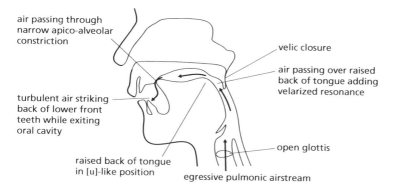

air passing through narrow apico-alveolar constriction

velic closure

air passing over raised back of tongue adding velarized resonance

turbulent air striking back of lower front teeth while exiting oral cavity

raised back of tongue in [u]-like position

open glottis

egressive pulmonic airstream

Ex 8.6.

Data	Approach-type	Release-type
Voiceless bilabial plosives [p]		
1 [dɪsˈpjuː-]	Fricativized median	Wide median
2 [ˈɹæpt]	Wide median	Masked (inaudible)
Voiceless alveolar plosives [t]		
1 [-uːtɪŋ]	Wide median	Wide median
2 [ˈstɹɒŋ]	Narrow median	Wide median
3 [ə ˈtɹævlə]	Wide median	Fricative median *([t] assimilates to postalveolar [ɹ] which undergoes devoicing because of the long VOT, resulting in local voiceless friction)*
4 [ˈɹæpt ɪn]	Wide median *(which takes place during hold-phase of [p])*	Wide median
Voiced alveolar plosives [d]		
1 [wɪnd ɔn]	Nasal	Wide median
2 [wə dɪs-]	Wide median	Wide median
Voiceless velar plosives [k]		
1 [ˈtɹævlə ˈkeɪm]	Wide median	Wide median
2a [wɔːm ˈkləʊk]	Nasalized	Lateralized
b	Wide median	*Either* Wide median (aspirated *or* unaspirated) *or* inaudible
Voiced velar plosive [g]		
[ˈstɹɒŋgə]	Nasal	Wide median

Chapter 9

Ex 9.1.

Spectrogram 1 *hijacks*

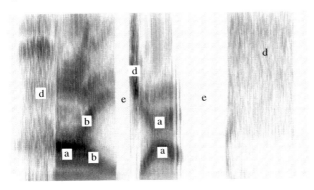

Spectrogram 2 *searches*

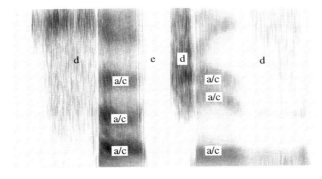

Ex 9.2.
The point of closure for the initial plosive consonant is much more advanced (further forward on the palate) for the initial consonants in *key* and *ghee* – the tongue anticipates the front close (palatal) position of the vowel and, accordingly, a part nearer to front than back rises and forms a pre-velar closure: [k̟] and [g̟]. (For some speakers, this might even be a pure palatal closure, involving the front of the tongue rather than a part between back and front.)

Again, for some speakers, the point of closure in *car* and *guard* might even be fractionally retracted, giving [k̠] and [g̠], while for almost everyone, the point of closure in *cur* and *girl* is pure velar.

Ex 9.3.

All changes are anticipatory in terms of direction.

1 Alveolar [d] at the end of *fried* anticipates the bilabial consonant [b] at the beginning of *banana*, becoming bilabial [b].

2 Alveolar [n] at the end of *town* anticipates velar [k] at the beginning of *crier*, becoming velar [ŋ].

3 Alveolar [t] at the end of *hit* anticipates dental [ð] at the beginning of *them*, becoming dental [t̪].

4 Alveolar [t] at the end of *court* anticipates bilabial [m] at the beginning of *martial*, becoming bilabial [p].

5 *Alveolar* [n] at the end of *corn* anticipates labiodental [f] at the beginning of *flakes* becoming labiodental [ɱ].

6 *Alveolar* [d] at the end of *red* anticipates postalveolar [ɹ] at the beginning of *rose*, becoming postalveolar [d̠].

7 Alveolar [nt] at the end of *front* anticipate velar [g] at the beginning of *gate*, becoming velar [ŋk].

8 Alveolar [s] at the end of *this* anticipates palatoalveolar [ʃ] at the beginning of *shop*, becoming palatoalveolar [ʃ].

9 Alveolar [ɬ] at the end of *well* anticipates dental [θ] at the beginning of *thought*, becoming dental [ɬ̪].

10 Alveolar [nt] at the end of *tent* anticipate bilabial [p] at the beginning of *pole*, becoming bilabial [mp].

The process involves a change in the ***place of articulation*** of an **alveolar** consonant such that it assumes the place of articulation of an immediately following consonant. (Note that the voice and the manner remain unchanged.)

Ex 9.4.

1 Perseverative nasalization at the beginning of [ẽɪ], caused by the immediately preceding [m].
Anticipatory palatalization of [lʲ], caused by the immediately following front close (palatal) vowel [iː].

2 Anticipatory labialization of [d̥ʷ], caused by the immediately following rounded [ɔː] vowel.
Perseverative nasalization at the beginning of [ᵇɒ], caused by the immediately preceding [n].

3 Anticipatory nasalization in [ə̃ũ], caused by the immediately following [ŋ].
Anticipatory labialization of [kʰʷ], caused by the immediately following rounded [ɔː] vowel.

4 Anticipatory velarization of ['fˠ], caused by the immediately following back close (velar) vowel [uː], and velarization of both consonants in the cluster [pˠɹ̥ˠ] in the fully 'velar' environment between the velarized lateral [ɫ] and the back close (velar) vowel [uː].

5   Anticipatory palatalization of both consonants in the cluster ['sʲtʲ] caused by the immediately following front close (palatal) [iĩ] vowel.
    Anticipatory nasalization of both [iĩ] and [ŭ], caused in both cases by an immediately following nasal, [m].
    Anticipatory velarization of [ĩˠ] caused by the immediately following back close (velar) vowel [ŭ].
    Nasalization of the sequence [ĩŭ] in the fully nasal environment between two tokens of [m].

Ex 9.5.

Observe here:

1   Preparation of the [ɹ] position during the hold-phase of the bilabial plosive [b] = *anticipatory lingual coarticulation.* (The tie bar and a superscript representation of [ɹ] has been used here to show the simultaneity of these two gestures at this point; transfer of the inherent labialization of English [ɹ] would also be implied here, making application of the labialization diacritic [ʷ] redundant = *anticipatory coarticulation of lip rounding.*

2   Lowering of the velum in anticipation of the up-coming [n] segment may start as early as the [ɹ] segment here and continue through the [æ] = *anticipatory coarticulation of nasality.*

3   The vowel [æ] is an open vowel and will usually have a wide jaw aperture; the opening movement of the jaw will begin at least by the release of [b] and continue right through [ɹ] being fully established in the beginning of [æ] itself = *anticipatory coarticulation of jaw opening.* (Compare the jaw action in a word like 'print'.)

Ex 9.6.

1

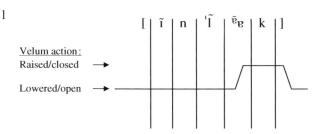

Note: the velum may start to rise earlier here, during the lateral, forming velic closure before the oral articulators reach the vowel segment. In that case, you would not indicate the presence of nasalization in the vowel. Whatever happens, the velum must be closed by the time the oral articulators form the final [k].

2

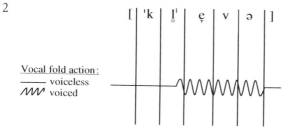

Vocal fold action:
—— voiceless
ⵑⵑⵑ voiced

3

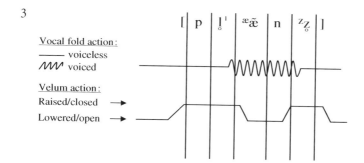

Vocal fold action:
—— voiceless
ⵑⵑⵑ voiced

Velum action:
Raised/closed →
Lowered/open →

Note: the velum could start to open earlier, at the very beginning of the vowel, for example, or even during the final voiced part of the lateral.

Ex 9.7.

1 /aɪskriːm/:   *I scream* [ˈaɪ ˌsʷkʷɹḭ̃ːm][1]   *ice-cream* [ˈa̰ɪs ˌkʷɹ̥ḭ̃ːm]
   open juncture   [aɪ] + [s]   [s] + [k]
   close juncture   [s] to [k] to [ɹ]   [ăɪ] to [s], and [k] to [ɹ̥]

2 /greɪteɪp/:   *grey tape* [ˈɡ̊ɹeɪ ˌtʰĕɪp]   *great ape* [ˈɡ̊ɹĕɪt˭ ˌʔĕɪp]
   open juncture   [eɪ] + [tʰ]   [t˭] + [ʔĕɪ]
   close juncture   [tʰ] to [ĕɪ]   [ĕɪ] to [t˭]

Note: The only unarguably distinctive detail in *great ape* is the pre-fortis clipping of the vowel in *great*. Unaspirated release of the final [t] in *great* and hard attack of the initial vowel in the stressed syllable *ape* are optional. They are, however, the kinds of features likely to be invoked when we try really hard to make the difference between the two utterances clear.

---

[1] Tonetic stress marks are being used here, adding some intonation information. [ˈ] tells us that this syllable is the nucleus – the most important stressed syllable in the utterance – and that a change in pitch occurs or begins here. [ˈ] is called a high fall and is typical of statements in MRP English – the pitch of the speakers voice starts high and falls to low.

3 /brɑːstræps/:   *bra straps* [ˈb̥ɹɑː sʷt̪ʷɹæps]   *brass traps* [ˈb̥ɹɑˑs ˈt̪ʷɹ̥æps]
   open juncture   [ɑː] + [s]   [s] + [t]
   close juncture   [s] to [t̪] to [ɹ]   [ɑˑ] to [s], and [t̪] to [ɹ]

4 /waɪtʃuːz/:   *white shoes* [ˈwăɪ̯ʔt̪ ˈʃuːz̥]   *why choose* [ˈwaɪ̯ ˈt͡ʃuːz̥]
   open juncture   [ʔt̪] + [ʃ]   [aɪ̯] + [t͡ʃ]
   close juncture   [aɪ̯] to [ʔt̪]   [t̪] to [ʃ]

Note: Apart from the clipping of the diphthong and the potential for glottal reinforcement of [t] in *white,* the distinctive characteristic here is likely to be the length of the voiceless palatoalveolar friction which will be longer in the [ʃ] of *shoes* than in the affricate [t͡ʃ] at the beginning of *choose.*

Chapter 10

In the following answers, any optional stresses are included in brackets.

Ex 10.1.

1 *He objected when the subject was raised.*
   /hi əbˈdʒektɪb wen ðə ˈsʌbdʒɪk wəz ˈreɪzd ‖/

2 *You need a written permit in order to return.*
   /ju (ˈ)niːd ə ˈrɪtəm ˈpɜːmɪt | ɪn ˈɔːdə tə rɪˈtɜːn ‖/

3 *It's a drop-in centre for dropouts.*
   /ɪts ə ˈdrɒpɪn (ˈ)sentə fə ˈdrɒpauts ‖/

4 *We got tickets for the fly-past and saw the Red Arrows fly over.*
   /wi ɡɒʔ ˈtɪkɪts fə ðə ˈflaɪpɑːst ‖ ən ˈsɔː ðə red ˈærəʊz flaɪ ˈəʊvə ‖/

5 *They found the runaway hiding near the runway, but he wouldn't say why he was running away.*
   /ðeɪ ˈfaʊn ðə ˈrʌnəweɪ | ˈhaɪdɪŋ nɪə ðə ˈrʌmweɪ ‖ bət i ˈwʊdn̩ seɪ ˈwaɪ i wəz (ˈ)rʌnɪŋ əˈweɪ ‖/

Ex 10.2.

1 /ði ˈɑːftənuːn ˈhændəʊvə | ˈweŋk kwaɪʔ ˈsmuːðli ‖/

2 • /hi ˈkɑːmp ˈpleɪ | ɪf iz ˈnɒʔ mætʃˈfɪt ‖/
   ○ /hiz əz ˈmætʃfɪʔ ˈnaʊ | əz ˈeniwʌn ˈɪz ‖/

3 /aɪ ɡɒʔ ˈtɒp kwɒləti ˈkɑːpɪts | ɪn a ˈpriː siːzn̩ ˈseɪl ‖ aɪ wʊd ˈəʊnli kənˈsɪdə tɒp ˈkwɒləti ‖/

4 /təˈmɒrəʊ ɑːftəˈnuːn | wil ɡet ə ˈtʃaɪniːz ˈteɪkəweɪ ‖/

5 /ɪts kɔːld ði ˈəʊvəsiːz ˈhaɪweɪ | bi(ˈ)kɒz ɪʔ ɡəʊz ˈəʊvə ðə ˈsiː ‖/

Ex 10.3.

1 /aɪ wəz 'ɡəʊɪŋ tə sɪt 'ɪn ɒn ðə 'lektʃə ‖ bət ɪ? wəz 'kænsl̩b bɪ'kɒz əv ðə 'sɪt ɪn ‖/

2 /hiz 'rɪəli 'ɡʊd ə? 'fraɪɪŋ 'steɪk ‖ səʊ aɪ bɔː? 'fraɪɪŋ steɪk | 'rɑːðə ðm̩ 'breɪzɪŋ steɪk | fə 'sʌpə ‖/

3 /aɪm 'ɡɪvɪŋ ðəm ə 'kriːm kʌləd 'dɪʃ | ənd ə 'mætʃɪŋ(')kriːm 'dʒʌɡ ‖ ðə 'dɪʃ ɪz fə 'ʃʊɡə | bət ðə 'dʒʌɡ kʊd bi ə 'mɪlk dʒʌɡ | ɔːr ə 'kriːm dʒʌɡ ‖/

4 /fər ə 'məʊmənt | aɪ 'θɔːt juːb bɔːt ə 'laɪt haʊs ‖ ju ment ɪts ə 'veri (')laɪt 'haʊs | wɪð 'lɒts əv 'wɪndəʊz ‖/

5 /aɪ 'dəʊn? (') nɔːməli 'drɪŋk ʃæm'peɪn ‖ bət ə 'ʃæmpeɪŋ 'kɒkteɪl əb bi 'naɪs ‖/

Ex 10.4.

A basic version using a minimum number of IPs (optional sentences stresses are shown in parentheses here) could be:

A 'heard any good 'jokes (')recently ‖[1]

B not 'really |[2] 'no ‖[3]

A 'didn't you hear the 'one about the 'man who went to the 'airport ‖[4]

B 'no ‖[5] (')how did it 'go ‖[6]

A well the 'airport (')didn't go 'anywhere |[7] but the 'man (')went by 'plane ‖[8]

B oh 'very 'funny ‖[9] I sup'pose you 'call that 'some kind of 'humorous 'take-off ‖[10]

Comments

IP1 Typically, a short inversion question like this will be produced as one IP. A slightly slower speech rate would probably result in a stress on *recently*, but more than that is very unlikely.

IP2, IP3 This is a fairly idiomatic sort of answer – a double negative! *Not really* could stand alone and occupies one IP. *No* is then added to reinforce this, having a second IP of its own.

IP4 As discussed in the chapter itself, the idiomatic introduction of a joke (as here: *Didn't you hear the one about the man who went to the airport*) is typically realised as a single IP – even if this does make it rather long! This is an example of idiomatic intonation and is almost always said this way – it will not be divided into shorter groups.

IP5 A monosyllabic negative statement, *No*, has its own IP.

IP6 A short, grammatically complete wh-question has its own IP.

IP7, IP8 Conjoined clauses. Conjoined items typically have their own IPs, the minor boundary occurring immediately before the conjunction (here: *but*). *Well* could stand alone, but it can also be absorbed into the following clause as here, functioning merely as an empty turn initiator, rather than as some kind of focus marker.

IP9 Exclamatory phrase rendered here as one IP. *Oh* could be treated as a separate exclamation, but this is not altogether appropriate in the context where the intention appears to be to communicate sarcasm rather than express surprise, so *Oh* is treated as an empty initiator, like *well* in IP7.

IP10 A grammatically complete statement. This is rather long for the average IP, and could be broken into two IPs (see further discussion below). However, it still sounds completely natural delivered here as one IP.

Further comments
More complex solutions are also possible, each involving more IPs. For example, alternative tonality here might consist of:

IP7 well the 'airport $|^{7a}$ 'didn't go 'anywhere $\|^{7b}$ but the 'man $|$ 'went by 'plane $\|$

In this case, the structural parallels are kept, but each clause is divided into two IPS, with the grammatical subject being given its own IP

One further possibility here would be to separate off *Well* into its own IP as in

IP7 'well $|^{7c}$ the 'airport $|^{7a}$ 'didn't go 'anywhere $\|^{7b}$

(Note that if this happens, *Well* becomes stressed – every IP must have at least one stress.)

Similarly, additional IPs can be introduced in IP9 and IP10. In IP9, the exclamatory *Oh* can be given its own IP:

IP9 'oh $|^{9a}$ 'very 'funny $\|^{9b}$

IP10 can be broken after *that,* but note that this also involves adjusting the rhythm and the sentence stresses in IPs 10a and 10b do not match exactly the stresses of the original IP10: I sup'pose you call 'that $|^{10a}$ 'some kind of 'humorous 'take-off $\|^{10b}$

Bibliography

JASA Journal of the Acoustical Society of America
JIPA Journal of the International Phonetic Association

Abe, Isamu, 1998, 'Intonation in Japanese', in Hirst and Di Cristo 1998, 360–375.

Abercrombie, David, Fry, D.B., MacCarthy, P.A.D., Scott, N.C. and Trim, J.L.M. (Eds), 1964, *In Honour of Daniel Jones*. London: Longman.

Adank, Patti, Van Hout, Roeland and Smits, Roel, 2005, 'An acoustic description of the vowels of Northern and Southern Standard Dutch' in *JASA* 116, 3: 1729–1738.

Akamatsu, Tsutomu, 1997, *Japanese phonetics. Theory and Practice*. München: Lincom Europa.

Armstrong, Lilias E., 1940, *The Phonetic and Tonal Structure of Kikuyu*. London: Oxford University Press.

Ashby, M.G., 1990, 'Articulatory possibilities for implosives' in *JIPA*, vol. 20, No. 2, pages 15–18.

Ashby, M., 2006 (2nd edition), 'Phonetic classification' in Brown, Keith (Ed.) *The Elsevier Encyclopedia of Language and Linguistics*. Oxford: Elsevier. Vol. 9: 364–372.

Ashby, M.G. and Maidment, J., 2005, *Introducing Phonetic Science*. Cambridge: Cambridge University Press.

Ashby, P., 2005 (2nd edition), *Speech Sounds*. London: Routledge.

Ashby, P. and Ashby, M., 1990, 'Generalizations on RP consonant clusters', in Ramsaran (Ed.), 1990.

Baugh, Albert C. and Cable, Thomas, 2002 (5th edition), *A History of the English Language*. London: Routledge.

Bloomfield, Leonard, 1933. *Language*. New York: Holt, Rinehart, & Winston.

Brosnahan, L.F. and Malmberg, B., 1970, *Introduction to Phonetics*. Cambridge: Heffer.

Bruce, G., 1977, *Swedish Word Accents in Sentence Perspective*. Lund: University of Lund.

Bruce, G. and Thelander, I., 2001, 'A pitch accent journey in southern Sweden' in *Working Papers* 49. Lund: Lund University, 14–17.

Butcher, A., 2004, '"Fortis/Lenis" revisited one more time: the aerodynamics of some oral stop contrasts in three continents', in *Clinical Linguistics and Phonetics*: 18, 547–557.

Bye, Patrik, 2004, 'Evolutionary typology and Scandinavian pitch accent.' Ms. University of Tromsø, at http://www.hum.uit.no/a/bye/Papers/pitch-accent-kluw.pdf. (Accessed 03 January 2010)

Castro, Obdulia, 2003, 'Pitch accent in Galician Spanish' in Sayahi, Lofti (Ed.), 2003, *Selected Proceedings of the First Workshop on Spanish Sociolinguistics*. Somerville, MA: Cascadilla Proceedings Project, 43–52.

Catford, J.C., 2001 (2nd edition), *A Practical Introduction to Phonetics*. Oxford: Oxford University Press.

Chapallaz, M., 1979, *The Pronunciation of Italian*. London: Bell & Hyman.

Childs, George Tucker, 2003, *An Introduction to African Languages*. Amsterdam: John Benjamins.

Chomsky, N., 1964, *Current Issues in Linguistic Theory*. The Hague: Mouton.

Chomsky, N. and Halle, M., 1968, *The Sound Pattern of English*. New York: Harper & Row.

Clark, John and Yallop, Colin, 1990, *An Introduction to Phonetics and Phonology*. Oxford: Basil Blackwell.

Collins, Beverley and Mees, Inger M., 1999, *The Real Professor Higgins. The Life and Career of Daniel Jones*. Berlin: Mouton de Gruyter.

Comrie, Bernard, 1981, *The Languages of the Soviet Union*. Cambridge: Cambridge University Press.

Conklin, H.C., 1959, 'Linguistic play in its cultural context' in *Language* 35: 631–636.

Cruttenden, A., 1997 (2nd edition), *Intonation*. Cambridge: Cambridge University Press.

Cruttenden, A., 2008 (7th edition), *Gimson's Pronunciation of English*. London: Hodder Education.

Crystal, D., 1969, *Prosodic Systems and Intonation in English*. Cambridge: Cambridge University Press.

Denes, P.B. and Pinson, E.N., 1983 (2nd edition), *The Speech Chain: The Physics and Biology of Spoken Language*. New York: W. H. Freeman and Company.

Dieth, E., 1950, *Vademecum der Phonetik*. Bern: Franke.

Donohue, Mark, 1999, 'Illustrations of the IPA: Tukang Besi' in *The Handbook of the International Phonetic Association*, 151–153.

Dow, Francis, D.M., 1972, *An Outline of Mandarin Phonetics*. Canberra: Australian National University Press.

Eaton, Helen, 2006, 'Illustrations of the IPA: Sandawe' in *JIPA*, Vol. 36, No. 2, pages 235–242.

Engstrand, Olle, 1999, 'Illustrations of the IPA: Swedish' in *The Handbook of the International Phonetic Association*, 140–142.

Eklund, Robert, 2008, 'Pulmonic ingressive phonation: diachronic and synchronic characteristics, distribution and function in animal and human sound production.' in *JIPA* vol. 38, No. 3, pages 235–324.

Elert, C.-C., 1972, 'Tonality in Swedish: rules and a list of minimal pairs.' in Firchow, E.S., Grimstad, K., Hasselmo, N. and O'Neil, W.A. (Eds), 1972, *Studies for Einar Haugen*. The Hague: Mouton, 151–173.

Fischer-Jørgensen, E., 1985, 'Some basic vowel features, their articulatory correlates, and their explanatory power in phonology' in Fromkin, V. A. (Ed), 1985, pages 79–100.

Fischer-Jørgensen, E., 1987, 'A phonetic study of the stød in Standard Danish' in *Annual Report of the Institute of Phonetics of the University of Copenhagen* 21, 55–265.

Foulkes, P. and Docherty, G.J. (Eds), 1999, *Urban Voices. Accent Studies in the British Isles*. London: Arnold.

Freeborn, Dennis, 2006 (3rd edition), *From Old English to Standard English. A Course Book in Language Variation across Time*. London: Macmillan.

Fromkin, V. A. (Ed.), 1985, *Phonetic Linguistics: Essays in Honour of Peter Ladefoged*. Orlando, Fl: Academic Press.

Fromkin, V., Rodman, R. and Hyams, N., 2006 (8th edition), *An Introduction to Language*. Boston, MA: Thompson Heinle.

Fry, D.B., 1955 'Duration and intensity and physical correlates of linguistic stress' in *JASA* 27, pages 765–768.

Fry, D.B., 1958, 'Experiments in the perception of stress' in *Language and Speech* 1, 126–152.

Fudge, E., 1984, *English Word-Stress*. London: Allen and Unwin.

Fuller, M., 1990, 'Pulmonic ingressive fricatives in Tsou' in *JIPA*, Vol. 20, No. 2, pages 9–14.

Greenberg, J.H., 1978, 'Some generalizations concerning initial and final consonant clusters.' in Greenberg, J.H., Ferguson, C.A. and Moravcsik (Eds), 1978, *Universals of Human Language*. Vol 2: *Phonology*. Standford: Stanford University Press, pages 243–79.

Gussenhoven, C. and Jacobs, H., 2005 (2nd edition), *Understanding Phonology*. London: Arnold.

Halliday, M.A.K., 1970, *A Course in Spoken English: Intonation*. London: Oxford University Press.

Haspelmath, Martin, Dryer, Matthew S., Gil, David and Comrie, Bernard (EDs), 2011, *The World Atlas of Language Structures Online*. Munich: Max Planck Digital Library. Available online at http://wals.info/ (Accessed: 03 January 2011)

Hayward, K., 2000, *Experimental Phonetics*. London: Longman.

Hayward, K. and Hayward, R.J., 1999, 'Illustrations of the IPA: Amharic' in *The Handbook of the International Phonetic Association*, 45–50.

Hirst, Daniel and Di Cristo, Albert, 1998, *Intonation Systems. A Survey of Twenty Languages*. Cambridge: Cambridge University Press.

Hoogshagen, S., 1959, 'Three contrastive vowel lengths in Mixe.' *Zeitschrift für Phonetik Sprachwissendschaft und Kommunikationsforschung* 12, 111–115.

Hualde, José Ignacio, 2005, *The Sounds of Spanish*. Cambridge: Cambridge University Press.

Hughes, A., Trudgill, P. and Watt, D., 2005 (4th edition), *English Accents and Dialects. An Introduction to Social and Regional Varieties of English in the British Isles*. London: Arnold.

Handbook of the International Phonetic Association, 1999. Cambridge: Cambridge University Press.

Jacewicz, Ewa, Fujimura, Osamu and Fox, Robert A., 2003, 'Dynamics in diphthong perception' in Solé, M., Recasens, D. and Romero, J. (Eds.) *Proceedings of the 15th international congress of phonetic sciences*. Universitat Autònoma de Barcelona: Barcelona, pages 993–996.

Jacobi, Irene, Pols, Louis C.W. and Stroop, Jan, 2007, 'Dutch diphthong and long vowel realizations as changing socio-economic markers.' in Trouvain, Jürgen and Barry, William (Eds) *Proceedings of the 16th international congress of phonetic sciences*. Saarbrücken: Universität des Saarlandes, 1481–1484.

Johnson, K., 2002 (2nd edition), *Auditory and Acoustic Phonetics*. Oxford: Blackwell.

JIPA. Cambridge: Cambridge University Press.

Jones, D.J., 1944, 'Chronemes and tonemes: a contribution to the theory of phonemes.' in *Acta Linguistica* Vol IV, fasc. I:1–10, reprinted in Jones & Laver 1973, 159–167.

Jones, D.J. and Ward, D., 1969, *The Phonemes of Russian*. Cambridge: Cambridge University Press.

Jones, W.E. and Laver, J., 1973, *Phonetics in Linguistics. A Book of Readings*. London: Longman.

Kent, R.D., 1983, 'The segmental organisation of speech.' in MacNeilage, P.F. (Ed.) *The Production of Speech*. New York: Springer-Verlag, 57–89.

Khozhevnikov, V.A. and Chistovich, L.S., 1966, *Speech: Articulation and Perception*. Washington: United States Department of Commerce.

Kingdon, R., 1958, *The Groundwork of English Intonation*. London: Longman.

Kohler, Klaus, 1999, 'Illustrations of the IPA: German' in *The Handbook of the International Phonetic Association*, 86–89.

Ladd, D. Robert, 1996, *Intonational Phonology*. Cambridge: Cambridge University Press.

Ladefoged, P., 1996 (2nd edition), *Elements of Acoustic Phonetics*. Chicago: University of Chicago Press.

Ladefoged, P., 1971, *Preliminaries to Linguistic Phonetics*. Chicago: University of Chicago Press.

Ladefoged, P., 2001 (4th edition), *A Course in Phonetics*. Orlando: Harcourt Brace.

Ladefoged, P., 2003, *Phonetic Data Analysis. An Introduction to Fieldwork and Instrumental Techniques*. Oxford: Blackwell.

Ladefoged, P., 2005 (2nd edition), *Vowels and Consonants. An Introduction to the Sounds of Languages*. Oxford: Blackwell.

Ladefoged, P. and Maddieson, I., 1996, *Sounds of the World's Languages.* Oxford: Blackwell.

Laver, J., 1980, *The Phonetic Description of Voice Quality.* Cambridge: Cambridge University Press.

Laver, J., 1994, *Principles of Phonetics.* Cambridge: Cambridge University Press.

Laufer, A., 1999, 'Illustrations of the IPA: Hebrew' in *The Handbook of the International Phonetic Association,* 96–99.

Leach, P., 1988, 'French intonation: tone or tune?' in *JIPA,* Vol. 18, No. 2, 125–139.

Lee, W.S. and Zee, E., 2003, 'Illustrations of the IPA: Standard Chinese (Beijing)'. in *JIPA,* Vol. 33, No. 1, 109–112.

Lee, W.S. and Zee, E., 2009, 'Illustrations of the IPA: Hakka Chinese.' in *JIPA,* Vol. 39, No. 1, pages 107–111.

Lehiste, Ilse, 1970, *Suprasegmentals.* Cambridge, MA: MIT Press.

Lerond, Alain, 1980, *Dictionnaire de la prononciation.* Paris: Larousse.

Lewis, M. Paul (Ed.), 2009 (Sixteenth edition), *Ethnologue: Languages of the World.* Dallas, Tex.: SIL International. Online version: http://www.ethnologue.com/. (Accessed: 07 May 2011)

Lindau, Mona, Norlin, Kjell and Svantesson, Jan-Olof, 1985, 'Cross-linguistic differences in diphthongs.' *UCLA Working Papers in Phonetics* 61, 40–44.

Lindblom, B. and Studdert-Kennedy, M., 1967, 'On the role of formant transitions in vowel recognition.' *JASA* 42, 830–843.

Lodge, K., 2009, *A Critical Introduction to Phonetics.* London: Continuum.

Lodge, R. Anthony, Armstrong, Nigel, Ellis, Yvette M.L. and Shelton, Jane F., 1997, *Exploring the French Language.* London: Arnold.

Lutz, Angelika, 1994, 'Vocalization of "post-vocalic r": an Early Modern English sound change' in Kastovsky, D. (Ed.), 1994, *Studies in Early Modern English.* Tiel: Mouton De Gruyter.

MacCarthy, Peter, 1975, *The Pronunciation of French.* London: Oxford University Press.

Maddieson, I., 1984, *Patterns of Sounds.* Cambridge: Cambridge University Press.

Maddieson, I., 2008a, 'Glottalized Consonants', in Haspelmath, Martin, et al. (EDs). Chapter 7. Available online at http://wals.info/feature/7 (Accessed: 03 January 2011)

Maddieson, I., 2008b, 'Tone', in Haspelmath, Martin, et.al. (EDs) Chapter 13. Available online at http://wals.info/feature/13 (Accessed: 03 January 2011)

Maddieson, I., 2008c, 'Absence of Common Consonants', in Haspelmath, Martin, et al. (EDs). Chapter 18. Available online at http://wals.info/feature/18 (Accessed: 03 January 2011)

Man, Chik Hon, 1985, *Everyday Cantonese.* Hong Kong: The Chinese University of Hong Kong.

Malmberg, Bertil, 1963, *Phonetics.* New York: Dover Publications Inc.

Martínez-Celdrán, Eugenio, Fernández-Planas, Ana Maria and Carrera-Sabaté, Josefina, 2003, 'Illustrations of the IPA: Castilian Spanish' in *JIPA,* Vol. 33, No. 2, pages 255–259.

Mees, I. and Collins, B., 1982, 'A phonetic description of the consonant system of Standard Dutch (ABN).' in *JIPA,* Vol. 12, No. 1, pages 2–12.

Mees, I. and Collins, B., 1983, 'A phonetic description of the vowel system of Standard Dutch (ABN).' in *JIPA,* Vol. 13, No. 2, pages 64–75.

Mitchell, T.F., 1962, *Colloquial Arabic.* London: Hodder and Staughton.

Mithun, Marianne, 2001, *The Languages of Native North America.* Cambridge: Cambridge University Press

Nakagawa, Hirosi, 1995, 'A preliminary report on the click accompaniments in |Gui.' in *JIPA,* Vol. 25, No. 2, pages 49–63.

National Geospatial-Intelligence Agency. *Romanization Systems and Policy,* at http://earth-info.nga.mil/gns/html/romanization.html (Accessed: 03 January 2011)

O'Connor, J.D., 1965, 'The perception of time intervals.' in *Progress Report,* September 1965. London: Phonetics Laboratory, University College London.

O'Connor, J.D., 1973, *Phonetics*. Harmondsworth: Penguin.

O'Connor, J.D. and Arnold, G.F., 1973 (2nd edition), *Intonation of Colloquial English*. London: Longman.

Ogden, Richard, 2006, *An Introduction to English Phonetics*. Edinburgh: Edinburgh University Press.

Ohala, Manjari, 1999, 'Illustrations of the IPA: Hindi' in *The Handbook of the International Phonetic Association*, pages 100–103.

Palmer, H.E., 1922, *English Intonation, with Systematic Exercises*. Cambridge: Heffer.

Pike, K.L.,1943, *Phonetics*. Ann Arbour: University of Michigan Press.

Pike, K.L.,1945, *The Intonation of American English*. Ann Arbor: University of Michigan Press.

Pike, K.L.,1947, *Phonemics*. Ann Arbor: University of Michigan Press.

Pike, K.L.,1948, *Tone*. Ann Arbor: University of Michigan Press.

Plag, Ingo, Kunter, Gero, Lappe, Sabine and Braun, Maria, 2007, 'Testing hypothese about compound stress assignment in English: a corpus-based investigation' in *Corpus Linguistics and Linguistic Theory*, 3.2, 199–223.

Plag, Ingo, Kunter, Gero, Lappe, Sabine and Braun, Maria, 2008, 'The role of semantics, argument structure, and lexicalization in compound stress assignment in English.' in *Language*, 84.4, 760–794.

Pring, Julian T., 1955, *A Grammar of Modern Greek. On a Phonetic Basis*. London: University of London Press.

Popperwell, R.G., 1963, *The Pronunciation of Norwegian*. Cambridge: Cambridge University Press.

Pullum, G.K. and Ladusaw, W.A., 1996 (2nd edition), *Phonetic Symbol Guide*. Chicago: The University of Chicago Press.

Ramsaran, Susan (Ed.) 1990, *Studies in the Pronunciation of English. A commemorative volume in honour of A.C. Gimson*. London: Routledge.

Raphael, Lawrence J., Borden, Gloria J. and Harris, Katherine, S., 2006 (5th edition), *Speech Science Primer. Physiology, Acoustics and Perception of Speech*. Baltimore: Williams and Wilkins.

Regueira, Xosé L., 1999, 'Illustrations of the IPA: Galician' in *The Handbook of the International Phonetic Association*, pages 82–85.

Roach, P.J., 1973, 'Glottalisation of English /p, t, k, tʃ/ – a re-examination', in *JIPA*, Vol. 3, pages 10–21.

Scurfield, Elizabeth, 1991, *Teach Yourself Chinese*. London: Hodder and Stoughton.

Shosted, Ryan K. and Chikovani, Vakhtang, 2006, 'Illustrations of the IPA: Georgian' in *JIPA*, Vol. 36, No. 2, 235–242.

Spencer, A., 2003, 'Does English have productive compounding?' in Booij, Geert E., Decesaris, Janet, Ralli, Angela and Scalise, Sergio (Eds), 2003, *Topics in Morphology: Selected Papers from the Third Mediterranean Morphology Meeting (Barcelona, September 20–22, 2001)*. Barcelona: Institut Universitari Lingüística Applicada, Universitat Pompeu Fabra.

Tench, P., 1978, 'On introducing parametric phonetics.' in *JIPA*, Vol. 8, 34–46.

Tench, P., 1996, *The Intonation Systems of English*. London: Cassell.

Tench, P., 2007, 'Illustrations of the IPA: Tera.' in *JIPA*, Vol. 37, No. 1, 228–234

Tingsabadh, M.R.K. and Abramson, A.S., 1999, 'Illustrations of the IPA: Thai' in *The Handbook of the International Phonetic Association*, 147–150.

Traill, A., 1985, *Phonetic and Phonological Studies of !Xóõ Bushman*. (Quellen zur Khoisan-Forschung 5.) Hamburg: Helmut Buske.

Traill, A., 1991, 'Pulmonic control, nasal venting and aspiration in Khoisan languages.' in *JIPA*. Vol. 21, No. 1, pages 12–18.

Tranel, Bernard, 1987, *The Sounds of French. An Introduction*. Cambridge: Cambridge University Press.

Watkins, Justin, W., 2001, 'Illustrations of the IPA: Burmese.' in *JIPA*, Vol. 31, No. 2, pages 291–295.

Wells, J.C., 1982, *Accents of English* Vols 1–3. Cambridge: Cambridge University Press.

Wells, J.C., 2006, *English Intonation. An Introduction*. Cambridge: Cambridge University Press.

Wells, J.C., 2008 (3rd edition), *Longman Pronunciation Dictionary*. London: Longman.

Westermann, D., 1930, *A Study of the Ewe Language*. London: Oxford University Press.

Yip, Moira, 2002, *Tone*. Cambridge: Cambridge University Press.

Zee, 1999, 'Illustrations of the IPA: Chinese (Hong Kong Cantonese).' in *The Handbook of the International Phonetic Association*, 58–60.

Language index

This index covers the 124 languages and language varieties referred to within *Understanding Phonetics*. All family, genus and geographical data are derived from Haspelmath, *et al.*

Language	Family, Genus	Geographical area	Pages
Agul	Nakh-Daghestanian, *Lezgic*	Russia	37, 42
Amharic	Afro-Asiatic, *Semitic*	Ethiopia, Egypt	72
Arabic (Modern Standard)	Afro-Asiatic, *Semitic*	Algeria, Bahrain, Comoros Islands, Egypt, Eritrea, Iraq, Israel, Jordan, Kuwait, Lebanon, Libya, Morocco, Oman, Palestinian West Bank & Gaza, Qatar, Saudi Arabia, Somalia, Sudan, Syria, Tunisia, United Arab Emirates, Yemen	2, 37, 42, 68, 128, 133–134, 142
Assamese	Indo-European, *Indic*	India	26
Basque	Basque	France, Spain	44
Bengali	Indo-European, *Indic*	Bangladesh, India	26, 45, 86
Bini	Niger-Congo, *Edoid*	Nigeria	175
Bosnian, *See* Serbo-Croat			
Burmese	Sino-Tibetan, *Burmese-Lolo*	Myanmar	28, 29, 53, 126, 127, 174
Cantonese	Sino-Tibetan, *Chinese*	China	28, 173–174, 176
Chatino	Oto-Manguean, *Zapotecan*	Mexico	28
Cherokee	Iroquoian, *Southern Iroquoian*	United States of America	2
Chinese (Modern Standard)	Sino-Tibetan, *Chinese*	China	2, 28, 68, 114, 117, 148, 173, 174–175, 176
Chipewyan	Na-Dene, *Athapaskan*	Canada	38, 74

Language	Family, Genus	Geographical area	Pages
Croatian, *See* Serbo-Croat			
Dafla	Sino-Tibetan, *Tani*	India	118
Dahalo	Afro-Asiatic, *Southern Cushitic*	Kenya	42
Danish	Indo-European, *Germanic*	Denmark	25, 125, 130
Dutch	Indo-European, *Germanic*	The Netherlands	2, 21, 57, 64, 86, 100, 116, 121–122, 123, 135, 136, 163, 171
Estonian	Uralic, *Finnic*	Estonian	104, 141
Ewe	Niger-Congo, *Kwa*	Ghana, Togo	46
Eyak	Na-Dene, *Eyak*	United States of America	38
Faroese	Indo-European, *Germanic*	Denmark (The Faroe Islands)	1, 127
Finnish	Uralic, *Finnis*	Finland	141, 161, 168
French	Indo-European, *Romance*	France, Switzerland	2, 21, 37, 40, 46, 49, 53, 64, 69, 86, 100, 122, 124, 125, 126, 140, 167
Fula	Niger-Congo, *Northern Atlantic*	Cameroon	131
Fuzhou Chinese	Sino-Tibetan, *Chinese*	China, Malaysia, Thailand	176–177
Galician Spanish	Indo-European, *Romance*	Spain	171
Georgian	Kartvelian	Georgia	2–3, 72
German	Indo-European, *Germanic*	Austria, Germany, Switzerland	37, 57, 61, 63, 64, 86, 100, 111, 121–122, 125, 128, 140, 163
Greek (Modern)	Indo-European	Greece	1, 5, 86, 134, 163
Gujarati	Indo-European, *Indic*	India	26, 118
ǀGui	Khoisan	Botswana	79
Hakka Chinese	Sino-Tibetan, *Chinese*	China	139
Hamtai	Trans-New Guinea, *Angan*	Papua New Guinea	72
Hausa	Afro-Asiatic, *West Chadic*	Niger, Nigeria	25, 28, 72, 74, 86, 128
Hawaiian	Austronesian, *Oceanic*	United States	168
Hebrew (Oriental)	Afro-Asiatic, *Semitic*	Israel	128

Language	Family, Genus	Geographical area	Pages
Hindi	Indo-European, *Indic*	India	26, 45, 49, 68, 123
Hokkien Chinese	Sino-Tibetan, *Chinese*	China	28
Hungarian	Uralic, *Ugric*	Hungary	124, 161
Icelandic	Indo-European, *Germanic*	Iceland	127
Igbo	Niger-Congo, *Igboid*	Nigeria	117, 174, 178
Ik	Nilo-Saharan, *Kuliak*	Uganda	118
Irish	Indo-European, *Celtic*	Ireland	11, 125, 127, 133, 190
Italian	Indo-European, *Romance*	Italy, Switzerland	2, 3, 53, 57, 64, 86, 136, 142, 157, 161, 162, 166, 179
Japanese	Japanese	Japan	8, 37, 60, 100, 118, 148, 168, 171–173, 179
Ju|'hoan	Khoisan, *Northern*	Angola, Botswana, Namibia	76
Kabardian	Northwest Caucasian	Russia	42
Kera	Afro-Asiatic, *East Chadic*	Chad	58
Korean	Korean	Korea	2, 100, 127, 139
Kurdish	Indo-European, *Iranian*	Iran, Iraq	42
Lak	Nakh-Daghestanian, *Lak-Dargwa*	Russia	42
Lao	Tai-Kadai, *Lao-Phutai*	Laos, Thailand	148
Latvian	Indo-European, *Baltic*	Latvia	171
Limburgse Dutch	Indo-European, *Germanic*	The Netherlands, Belgium, Germany	171
Lithuanian	Indo-European, *Baltic*	Lithuania	171
Luganda	Niger-Congo, *Bantoid*	Uganda	168
Malay	Austronesian, *Malayic*	Malaysia	2
Malayalam	Dravidian, *Southern Dravidian*	India	58
Mandarin, *See* Chinese (Modern Standard)			
Mangbetu	Nilo-Saharan, *Mangbetu*	Democratic Republic of Congo	58
Margi	Afro-Asiatic, *Biu-Mandara*	Nigeria	25

World Englishes index

Subject index

abduction (of vocal folds) 16 *See also* speech organs/vocal folds
ABN 116
accent, regional
  Australian 28, 198
  Birmingham 198
  broad London 198
  Cockney 198
  g-dropping 6
  general 4, 5, 6, 11–12, 40, 43, 54, 128, 171, 183, 188
  General American (GAm) 11, 12, 13, 37, 45, 116, 131, 197
  h-dropping 43
  h-pronouncing 43
  Irish English 40, 188
  Japanese Standard (Tokyo) 172
  Liverpool (Scouse) 135, 189
  midlands 189
  Modern Received Pronunciation (MRP) 11, 125, 128, 132, 198
  Multicultural London English (MLE) 11
  northern (English) 198
  northern Dutch 116
  popular London 43
  Scottish English 11, 57, 99, 131, 188, 197, 198
  Standard Indian English 45
  South African English 57, 188
  urban 11, 188
  Yorkshire 99, 126, 183
accent
  pitch 170–173
  stress 7, 159ff, 168–170, 179, 181
  tone 25
  word 179
accent coaching 10
accentism 11
acoustic
  guitar 93
  measurements 10
  signal 62
  viewpoint 13, 52
acoustic correlates *See also* acoustic representations
acoustic cues 144–151, 157, 169–170

acoustic phonetics 1, 9–10
acoustic representations
  English /l/ and /r/ 117
  general xii
  vowels 90–95
  consonants (*including* fotis *and* lenis) 117, 120, 144–151, 158
acute accent 7, 25, 172
active articulators *See* articulators, active
Adam's apple 15
adduction (of vocal folds) 16 *See also* speech organs/vocal folds
adjective 70, 163–164
advanced xvi, 41, 45, 196, 202 *See also* diacritics, advanced
Advanced Tongue Root ([ATR]) 116–117
affricate *See* manner of articulation
affrication 135
a/f spectrum *See* amplitude/frequency spectrum
airflow 19, 32, 48–51, 53, 54, 56, 57, 58, 59, 62–63, 68, 69, 70, 71, 73, 76, 78, 102, 120, 129, 134, 135, 140, 146, 154, 192
  central 50, 59, 140
  lateral 50, 59
air pressure 54, 59, 61, 62–63, 74, 75, 76–77, 82, 139, 193
airstream (pulmonic) 18–19, 25, 29, 31–32, 48, 50, 52, 53, 54, 57, 59, 63, 93, 117, 132, 138, 140, 146
airstream initiators 18, 69–70, 75, 80, 127
airstream mechanisms 68–83
  glottalic 69–75
  oral 75 *See* velaric airstream
  pharyngeal 70 *See* glottalic airstream
  pulmonic 18–19, 68–69
  velaric 75–81
allophone 12, 104, 178 (*See also* phoneme)
  aspirated 129, 156
  diphthongal 116
  glottalized 129
  major 151–152
  norm 104, 110–112, 144, 197
  unaspirated 157
  velarized 152, 200
allotone 177 (*See also* toneme)

Printed in Great Britain
by Amazon